Springer Series

FOCUS ON WOMEN

Violet Franks, Ph.D., Series Editor

Confronting the major psychological, medical, and social issues of today and tomorrow, *Focus on Women* provides a wide range of books on the changing concerns of women.

VIOLET FRANKS, Ph.D., received her Doctorate
from the Institute of Psychiatry, University of London,
London, England in 1959. She is Director of Psychology at the Carrier Foundation in Belle Mead, New
Jersey, and also a member of the Adjunct Faculty of
Rutgers University at the Graduate School of Applied
and Professional Psychology. She has lectured and
conducted workshops extensively on therapy issues
relevant to women, both nationally and internation-
ally, and has published widely in this and related
areas. Her two previous books are *Women and
Therapy* and *Gender and Disordered Behavior*.

ESTHER D. ROTHBLUM, Ph.D., received her Doctorate in clinical psychology from Rutgers University,
New Brunswick, New Jersey, in 1980. She completed
her pre-doctoral internship at the University of
Mississippi Medical Center, Jackson Mississippi, and
her post-doctoral fellowship at the Yale University
Depression Research Unit. She is the author of numerous papers, and has conducted workshops and
symposia on depression, women's mental health, and
therapy for women. She is co-chair of the Feminist-
Research Committee of the Association for Women in
Psychology. Dr. Rothblum is currently on the faculty
of the University of Vermont Department of Psychology, Burlington, Vermont.

The Stereotyping of Women
Its Effects on Mental Health

Violet Franks, Ph.D.
Esther D. Rothblum, Ph.D.
Editors

SPRINGER PUBLISHING COMPANY
New York

Springer Publishing Company, Inc.
200 Park Avenue South
New York, New York   10003

83 84 85 86 87 / 10 9 8 7 6 5 4 3 2 1

Library of Congress Cataloging in Publication Data

Main entry under title:

The Stereotyping of women.

    (Springer series, focus on women ; v. 5)
    Includes bibliographies and index.
    Contents: Introduction / Esther D. Rothblum and Violet Franks — Sex-
role stereotypes and mental health / Jeffrey A. Kelly — The development of sex-
role stereotypes in children / Marsha Weinraub and Lynda M. Brown — [etc.]
    1. Women — Mental health — Addresses, essays, lectures.   2. Sex role —
Addresses, essays, lectures.   3. Sexism — Addresses, essays, lectures.   I.
Franks, Violet.   II. Rothblum, Esther D.   III. Series. [DNLM: 1.
Women — Psychology.   2. Stereotyping.   3. Identification (Psychology)
W1 SP685KD v. 5 / HQ 1206 S838]
RC451.4.W6S78   1983   616.89'0088042   82-19207
ISBN 0-8261-3820-9

Printed in the United States of America

Contents

Preface

The idea for this book germinated at a cocktail party in Mississippi in 1979, when a group of five female psychology students — Kathy Brehony, Laura Solomon, Marilyn Zegman, Charlene Muehlenhard, and Esther Rothblum — were discussing their research areas. Each woman began to realize that in her area of clinical research (agoraphobia, stress, obesity, assertion, and depression) women were overrepresented as patients. We hypothesized that sex-role stereotypes contributed to the relevance to women of each of these research topics. By the end of the gathering, we had decided to present a symposium in which each of us would delineate the prevalence of the clinical area for women, the contribution of sex-role stereotypes, the research to date, and implications for future research and therapy with women. We knew that some research already existed on women and psychopathology, and we asked Violet Franks, who had edited two books in the area of women and emotional distress (*Women in Therapy*, 1974; *Gender and Disordered Behavior*, 1979), to chair our symposium. We wanted to know what the implications of the past were, and Violet had been part of the women's mental health movement since its beginning in the early 1970s.

The symposium was a tremendous success, and we decided to publish the current book on sex-role stereotypes and women's mental health. Each member of the original panel suggested a well-known researcher in yet another area of clinical psychology in which women had special needs: Patricia Resick on rape and spouse-abuse victims, Sandra Leiblum on sexual dysfunction, and Judith Worell on the single-again woman. Furthermore, we invited Jeffrey Kelly, because of his expertise in the research area of androgyny, to contribute a general introductory chapter on sex-role stereotypes, and Marsha Weinraub to contribute a chapter on her area of expertise, the development of sex-role stereotypes. Finally, we invited Barbara Kirsh to contribute a chapter on sex roles and language use. Thus, the final selection of contributors for the book consisted equally of fledgling psychologists who were just beginning research and well-known psychologists who had written extensively on their topic area.

The editors also represent two generations. One of us (VF) had been influenced by the era of the feminine mystique; the other (ER) had grown up with the feminist movement. Even our expectations differed concerning the conclusions that various contributors would reach. VF had felt in the 1970s that opportunities for women were burgeoning and that a paradigm shift had occurred. By 1980, however, she did not regret having been born earlier; she felt that young women today face equally difficult conflicts regarding career and family choices. ER was aware that women's roles have not changed much in the past decade; however, she felt optimistic that the book would indicate where changes could be made for future research and treatment in mental health. The following chapters, therefore, will help to establish the reality.

The topics of this book fall into three categories: (1) introductory chapters on sex-role stereotypes (Kelly), the development of sex-role stereotypes in children (Weinraub and Brown), and sex roles and language use (Kirsh); (2) traditional categories of psychopathology listed in the *Diagnostic and Statistical Manual of the American Psychiatric Association* (DSM III), including depression (Rothblum), agoraphobia (Brehony), and sexual dysfunction (Tevlin and Leiblum); and (3) special problems of living, including lack of assertion (Muehlenhard), obesity (Zegman), resocialization of the single-again woman (Worell and Garret-Fulks), and violence against women (Resick). All are topics of concern to both men and women; however, our focus is on women.

The book has four aims: (1) to describe the prevalence of each disorder, with particular emphasis on women; (2) to discuss the contribution of sex-role stereotypes to the disorder; (3) to review relevant research on women in each area of mental health; and (4) to describe future implications for research and intervention in women's mental health. In sum, as we begin the 1980s, we ask: What are the new components operating for women?

It is difficult to convey in writing the sense of excitement, novelty, and camaraderie that has accompanied the entire process of this book since its conception. Perhaps because of the relative youth of so many of the contributors or perhaps because of the contrast this book provides to the mental health plans of the current conservative administration, there was tremendous enthusiasm and cooperation among us. This book has profited from the support and encouragement of numerous individuals. We would like to thank the faculty and staff of The Carrier Foundation and of the Rutgers University Graduate School of Applied and Professional Psychology for their interest and enthusiasm. We owe particular gratitude to Dr. Cyril Franks for his incisive comments and his moral support. The faculty and staff of the Department of Psychiatry and Human Behavior of the University of Mississippi Medical Center provided generous support for this project since its inception as a symposium. This book was written while the second editor was supported by NIMH Training Grant MH 14235. We would like to thank the faculty and staff at the Yale University Depression Research Unit, particularly the director, Dr. Myrna Weissman, for helpful comments. Barbara Watkins from Springer Publishing Company provided generous assistance and editorial advice. Finally, we would like to thank Laura Solomon, who has truly been a part of the spirit of this book since its beginning, for her encouragement and her great support as a friend.

Violet Franks, Ph.D.
Esther D. Rothblum, Ph.D.

Contributors

Kathleen A. Brehony, Ph.D., Department of Psychology, Virginia Polytechnic Institute and State University, Blacksburg, Virginia.

Lynda M. Brown, M.Ed., Department of Educational Psychology, Temple University, Philadelphia, Pennsylvania.

Violet Franks, Ph.D., Chief Psychologist, The Carrier Foundation, Belle Mead, New Jersey.

Nikki Garret-Fulks, Doctoral Intern in Counseling Psychology, Department of Educational and Counseling Psychology, University of Kentucky, Lexington, Kentucky.

Jeffrey A. Kelly, Ph.D., Department of Psychiatry and Human Behavior, University of Mississippi Medical Center, Jackson, Mississippi.

Barbara Kirsh, Ph.D., Associate Research Scientist, Educational Testing Service, Princeton, New Jersey.

Sandra Risa Leiblum, Ph.D., Director, Sexual Counseling Service, Department of Psychiatry, Rutgers Medical School, Piscataway, New Jersey.

Charlene L. Muehlenhard, Ph.D., Department of Psychology, Texas A&M University, College Station, Texas.

Patricia A. Resick, PhD., Department of Psychology, University of Missouri, St. Louis, Missouri.

Esther D. Rothblum, Ph.D., Department of Psychology, University of Vermont, Burlington, Vermont.

Helen E. Tevlin, Ph.D., Clinical Psychologist in private practice. Portland, Oregon.

Marsha Weinraub, Ph.D., Director, Infant Behavior Laboratory, Department of Psychology, Temple University, Philadelphia, Pennsylvania.

Judith Worell, Ph.D., Department of Educational and Counseling Psychology, University of Kentucky, Lexington, Kentucky.

Marilyn Ann Zegman, Ph.D., Department of Psychology, University of Central Florida, Orlando, Florida.

■ one
INTRODUCTION

■ 1
Introduction: Warning!
Sex-Role Stereotypes
May Be Hazardous to Your Health

ESTHER D. ROTHBLUM and VIOLET FRANKS

> Melissa! Help the other children tidy up the classroom. You said you want
> to be a mommy when you grow up, and MOMMIES CLEAN! Comment
> given to kindergarten girl by her teacher, 1980, overheard by one of the
> editors.

Why devote a book to the impact of sex-role stereotypes on women's
mental health? The 1980s follow a decade of increasing change in wom-
en's roles. Many women have profited from equal opportunities with
men in employment, in legal issues, and in marital relationships, to
mention just a few examples. The women's movement has attempted to
break down traditional stereotypes about men and women in society.
Why, then, focus on "troubled" women in such an era of progress?

We, the editors, are feminists. We have experienced the proliferation of "women's liberation" in the 1970s through the use of television,
popular books, workshops, and other media to "raise women's consciousness." We are also clinical psychologists. Despite the changes in
society, we continue to find women overrepresented as patients in certain clinical problem areas, such as depression, agoraphobia, sexual
dysfunction, and lack of assertion. These problem areas seem "passive," in

3

contrast to the "acting out" areas in which men predominate, such as alcoholism, drug abuse, and certain personality disorders. The purpose of this book is to examine the discrepancy between the *rhetoric* presented by the media and the *reality* experienced by women in their everyday lives.

WHY GENERALIZE — A DEFINITION OF SEX-ROLE STEREOTYPES

> How we are fallen! Fallen by mistaken rules
> And Education's more than Nature's fools;
> Debarred from all improvement of the mind
> And to be dull, expected and designed
> And if someone would soar above the rest,
> With warmer fancy and ambitions pressed,
> So strong the opposing faction still appears,
> The hopes to thrive can ne'er outweigh the fears.
>
> *Lady Winchilsea,*
> *seventeenth-century Englishwoman*

It would be nice if just once we could read a volume that began, "When the first ancestor of the human race descended from the trees, she had not yet developed the mighty brain that was to distinguish her so sharply from all other species . . ." [Elaine Morgan,[1] *The Descent of Women*]

A stereotype is a set of beliefs about the nature of a particular group of individuals; thus, sex-role stereotypes are beliefs about the nature of women and men. These beliefs are ascribed to most men and women and are widely held by members of society (Deaux, 1976). Sex-role stereotypes do not describe how women and men *actually* differ, but how society *thinks* they do. Stereotypes about men and women often refer to personality traits such as "men are tough, rational, and adventurous," or "women are nurturant, tactful, and emotional." But stereotypes can describe any situation, such as "women go to college to find a husband,"

---

[1]The poem and the quotation are from an anthology by L. W. Clark, *Women, Women, Women: Quips, Quotes, and Commentary*. New York: Drake Publishers, 1977.

or "men feel threatened if their wives make a higher income than their's." Sex-role stereotypes are so familiar to us that, given no additional information other than the sex of a person, we are likely to ascribe certain traits and behaviors to him or her. Furthermore, sex-role stereotypes govern our own behavior. To varying degrees, we have learned to be good observers of human nature as we attempt to "fit in" to roles at school, at work, and in social situations.

Why make generalizations? Most people are aware that all rules have exceptions, and they can point out variations or extremes. Yet readers of this chapter may not be aware that they bought this book with the assumption that it would be written in English, that each copy of this book would contain the same information, and that the content, judging by the title, would not focus on math or Southeast Asia. Similarly, generalizations about people may indeed be true. Men, as a whole, do seem more aggressive, self-confident, and dominant than women. Women, in general, seem more nurturant, dependent, and self-devaluating than men. Within-group differences are greater than between-group differences; thus, some men are more nurturant than most women and some women are more self-confident than most men. Sex-role stereotypes, like other generalizations, do not allow for flexibility and are often deleterious. Thus, an employer who assumes women are not ambitious will refuse to hire a woman for a position that has good opportunities for advancement. A parent who believes that "boys don't cry" will encourage a son not to express certain emotions. Whenever we say (or imply) *"all* women . . ." in describing a characteristic that applies to 97 percent of women, we are ignoring an important three percent of exceptional women.

Even mental health professionals are not immune from sex-role stereotypes. Much has been written (see Menaker, 1974; Kaplan & Yasinki, 1980) on Sigmund Freud's "phallocentric" or penis-centered theory of personality, with its limited conceptions of women's roles. Menaker states:

Undoubtedly Freud observed penis envy in his female patients, and little wonder in a culture in which men were preferred. Freud's own familial situation in which he was so clearly favored by his mother as against his sisters is stereotypic for the culture and period in which he grew up (Jones, 1953) and [in which he] had much more freedom, many more rights, privileges, and opportunities for self-fulfillment. The women who consulted

Freud were indeed thwarted — thwarted by the values and sexual mores of their society and by the denigrated image of them which the male dominated culture projected onto them. For many of them their frustrations (and Freud was concerned primarily with sexual frustration) were expressed in neurotic symptoms, often of a hysterical nature, and it was for these that they sought help. Thus Freud's theories of feminine sexuality arose out of his therapeutic work with a specific population in a specific time and place. [1974, p. 233]

Thus, adhering to sex-role stereotypes can have harmful effects on the lives of the members of the stereotyped group. Stereotypes about women's passivity and dependence might lead to depression, rather than action, in stressful situations. Agoraphobia, or fear of leaving the home, may be the result of stereotypes and conflicts concerning women's roles as housewives. Sexual problems and problems in socializing after divorce and widowhood may be related to stereotypes about women's passive roles in interpersonal situations. This book will examine the relationship between traditional sex-role stereotypes about women and those clinical problems that affect women with greater preponderance than men.

WHAT THIS BOOK IS NOT ABOUT

It occurred to me when I was thirteen and wearing white gloves and Mary Janes and going to dancing school, that no one should have to dance backwards all their lives. [Jill Ruckelshaus, 1973[2]]

But what about women like myself? [Ursula Springer, Springer Publishing Company, personal communication to the editors, 1981.]

This book is not about the exceptional woman — the woman who is successfully pursuing a career in which few of her predecessors were female. We are living in an age during which a few women are beginning to receive tenure at prestigious universities, serve as chairpersons of the boards of large companies, be elected to the United States Senate, direct an orchestra, or — very recently — be appointed Supreme

[2]Taken from Clark, op cit.

Court Justice. Perhaps these women have advanced to positions usually reserved only for men because of unique constitutional or personality factors. Perhaps they have avoided potential difficulties through non-traditional childrearing or other environmental factors. Their lives present a fascinating account but do not provide the subject matter of this volume.

Nor is this book about the woman who has made the decision to become a mother and homemaker and is pursuing this goal with happiness and without difficulty. Traditional sex-role stereotypes about women do not conflict unduly with the roles of childrearing and housework; thus, women in these roles may not identify with the problems discussed in the following chapters.

Ironically, we too, the authors of this book, may seem to be categorizing or stereotyping women when we make unqualified statements in the following chapters. It must be kept in mind, consequently, that our focus is not on content, successful women who are pursuing life to its fullest potential. Individual differences are great, so when we say "women" we do not imply "every woman" or "all women;" rather, we are appraising and reporting trends.

Finally, this book is not about men. It is evident that sex-role stereotypes about men also result in problems of living; however, it is our opinion that until recently most research and theory in psychopathology has focused primarily on men. "Women's problems," when discussed at all, were included only as a chapter or subsection. Thus, it is our goal to concentrate on women's lives and the experiences that result in their psychopathology. Data on men will be described only as a means of comparison with women.

WHAT THIS BOOK IS ABOUT:
TROUBLED WOMEN

The phrase "to act like a lady" implies: (a) to be graceful, courteous, refined, and well-mannered; (b) to behave with overt forceful action, bold self-confidence, and ambition; (c) all of the above; (d) none of the above.

This book focuses on the negative effects of sex-role stereotypes about women. It is thus a discussion of mental health problems; of "troubled women." We shall examine how the pressures to be "normal" by conforming to sex-role stereotypes result in depression, sexual dysfunction, obesity, and other clinical problems. If traditional stereotypes conflict with a changing society, is a large proportion of women becoming dysfunctional? Even "liberated" women may conform to sex-role stereotypes more than is commonly believed. If they were raised to assume the responsibilities of childcare and housework, they now struggle to combine these with a career, resulting in new stresses and conflicts.

This book is directed at mental health professionals and students. It attempts to alert members of the mental health professions, who are working with women, to the dilemmas resulting from traditional sex roles. It evaluates the clinical problems that women are likely to experience as a consequence of societal forces. We hope that a fuller understanding of women's mental health problems will contribute to clinicians' understanding and expertise about sex-role "traps" and help them question their own belief systems.

The book summarizes current research on women and mental health. A decade ago, there was little research on environmental factors related to women's mental health problems. Recently, political interest in women's issues has resulted in some research; however, it has not focused equally on all areas of psychopathology and other problems affecting women, and so there are ample data in some areas and only preliminary information about others. The following chapters will discuss the research concerning specific mental health problems.

The book devotes considerable emphasis to future implications of sex-role stereotypes and women's mental health. While much can be criticized about current societal issues facing women, it is more difficult to provide recommendations for change. Thus, each chapter will conclude with suggested future implications involving research, treatment, or societal change.

OUR GOALS

Make policy, not coffee. [Motto of the Women's Political Caucus[3]]

The next three chapters in this, the introductory, section (Part One) of the book will address the following topics:

[3]Taken from Clark, op. cit.

Chapter 2. A more detailed introduction to the concepts of sex-role stereotypes, including a summary of theory and research in this area, will be given. The term *androgyny*, describing a balance between male and female characteristics, will be introduced and discussed in relation to adjustment and mental health (Kelly).

Chapter 3. This chapter, subtitled "crushing realities" will examine the development of sex-role stereotypes in children. The authors (Weinraub and Brown) will review the evidence for children's knowledge of and conformity to sex-typed behavior and some of the factors that contribute to the development of this behavior.

Chapter 4. Sex-role stereotypes will be described that are inherent in our language. We will discuss how they reflect psychological sex differences and what their implications for mental health are (Kirsh).

Now that society has focused attention on women's roles, it is time to analyze whether or not sex-role stereotypes reinforce conflict and dysfunction. In order to investigate the relationship between sex-role stereotypes and mental health problems, we purposely have selected problem areas in which women are overrepresented. Furthermore, we have chosen areas that are of fairly high prevalence, rather than rare or unusual phenomena. These problem areas will be discussed in the next two sections. Thus, Part Two includes traditional categories of psychopathology listed in the *Diagnostic and Statistical Manual of the American Psychiatric Association* (DSM III), including *depression* (Rothblum, Chapter 5), *agoraphobia* (Brehony, Chapter 6), and *sexual dysfunction* (Tevlin and Leiblum, Chapter 7). Part Three focuses on special problems of living, including *lack of assertion* (Muehlenhard, Chapter 8), *obesity* (Zegman, Chapter 9), *resocialization of single-again women* (Worell and Garret-Fulks, Chapter 10), and *violence against women* (Resick, Chapter 11).

Each chapter is designed to incorporate four goals: (1) to describe the prevalence of each disorder, with particular emphasis on women; (2) to discuss the contribution of sex-role stereotypes to the disorder; (3) to review relevant research on women in each area of mental health; and (4) to describe future implications for research and intervention in women's mental health. In sum, as we begin the 1980s, we ask: What is the reality and what are some solutions for the new woman?

Every decade in history has been accompanied by specific pressures to conform. Even during this century, there have been periods in the United States when women's traditional roles were questioned: the 1920s, the 1940s, and the 1960s. It is presumptuous of us to assume that the past decade is unique in the women's movement, yet none of these reappraisals or these attempts to liberalize women's roles can eliminate generations of stereotypes. In each period, *most* of society appears to remain unaffected by, if not unaware of, change.

In a computerized epoch, women are urged to seek out nontraditional careers and aspire to positions of status and power. But women continue to be socialized to be dependent and passive and to take care of the home and children. Feminists have raised women's awareness of this dilemma. Yet how many women are so strong that they can oppose societal pressures and cope with emotional cost? A shining new house in the suburbs may have a trap door, but will the townhouse of this decade fare any better? Which stereotypes should we cherish and which should we discard? Do androgynous women experience less stress and mental distress? What recommendations are optimal for permanent change in women's adjustment? These are the vital issues that will be the focus of this volume.

REFERENCES

Deaux, K. *The Behavior of Men and Women*. Monterey, Calif.: Brooks/Cole, 1976.

Kaplan, A. G., & Yasinski, L. Psychodynamic perspectives. In A. M. Brodsky & Hare-Mustin (Eds.), *Women and Psychotherapy*. New York: Guilford Press, 1980.

Menaker, E. The therapy of women in the light of psychoanalytic theory and the emergence of a new view. In Franks, V., & Burtle, V. (Eds.) *Women in Therapy: New Psychotherapies*. New York: Brunner/Mazel, 1974.

■ 2
Sex-Role Stereotypes and Mental Health: Conceptual Models in the 1970s and Issues for the 1980s

JEFFREY A. KELLY

The decade of the 1970s witnessed a tremendous proliferation of psychological research interest in the adjustive consequences of human sex-role orientation. Paralleling, or perhaps more accurately as a result of, feminist social and political activities, psychologists in the 1970s examined the adequacy of traditional theories of sex-role orientation, advanced new formulations of sex roles, devised measurement instruments to assess these new conceptual models, and began lines of empirical research to examine relationships between sex roles and lifestyle adjustment. This period of time has been an extremely productive one, both in terms of new conceptual models and empirical investigation; however, it is also a decade now behind us and, as such, it appears appropriate to comment on new directions for research in the 1980s. The purpose of this

The author extends appreciation to Andrew Bradlyn for his comments on this manuscript. Requests for reprints should be sent to Jeffrey A. Kelly, Department of Psychiatry and Human Behavior, University of Mississippi Medical Center, 2500 North State Street, Jackson, MS 39216.

paper is, first, to summarize briefly previous research on sex-role stereotypes and to then examine several promising avenues for future investigation. It is not possible to review exhaustively the entire body of sex-role
research in a relatively short article; instead, we will consider several
key developments that have given rise to new areas of investigation, focusing attention on sex roles as they relate to adjustment and mental health
issues.

TRADITIONAL MODELS
OF SEX-ROLE DEVELOPMENT

Historical formulations of sex roles have relied on two major assumptions. The first is that there exists a collection of behaviors, characteristics, attitudes or competencies that are associated strongly with one's
biological gender. Thus, knowing only the sex of a person, it would be
possible to predict, with some accuracy, how that individual would act,
feel, think, or approach certain situations. A second assumption underlying traditional models of sex-role orientation is that an individual
should exhibit these attributes that are associated with her or his gender
in order to be ideally adjusted. From this perspective, appropriate sex-
role orientation traditionally has been defined in terms of the "match"
between one's gender and those characteristics that are correlated with
being a male or a female. To the degree that this match is present, the
person would be considered sex typed.

At least three aspects of historical formulations of sex roles merit
comment. The first is that traditional theories of "appropriate" sex typing seem to have relied on a "normalcy equals the average" assumption.
Specifically, if one were to examine the behavior of *most* males and
most females, and if one were to find that persons of one gender more
frequently exhibited some characteristic, a sex difference on that characteristic would be established. If one takes this a step further and postu-
lates that normal behavior can be defined as that which the majority of
people exhibit, it becomes possible to define normal or appropriate female roles in terms of the average behavioral characteristics exhibited by
most women and normal, appropriate male roles in terms of the characteristics most frequently exhibited by most men. The "normalcy equals
the average" assumption has been relied upon quite frequently in the
psychological literature; within the historical sex-typing literature, this

assumption led to the seeming conclusion that because males are described more often as assertive, forceful, cognitive, and vocation or construction oriented, these characteristics are normal or appropriate in
males. Because females are described more often as nurturant, self-sub-
ordinative, emotional, unassertive, and home-oriented, these characteristics could be viewed as normal roles for females and the individual
who exhibits them would be considered appropriately sex typed (cf. discussions by Kagan, 1964; Kohlberg, 1966; Mussen, 1969). However,
there are a number of unfortunate consequences associated with normalcy
defined as an average. These include a perpetuation of the status quo in
relation to sex-stereotyped roles, a disregard for the possibility that even
highly sex-typed behaviors exhibited by persons of one gender may be
less than maximally adaptive for them, and so on. Nonetheless, historical formulations of "appropriate" sex roles appear to have relied very
heavily on this assumption.

A second aspect of traditional sex-role conceptualizations involves
the construal of masculinity and femininity as psychological "opposites."
In a now-classic paper, Constantinople (1973) reviewed many psycho-
metric scales intended to measure psychological masculinity and femininity (M–F), including those of the Minnesota Multiphasic Personality
Inventory, the California Psychological Inventory, and the Strong Vocational Interest Blank. Each of these inventories assesses masculinity
and femininity such that one direction of response to a scale item (i.e.,
"true") is indicative of masculinity, while the opposite direction of response ("false") to the same item indicates femininity. The items included in M–F scales are usually those which yield the clearest sex differentiation in direction of item endorsement. Thus, Constantinople (1973)
argued, traditional M–F scales create a bipolar sex-role continuum with
masculinity placed at one end of the range and femininity at the other.
Because of this bipolar construction, masculinity and femininity became
defined as mutually exclusive opposites. Under the scoring criteria used
for most M–F scales, the "ideal" profile for males is to achieve highly
masculine scores (i.e., to respond to scale items as most males do) and the
"ideal" female profile is to respond to the same items in the same direction as did most females in the scale's normative sample. The individual
not so sex stereotyped presumably would score somewhere in the midrange of the M–F scale continuum. Rather than reflecting adjustment or
some sense of positive personal liberation, however, midrange scores on
a bipolar M–F scale do not have clear meaning other than indicating sex-

role confusion, since the individual is responding *neither* as most males *nor* as most females, within the limitations of the scale's bipolar construction properties.

A third aspect of traditional sex-role formulations involves the development antecedents of sex typing. Almost all major personality theories have stressed the importance of developmental experiences that promote a child's adoption of an "appropriately" typed sex-role identity (i.e., the acquisition of masculine characteristics in males and feminine characteristics in females). Psychoanalytic theories, in particular, have relied heavily on the notion of necessary identification in early childhood with the same-sex parent to achieve sex typing and have viewed outcomes other than masculine typing in males or feminine typing in females to be symptomatic of developmental pathology (Freud, 1949; Mussen & Distler, 1959; Sears, 1957; Whiting & Child, 1953). Other theories have postulated different mechanisms to account for sex typing in childhood, including the incorporation of appropriate sex-role stereotypes into children's cognitive schema (Kohlberg, 1966) and behavioral contingencies that differentially reinforce sterrotypically masculine behaviors in boys and stereotypically feminine behavior in girls and punish any "cross-typed" responses that may occur (Bandura, 1969; Grusec & Brinker, 1972). Regardless of the principles used to account for the sex typing of social behavior in childhood, however, it appears that traditional personality development theories have assumed widely that rigid role typing is a normal and desirable aspect of early life socialization and that the failure to acquire either a masculine-typed or feminine-typed role style is both indicative of past developmental disturbance and predictive of future life-adjustment problems.

As we will see, theorists in the 1970s challenged each of these traditional sex-role assumptions. Specifically, recent research has (1) questioned whether optimal developmental experiences should result in rigid sex-role stereotyping, (2) questioned the utility of a bipolar conceptualization of femininity and masculinity, and (3) examined how sex typing can inhibit adaptive, adjusted behavior in females and males.

NEW FORMULATIONS OF SEX-ROLE STYLE

Following Constantinople's critique (1973) of bipolar M–F scales, a number of investigators proposed an alternative sex-role formulation that treats femininity and masculinity as nonmutually exclusive psychological domains (Bem, 1974; Spence, Helmreich, & Stapp, 1975; Berzins, Welling, & Wetter, 1978). This has been accomplished psychometrically by creating sex-role self-report inventories that include separate, nonoverlapping scales for femininity and masculinity. Examples are the Bem Sex-Role Inventory (BSRI; Bem, 1974), the Personal Attributes Questionnaire (PAQ; Spence et al., 1975) and the PRF ANDRO Scale (Berzins et al., 1978). Masculinity has been construed generally to include such characteristics as assertiveness, instrumentality, social ascendance, forcefulness, and a cognitive task orientation; femininity has been defined to include such characteristics as affectivity, sensitivity, supportiveness, self-subordination, tenderness and kindness (see Kelly & Worell, 1977). However, in contrast to traditional sex-role models, femininity and masculinity are conceptualized and measured as independent dimensions. Thus, a person could be considered sex typed masculine if she or he is high in masculine characteristics and low in feminine characteristics, sex typed feminine if she or he is high in feminine characteristics and low in masculine ones, or androgynous if there is a balance between the two (Bem, 1974). Following some debate in the research literature, androgynous roles generally have become defined in terms of not only a proportional balance between masculinity and femininity, but also the presence of each characteristic at high levels (high masculine–high feminine) (Bem, 1977; Berzins et al., 1978, Kelly & Worell, 1976; Spence et al., 1975; Strahan, 1975). The endorsement of few masculine and feminine characteristics reflects neither a sex-typed role (since the individual is high in neither) nor an androgynous role (since the individual is not high in both); hence it has been termed "undifferentiated" or "indeterminate" in orientation.

Perhaps the most striking implication of sex-role formulations advanced in the 1970s is the suggestion that an ideally adjusted individual will not be sex typed, but instead androgynous, in his or her role orientation. Bem, for example, has argued that while highly sex-typed persons will exhibit effective behavior in situations requiring responses consistent with their sex typing (e.g., assertiveness for a highly masculine individual and compassion for a highly feminine individual), they also will exhibit behavioral *deficits* in situations calling for opposite-typed responses (Bem, 1974, 1975; Bem & Lenney, 1976; Bem, Martyna, & Watson, 1976). As an example, the highly feminine-typed woman may handle effectively interactions that require kindness, tenderness, and compassion but fail to exhibit assertion, forcefulness, and cognitive task orientation even when these characteristics are appropriate. On the other hand, the androgynous individual (regardless of that person's gender) should be in a position to handle effectively a wide range of situations and exhibit adaptive behavioral flexibility by virtue of a psychological makeup that includes both desirable masculine *and* desirable feminine response capabilities (cf. Bem, 1975; Kelly, O'Brien, & Hosford, 1981; Kelly & Worell, 1977). Presumably, undifferentiated orientations (reflecting the relative absence of either masculine or feminine characteristics) should be related to the ineffective handling of situations, since the individual is endorsing few desirable attributes of either kind.

A great deal of recent research literature has been devoted to validating the constructs of sex-typed, androgynous, and undifferentiated sex roles. Bem and her associates, for example have compared the performance of persons categorized as feminine typed, masculine typed, or androgynous (based upon the BSRI) on tasks that require the expression of stereotypically masculine behavior (such as social-attitudinal nonconformity) and stereotypically feminine behavior (such as play with a kitten or a human infant or nurturance exhibited to an unhappy-appearing confederate in a conversation) (Bem, 1975; Bem & Lenney, 1976; Bem et al., 1976). In these studies, persons describing themselves as androgynous have exhibited the general behavioral competence conceptually ascribed to this role orientation, while sex-typed roles were related to performance deficits in tasks calling for adaptive but cross-typed responses. One exception to this pattern involved feminine roles in females, which have not been associated consistently with behavioral competence even in situations where stereotypically nurturant responses were required (Bem, 1975; Bem et al., 1976). In similar assessment paradigms, Rodriquez, Nietzel, & Berzins (1980) and Kelly, O'Brien, & Hosford (1981) related self-report sex-role categorization to performance in role-play situations requiring assertiveness. Both of these recent projects found that androgynous roles were associated with effective social skills and undifferentiated roles were connected with ineffective skills. The Rodriquez et al. (1980) study also confirmed the expected relationship between masculine typing and the ability to assert oneself when confronted with a portrayed antagonist's unreasonable behavior.

A substantial body of research also has related sex-role orientation, assessed by the BSRI, PAQ, or PRF ANDRO scale, to other self-report measures of adjustment or personality. For example, high self-esteem scores have been associated frequently with both androgynous and masculine typed sex roles in females and males; significantly lower self-esteem is reported by persons classified as feminine typed or undifferentiated (cf. Antill & Cunningham, 1979; Bem, 1977; Jones, Chernovetz, & Hansson, 1978; O'Connor, Mann, & Bardwick, 1978; Spence et al., 1975). Since elevated self-esteem is related consistently to the endorsement of masculine characteristics occurring in masculine-typed and androgynous roles, several investigators have suggested that it is principally the presence of masculinity in both females and males that contributes to their improved evaluations of self-worth (Antill & Cunningham, 1979; Jones et al., 1978). In fact, in an unusually comprehensive program of studies relating sex-role orientation to both behavioral and self-report measures of adjustment, Jones et al. (1978) concluded that flexibility and adaptive responses almost always were associated with masculinity and that feminine-typed persons (regardless of their gender) indicated a preference for exhibiting more masculine sex-role traits if that were possible. Other studies have established relationships between androgynous (or androgynous and masculine-typed) roles and self-report indices of personality adjustment (Berzins et al., 1978), autobiographical life-adjustment (Helmreich, Wilhelm, & Stapp, 1975; Woods, 1975), and positive child-rearing practices (Kelly & Worell, 1976). However, it is important to note that the methodology used to establish many of these findings relied only upon correlating self-report scales with one another, a potentially serious research limitation since it leaves open the possibility of substantial variance attributable to the method of self-report assessment alone and evaluates only subject self-reports of behavior (Campbell & Fiske, 1959; Kelly & Worell, 1977; Worell, 1978).

If we were to summarize several of the major developments in the sex-role research of the 1970s, they might well include the following. First, the traditional bipolar conceptualization of masculinity–femininity has been replaced gradually with the notions that both of these domains of positively valued characteristics represent orthogonal, unrelated dimensions and are not psychological opposites. Second, and following from this, new sex-role formulations hypothesize that optimal adjustment will be achieved by persons of either gender who exhibit the ability to combine masculine- and feminine-stereotyped responses, depending upon the situation in which they are engaged. This "androgyny equals adjustment" assumption has received mixed empirical support in the research, since it appears that masculinity in both females and males primarily contributes to positive adjustment indices, leaving unclear the manner in which stereotypic femininity independently contributes to enhanced adjustment. With respect to females, however, the research does seem to indicate clearly that rigid, stereotypically feminine sex roles are *not* those maximally associated with psychological well-being. Perhaps demonstrating this with empirical data and thus extending the issue beyond that of a social cause was one of the major contributions of sex-role research in the past decade.

On the other hand, one might argue that recent directions of sex-role research, while conceptually promising, now may be moving toward some empirical impasses. One of them is that the sex-typed-versus-androgyny literature has focused almost exclusively on examining self-report, personality, and behavioral correlates to paper-and-pencil measures of sex-role style (such as the BSRI, PAQ and PRF ANDRO scales). A very common research strategy has been to administer a brief sex-role scale to a large sample of college students, assign subjects into sex-role categories (sex typed, androgynous, or undifferentiated) based on their scale scores, and then compare the resultant categories on some self-report or, perhaps, behavioral measure. This methodological approach can serve initially to validate new sex-role constructs (such as androgyny) and provide validation for sex-role self-report inventories. It is also a relatively "easy" research strategy. However, defining, categorizing, and labeling an individual's sex-role orientation based upon item endorsements on an inventory also can divert important attention from the fact that the sex-roles actually represent relatively complex, situationally determined, behavioral skill repertoires. To this point, much of the sex-role literature has been confined to the assignment of individuals to typological categories and the creation of labels to describe the personality makeup of persons within a given category. Constructs such as "masculinity," "femininity," or even "androgyny" have been used as trait labels and as though they were characteristics that people possess." Are there alternative ways to examine sex-role style which carry greater clinical and applied relevance?

SEX ROLES AS BEHAVIORAL SKILL REPERTOIRES: AN ALTERNATIVE TO TRAIT LABELS

Elsewhere, we have observed that the items comprising most sex-role inventories concern the respondent's perception of her or his own social behavior or interpersonal competence (Kelly, O'Brien, & Hosford, 1981; Kelly, Wildman, & Urey, unpublished; Kelly & Worell, 1977). Self-descriptors such as assertive, forceful, independent, kind, tender, and emotional all have, as their behavioral referents, the interpersonal conduct of the respondent. Consequently, one might argue that what we term "sex roles" actually represent the strategies, often interpersonal, that persons use to obtain (or maintain) reinforcement from their environment. At this level of analysis, individuals who have been called masculine typed are those who exhibit well-developed social competencies in assertion, forcefulness, decision making, leadership, and so on; while feminine-typed persons should exhibit competence in more affective, commendatory, sensitive, and emotional social skills. Individuals termed adrogynous are those who apparently have learned to exhibit a wide range of qualitatively and functionally diverse skills and thus have the most elaborated repertoire of behavioral competencies for obtaining reinforcement. Individuals with undifferentiated roles exhibit pervasive social incompetence.

Interestingly, one then might question whether trait labels such as masculine, feminine, or androgynous will continue to serve a useful purpose in the sex-role literature and whether brief sex-role inventories represent a behaviorally or clinically useful method from which to approach and measure sex-role orientation. If we reflect on the recent history of personality assessment in clinical psychology, it is apparent that traditional trait-or typology-based global personality descriptors derived from self-report inventories increasingly are criticized for their imprecision, lack of behavioral validity, and limited relevance to clinical treatment (Mischel, 1968). In similar fashion, taking too literally the notion that a person's sex-role orientation can be "discovered," quantified, and meaningfully labeled from responses to sex-role scale items may prevent future research from focusing attention on the behaviors these labels represent and the adjustive consequences of those competencies. Sex-role research in the 1980s might retain the important conceptualizations of masculinity, femininity, and androgyny advanced by Constantinople (1973), Bem (1974), Spence et al. (1975), and others, but it should explore alternative methods to self-report scales to assess them.

PSYCHOLOGICAL DISORDERS
IN RELATION TO SEX ROLES

An area that is only beginning to receive research attention involves the relationship between psychological disorders and sex roles. As other chapters in this book elaborate, there are a number of behavioral and psychological difficulties that have been associated with one's sex or, perhaps more accurately, with one's sex-role orientation. For example, depression (Radloff, 1975; Woodruff, Goodwin, & Guze, 1974), agoraphobia (Davison & Neale, 1978; Marks, 1969), and lack of assertiveness (Alberti & Emmons, 1974; Hollandsworth & Wall, 1977) have each been reported as far more problematic for females than for males; aggressive disorders and violent behavior are reported more commonly among males than females (Feshbach & Feshbach, 1973; Heterington & Parke, 1979; Maccoby & Jacklin, 1974). Even in these allegedly liberated times, however, the largest proportion of females are feminine typed and most males are masculine typed in their sex-role orientation (Bem, 1974; Berzins et al., 1978). Thus, behavioral disorders that occur more frequently among females than males, or vice versa, may not be associated with gender but instead with the sex-role typing that predominates among persons of that gender. In some cases, behavioral difficulties *have* been related empirically to sex-role style rather than gender; for example, the Rodriquez et al. (1980) finding that women with a highly feminine sex-role orientation are less assertive than nonfeminine-typed women when handling an unreasonable antagonist in a role-play situation illustrates such a relationship. For the most part, however, studies of sex differences in psychological disorders have not yet systematically taken into account the effect of sex-role orientation independent of the person's biological gender. When this is done, we may find that rigidity of sex-role orientation more strongly predicts some sex-differentiated disorders than does gender.

From the previously described response repertoire formulation of sex roles, one might hypothesize certain relationships between role orientation and maladjustments. As noted earlier, an individual who is not sex-role stereotyped presumably has a wide array of behavioral response options for dealing with various life situations. These could include multiple strategies for obtaining reinforcement from the environment, a range of ways to resolve conflict, various behaviors that can be used to deal with threats to one's self-esteem, and the perception of diverse solutions to problem areas that are encountered. On the other hand, rigid sex typing implies that an individual utilizes a relatively restricted set of behaviors when interacting in the environment and has, therefore, fewer response options at her or his disposal in a given situation. To illustrate how this may relate to behavior disorders, let us consider the examples of depression, unassertiveness, agoraphobia and other anxiety disorders, and aggression.

Depression

While there are many theories on the development of depression, some recent behavioral theories have focused on deficits in the individual's instrumental capacity to obtain reinforcement from the environment (Lewinsohn, 1974; Lewinsohn & Libet, 1972). When avenues for obtaining significant reinforcers are limited or ineffective, the probability of depression increases. Further, once depressed and inactive, an individual then will be even less likely to engage in behaviors that can lead to reinforcing outcomes, and the depression becomes perpetuated.

From a behavioral-repertoire perspective of sex roles, both highly masculine- and feminine-sex-typed persons utilize relatively restricted strategies for obtaining environmental reinforcers compared to their nonsex-typed counterparts. Thus, in theory, the stereotypically masculine man and the stereotypically feminine woman *each* should have quantitatively fewer response options to reinforcement than persons not so inhibited by role stereotypes, and they should be equally prone to depression if this behavioral model is correct. The reality is, however, that the incidence of depression is higher among females. One possible explanation is that masculine and feminine roles or behaviors have different "utility values" (Kelly & Worell, 1977); specifically, stereotypically feminine responses such as kindness, emotionality, self-subordination, or gentleness may be less effective for obtaining reinforcement in this society than stereotypically masculine responses such as assertiveness, forcefulness, leadership ascendancy, and social dominance (Jones et al., 1978). Consequently, the woman whose behavioral repertoire is limited to feminine-typed behaviors would be likely to reach fewer reinforcing goals than the male whose repertoire is similarly restricted to masculine-typed behaviors. An increased proneness to depression thereby would be predicted for females.

Unassertiveness

Assertiveness refers to the ability to effectively and appropriately express one's beliefs, opinions, or viewpoints to others. While there are many types of assertiveness, the form that has received the greatest attention in the literature is refusal assertion; this includes such competencies as dealing effectively with antagonists who would otherwise thwart one's own goal-directed behavior, expressing disagreeing viewpoints, or defending one's own position in interpersonal conflict situations. Presumably, by failing to develop these competencies, an individual would be more susceptible to frustration, reduced self-esteem, and increased inappropriate imposition by others.

Women, in general, have been found to be less assertive than men with respect to refusal assertiveness (cf. Alberti & Emmons, 1974; Hollandsworth & Wall, 1977), and it appears that traditional sex-role expectations reinforce assertive responding in males but fail to reinforce (or may even punish) the development of similar behavior among females. To illustrate this, in one of our recent studies (Kelly, Kern, Kirkley, Patterson, & Keane, 1980), college students were shown videotapes of a male or a female behaving assertively or passively when confronted with the unreasonable behavior of another person. Videotape model behavior was matched such that the assertive females and assertive males behaved in an identical manner, while the passive males and passive females also behaved comparably. When college student observers were asked to evaluate the "personality" of the model they just saw, the observers consistently rated assertive female models *lower* than the identically behaving assertive male models on indices such as thoughtfulness, kindness, warmth, likability, friendliness, being open-minded, being good-natured, being considerate, and so on. One interpretation of this finding is that when the female models were exhibiting appropriate refusal assertion skills, they also were exhibiting a competence inconsistent with the stereotyped feminine sex role. The problem, of course, is that in situations where refusal assertiveness is appropriate, adaptive, and necessary, traditional role stereotypes may operate to punish differentially women's skills for behaving assertively and forthrightly. Reduced self-esteem and frustration of goal-directed behavior then would follow.

Agoraphobia and Similar Anxiety Disorders

Increased clinical attention now is being focused on agoraphobia, a disorder characterized by (1) extreme fearfulness and panic in open situations requiring independent social behavior, (2) a housebound activity lifestyle, (3) helplessness, (4) feelings of being trapped, and (5) excessive passivity. Once again, the incidence of agoraphobia is much higher among females than males. Brehony (1980) has pointed out that there is a high similarity between the characteristics that agoraphobic individuals use to describe themselves and those characteristics associated with a highly feminine-typed sex-role orientation. Indeed, agoraphobia often appears to represent an extreme adoption of a rigidly feminine-typed sex role, with many of its victims virtually incapacitated in situations outside the home and other familiar settings. It would appear that agoraphobics lack, or in any event fail to use, effective coping skills to deal with anxiety in situations where they are the focus of attention, will need to behave independently, or are in the open. However, although agoraphobia seems, on a descriptive level, to reflect an exaggerated version of feminine role stereotyping, the development of the disorder has yet to receive definitive empirical attention.

Aggression

Depression, unassertiveness, and agoraphobia are all disorders that are found more frequently among females; aggressive and violent behavior are reported widely to be more common among males (Feshback & Feshback, 1973 Hetherington & Parke, 1979; Maccoby & Jacklin, 1974). Just as extreme passivity and depression may be the byproducts of extreme feminine typing in some women, aggressiveness appears to be an unfortunate consequence of exaggerated self-definitions of masculinity in some men. It is important to note that most formulations of masculinity do *not* include overt aggression and violence as part of an acceptable masculine role, any more than socially acceptable feminity includes extreme helplessness and proneness to depression. However, if an individual's social skills repertoire is largely limited to certain types of acceptable masculine behavior such as assertiveness, forcefulness, and dominance, those responses might escalate to less socially acceptable aggression under circumstances when (1) aggressiveness is likely to be reinforced by one's peers or by people one respects (2) the individual perceives that aggression is consistent with a masculine sex-role "identity," or (3) the individual does not have the competencies to handle conflict situations in ways other than through aggressive or violent behavior. In each of these cases, aggression would be more likely to accompany rigid masculine-typed-roles.

While a number of behavioral disorders can be conceptualized plausibly in relation to sex-role style, there has been very little empirical research in this area. Further, even if one were to establish objectively correlational relationships between sex-role rigidity and proneness to certain behavioral disorders, it would require more elaborate methodologies to demonstrate casual relationships between sex roles and indices of adjustment or maladjustment. In the 1970s, much of the sex-role and androgyny literature has relied upon "normal" college student samples and has used analogue adjustment paradigms. An important goal for the 1980s may be to integrate more directly sex-role "personality" research with research on clinical disorders.

PSYCHOLOGICAL TREATMENT AND SEX-ROLE CHANGE

Another conceptual rapprochement can be made between sex-role research and clinical treatment, especially with respect to women's mental health issues. Many of the behavioral treatments now used for emotional problems reported by women seem, most fundamentally, to increase the behavioral repertoire of the female client. Often, treatment takes the form of enhancing behaviors that might be considered as traditionally masculine. Assertiveness training for women is one of the clearest examples, since it attempts directly to build and reinforce important interpersonal competencies that are excluded by traditionally feminine sex roles (cf. Bloom, Coburn, & Pearlman, 1975; Jakubowski-Spector, 1973). While most past research on dating skills has focused primarily on teaching males to initiate date interactions, attention now has been given to specifically equipping females with similar date-initiation competencies (Muehlenhard & McFall, 1981). The treatment of depression (and, in similar fashion, of agoraphobia) often includes such procedures as assertiveness training, teaching the client to identify a wide range of possible solutions to problems, instruction on assuming greater personal control over one's behavior and feelings, and increasing the sheer number of effective response skills available to the individual. All of these are therapy techniques that can add behavioral flexibility to formerly narrow sex roles and encourage the female client to develop nonsex-stereotyped ways of handling difficult situations.

Viewing such clinical treatment as the alteration of a client's own sex-role rigidity raises the therapy issue that may become increasingly relevant in the coming decade. Therapists who treat women will often find themselves addressing adjustive problems that have been brought about, or at least perpetuated, by past and current sex-role stereotypes. Effective treatment may well involve teaching the client to exhibit new behaviors or competencies that are inconsistent with sex-role stereotypes traditionally reinforced in our society. This, of necessity, will place the therapist not only in the usual role of clinician or treatment provider but also in the role of social change agent. It is important to recognize that sex-role stereotypes are not simply minor but annoying anachronisms that have carried over from the past; instead, they represent strong contingencies that differentially reinforce certain important behaviors in women and men. Because these sex-role stereotypes *do* continue to exist, the client who first learns to exhibit nontraditional competencies may be in a position not only for greater growth but also greater social risk in the form of potentially negative responses from others. The previously described study showing differential reactions to assertiveness exhibited by males and females illustrates such a possibility (Kelly et al., 1980). To extrapolate this finding to the issue of treatment, it would appear that women learning to behave assertively will encounter less social reinforcement (or more social punishment) than will men. Here, the potential benefit of exhibiting a new behavior inconsistent with stereotyped sex roles is an increase in the female client's ability to express opinions, offer disagreeing viewpoints, and resist unreasonable behavior; the potential social risk is that by exhibiting these very competencies, the client may elicit negative evaluations in a society that still reinforces sex-role stereotypes. This issue potentially holds true not only for assertiveness training but for any behavior change that brings client competencies into conflict with existing societal sex-role expectations.

The therapist treating clients under these circumstances might consider the following several issues that can facilitate behavior change. Although these issues are relevant to any form of therapy, they may be especially important when working with individuals whose adaptive behavior is inhibited by the existence of sex-role stereotypes.

Use of Treatment Techniques That Increase the Skills Repertoire of the Client. We might postulate that some clients have not learned important competencies because the acquisition of those behaviors was hindered due to sex-role stereotypes. Examples among some women include refusal assertiveness, forceful problem solving, active decision making, or the development of athletic leisure-time pursuits; among men, feeling-oriented communication styles, commendatory assertion, and emotional tenderness are skills that are inconsistent with traditionally masculine sex typing. If an individual does, indeed, lack such important competencies, one goal of treatment may be to train them directly. Presumably, most people learn adaptive skills naturally as a result of observing skilled models, having opportunities to practice responses in the natural environment, and receiving feedback and reinforcement from others. Sex-role stereotyping can function to prevent the natural learning of skills that have been considered traditionally "appropriate" for persons of the other sex. Consequently, treatment consisting of modeling, behavior rehearsal, feedback, and therapist-administered reinforcement may be particularly useful for establishing new skills in the individual's adaptive repertoire.

Cognitive Techniques to Expand the Client's Perception of Possible Response Options. Rigid sex-role stereotyping implies not only that the client's *behavioral* repertoire is limited in accordance with social expectations, but also that the individual *believes* that only certain responses are acceptable for persons of her or his gender. If an individual's behavior is restricted sufficiently to be causing emotional distress, clinical techniques that challenge a narrow view of oneself may be useful. Possible strategies include having the client "brainstorm" many possible ways to handle troublesome situations (regardless of their presumed appropriateness for males or females), analyzing with the client the potential benefits versus risks of various responses (such as behaving assertively or unassertively in a specific situation), or assisting the client in changing unadaptive or irrational behavior-inhibiting beliefs about sex roles. It is crucial, of course, that individuals first have acquired the skills to actually handle situations in a new manner.

Further Attention to Efforts to Prevent or Alter the Negative Effects of Sex-Role Stereotyping. While clinical treatment often must be directed to the individual client, there appears to be an emerging consensus in the professional community that rigid sex-role stereotypes inhibit the growth and functioning of a large number of people. During the past decade, one can identify a variety of attempts to correct this stereotyping, including the advocacy of nonsexist language, media portrayals of women and men in nontraditional roles, challenges to vocational and educational sex-based "tracking," affirmative-action programs, and so on. Assessing the impact of these efforts and developing other larger-scale social change projects to reduce sex-role stereotypes are areas that will become increasingly important in the decade before us.

REFERENCES

Alberti, R. E., & Emmons, M. L. *Your perfect right: A guide to assertive behavior.* San Luis Obispo, California: Impact, 1974.

Antill, J. K., & Cunningham, J. D. Self-esteem as a function of masculinity in both sexes. *Journal of Consulting and Clinical Psychology,* 1979, *47,* 783–785.

Bandura, A. Social learning theory of identificatory process. In D. A. Goslin (Ed.), *Handbook of socialization theory and research.* Chicago: Rand McNally, 1969.

Bem, S. L. The measurement of psychological androgyny. *Journal of Consulting and Clinical Psychology,* 1974, *42,* 155–162.

Bem, S. L. Sex role adaptability: One consequence of psychological androgyny. *Journal of Personality and Social Psychology,* 1975, *31,* 634–643.

Bem, S. L. On the utility of alternative procedures for assessing psychological androgyny. *Journal of Consulting and Clinical Psychology,* 1977, *45,* 196–205.

Bem, S. L., & Lenney, E. Sex typing and the avoidance of cross-sex behavior. *Journal of Personality and Social Psychology,* 1976, *33,* 48–54.

Bem, S. L., Martyna, W., & Watson, C. Sex typing and androgyny: Further explorations of the expressive domain. *Journal of Personality and Social Psychology,* 1976, *34,* 1016–1023.

Berzins, J. I., Welling, M. A., & Wetter, R. E. A new measure of psychological androgyny based on the Personality Research Form. *Journal of Consulting and Clinical Psychology,* 1978, *46,* 126–138.

Bloom, L. Z., Coburn, K. L., & Pearlman, J. C. *The new assertive woman.* New York: Delacorte Press, 1975.

Brehony, K. A. Agoraphobia. In V. Franks (Chair), *Sex differences in psychological/behavioral problems: Research issues and implications for behavior therapy.* Symposium presented to the Annual meeting of the Association for the Advancement of Behavior Therapy, New York, November 1980.

Campbell, D. T., & Fiske, D. W. Convergent and discriminant validation by the multitrait–multimethod matrix. *Psychological Bulletin,* 1959, *56,* 81–105.

Constantinople, A. Masculinity–femininity: An exception to the famous dictum. *Psychological Bulletin,* 1973, *80,* 389–407.

Davison, G. C., & Neale, J. M. *Abnormal psychology: An experimental clinical approach.* New York: John Wiley & Sons, 1978.

Feshbach, S., & Feshbach, N. The young aggressors. *Psychology Today,* 1973, *6,* 90–95.

Freud, S. *An outline of psychoanalysis.* New York: Norton, 1949.

Grusec, J. E., & Brinker, D. B. Reinforcement for imitation as a social learning determinant with implications for sex-role development. *Journal of Personality and Social Psychology*, 1972, *21*, 149–158.

Helmreich, R., Wilhelm, J., & Stapp, J. Life History Questionnaire (short form): Instrument, norms, and intercorrelations. *JSAS Catalog of Selected Documents in Psychology*, 1975, *5*, 327 (Ms. no. 1098).

Hetherington, E. M., & Parke, R. D. *Child psychology: A contemporary viewpoint.* New York: McGraw-Hill, 1979.

Hollandsworth, J. G., & Wall, K. E. Sex differences in assertive behavior: An empirical investigation. *Journal of Counseling Psychology*, 1977, *24*, 217–222.

Jakubowski-Spector, P. Facilitating the growth of women through assertive training. *The Counseling Psychologist*, 1973, *4*, 75–86.

Jones, W. H., Chernovetz, M. E., & Hansson, R. O. The enigma of androgyny: Differential implications for males and females? *Journal of Consulting and Clinical Psychology*, 1978, *46*, 298–313.

Kagan, J. Acquisition and significance of sex-typing and sex-role identity. In M. L. Hoffman & L. W. Hoffman (Eds.), *Review of child development Research.* New York: Russell Sage Foundation, 1964.

Kelly, J. A., Kern, J. M., Kirkley, B. G., Patterson, J. N., & Keane, T. M. Reactions to assertive versus unassertive behavior: Differential effects for males and females, and implications for assertive training. *Behavior Therapy*, 1980, *11*, 670–682.

Kelly, J. A., O'Brien, C. G., & Hosford, R. Sex roles and social skills: Considerations for interpersonal adjustment. *Psychology of Women Quarterly*, 1981, *5*, 758–766.

Kelly, J. A., Wildman, H., & Urey, J. R. Gender and sex role differences in group decision-making social interactions: A behavioral analysis. Unpublished study, 1978.

Kelly, J. A., & Worell, L. Parent behaviors related to masculine, feminine and androgynous sex role orientations. *Journal of Consulting and Clinical Psychology*, 1976, *44*, 843–851.

Kelly, J. A., & Worell, J. New formulations of sex roles and androgyny: A critical review. *Journal of Consulting and Clinical Psychology*, 1977, 45, 1101–1115.

Kohlberg, L. A cognitive-developmental analysis of children's sex role concepts and attitudes. In E. E. Maccoby (Ed.), *The development of sex differences.* Stanford, Calif.: Stanford University Press, 1966.

Lewinsohn, P. H. A behavioral approach to depression. In R. J. Friedman and M. M. Katz (Eds.), *The psychology of depression: Contemporary theory and research.* Washington, D.C.: Winston-Wiley, 1974.

Lewinsohn, P. H., & Libet, J. M. Pleasant events, activity schedules and depressions. *Journal of Abnormal Psychology*, 1972, 79, 291–295.

Maccoby, E. E., & Jacklin, C. N. *The psychology of sex differences.* Stanford, Calif.: Stanford University Press, 1974.

Marks, I. M. *Fears and phobias.* New York: Academic Press, 1969.

Mischel, W. *Personality and assessment.* New York: Wiley, 1968.

Muehlenhard, C. L., & McFall, R. M. Dating initiation from a woman's perspective. *Behavior Therapy*, 1981, *12*, 682–691.

Mussen, P. H. Early sex-role development. In D. A. Goslin (Ed.), *Handbook of socialization theory and research.* Chicago: Rand McNally, 1969.

Mussen, P. H., & Distler, L. Masculinity, identification and father–son relationships. *Journal of Abnormal and Social Psychology*, 1959, 59, 350–356.

O'Connor, K., Mann, D. W., & Bardwick, J. M. Androgyny and self-esteem in the upper-middle class: A replication of Spence. *Journal of Consulting and Clinical Psychology*, 1978, *46*, 1168–1169.

Radloff, L. Sex differences in depresion: The effects of occupation and marital status. *Sex Roles*, 1975, *1*, 249–265.

Rodriquez, R., Nietzel, M. T., & Berzins, J. I. Sex role orientation and assertiveness among female college students. *Behavior Therapy*, 1980, *11*, 353–366.

Sears, R. R. Identification as a form of behavioral development. In D. B. Harris (Ed.), *The concept of development.* Minneapolis: University of Minnesota Press, 1957.

Spence, J. T., Helmreich, R., & Stapp, J. Ratings of self and peers on sex role attributes and their relation to self-esteem and conceptions of masculinity and femininity. *Journal of Personality and Social Psychology*, 1975, *32*, 29–39.

Strahan, R. F. Remarks on Bem's measurement of psychological androgyny: Alternative methods and a supplementary analysis. *Journal of Consulting and Clinical Psychology*, 1975, *43*, 568–571.

Whiting, J. W. M., & Child, I. L. *Child training and personality.* New Haven: Yale University Press, 1953.

Woodruff, R. A., Goodwin, D. W., & Guze, S. B. *Psychiatric diagnosis.* New York: Oxford University Press, 1974.

Woods, M. M. The relation of sex role categories to autobiographical factors. Paper presented to the Annual Meeting of the American Psychological Association, Chicago, August 1975.

Worell, J. Sex roles and psychological well-being: Perspectives on methodology. *Journal of Consulting and Clinical Psychology*, 1978, *46*, 777–791.

■ 3
The Development of Sex-Role Stereotypes in Children: Crushing Realities

MARSHA WEINRAUB and LYNDA M. BROWN

A question frequently asked of young children is "What do you want to be when you grow up?" The replies are disquieting. "When I grow up I want to fly like a bird. But I'll never do it because I'm not a boy." "A girl? Oh, if I were a girl I'd have to grow up to be nothing."

Are these answers from long ago, replies from an unenlightened era? Unfortunately, they are not. These answers are from interviews conducted in 1973 with middle-class children from 3 to 6 years of age (Beuf, 1974). More recent studies, as well as simple observations of young children today, suggest that these replies are not outmoded. They reflect cultural realities as well as sex-role stereotypes of adults in our society.

This article reflects the equal contributions of both authors and was prepared while both authors were supported by Grant number R01 MH/HD32189 from the National Institute of Mental Health. Requests for reprints should be sent to Marsha Weinraub, Infant Behavior Laboratory, Department of Psychology, Temple University, Philadelphia, Penn. 19122.

The development of sex-role stereotypes is a relatively recent area of interest to psychologists. Previous psychological research in the area of sex-role development focused on children's sex-role preference, sex-typed preferences, perceived sex-role similarity, sex-role adoption, sex-role identification, and sex-role orientation (Lynn, 1969; Biller, 1976). What children consider appropriate for their sex has been of little concern. Over the last decade, however, two factors have fostered interest in children's sex-role stereotypes. First, psychologists are becoming more and more aware not only of the pervasiveness of adult sex-role stereotypes, but also of the impact of these stereotypes on adult behavior. Second, psychologists are coming to appreciate the intricate interaction between cognitions and social behavior, particularly in a developmental context. Not only does experience in the social world seem to foster cognitive development (e.g., Lewis & Weinraub, 1976), but also the child's increasing cognitive development may have important implications for social behavior (Kohlberg, 1966; Weinraub & Lewis, 1977). For individuals of all ages, what the individual believes is increasingly being recognized as an important determinant of what the individual does.

A number of studies have demonstrated that adults in our society have sex-role stereotypes (Broverman, Broverman, Clarkson, Rosenkrantz, & Vogel, 1972; Deaux, 1976; MacBrayer, 1960; Rosenkrantz, Vogel, Bee, Broverman, & Broverman, 1968) and, in addition, that adults modify their behaviors and their perceptions in a variety of situations in accordance with these sex-role stereotypes (Bem, in press; Schaffer & Wegley, 1974; Spence & Heimreich, 1972). There is also evidence that even preschool children in our culture have sex-role stereotypes similar to those of adults (Fauls & Smith, 1956; Garret, Ein & Tremaine, 1977; Nadelman, 1974; Schlosberg & Goodman, 1975; Vener & Snyder, 1966; Williams, Bennet, & Best, 1975). Certainly, by elementary school, children have very definite ideas about what toys, what activities, and what occupations our society considers appropriate for men and women, boys and girls.

In order to facilitate our discussion of children's sex-role stereotypes, some definitions will be helpful. Both sex differences and children's awareness of sex differences are related to the sex roles defined by society. *Sex roles* may be defined as "any pattern that a given individual in a specified set of situations is expected and required to perform"

(O'Leary, 1977, p. 119). A *sex-typed behavior* is a behavior for which sex differences are expected, in conformity with sex roles. A *sex-typed individual* is one who conforms to these required sex differences. The *sex-typing process* is some hypothetical process usually offered to account for the acquisition of sex differences. *Gender identity* is the assignment of the self to one of the sex categories. *Gender constancy* refers to the child's ability to maintain a stable concept of someone's sexual identity, including his or her own, despite changes in the person's appearance or behavior. *Empirical sex differences* are traits, abilities, and behaviors on which males and females are shown to differ. These differences are frequently, but not necessarily, related to sex roles and sex-typed behaviors.

Children's awareness of sex roles and sex differences contribute to children's sex-role stereotypes. A distinction should be drawn between children's *knowledge* of sex-role stereotypes and their *conformity* to them. *Sex-role stereotypes* can be thought of as culturally shared assumptions and expectations about sex differences in abilities, personality traits, activities, and roles. Stereotyping occurs when an individual is categorized according to these assumptions — whether or not the individual possesses these abilities and traits or engages in these activities or roles. Children may be aware of sex-role stereotypes but not necessarily act in conformity with them. For example, an 8-year-old girl may believe that nursing is a feminine profession and doctoring a male profession. Although she knows she is a girl and has secure gender identity and constancy, she may nevertheless want to become a doctor when she grows up. In contrast, another girl, also with gender identity and gender constancy but confined by her awareness of sex-role stereotypes, may consciously decide not to become a doctor because she feels doctoring is inappropriate for girls. Thus, a child may hold sex-role stereotypes but may not necessarily be a sex-typed individual.

In this paper, we review the literature on the development of what children know about sex differences in behavior and how early they show sex-typed interests. We also consider the evidence on the relationship between this knowledge and conformity to it in personal preferences. In addition, we discuss some of the factors that contribute to the development of children's sex-role stereotypes and sex-typed interests. Finally, we explore the implications of sex-role stereotyping for child rearing and for the dilemmas women face today.

AWARENESS OF SEX DIFFERENCES

Adult Possessions and Children's Toys

How early are children aware of sex differences in possessions and activities in our society? Do they associate certain toys with boys and others with girls? Are they aware of adult sex differences in possessions and activities?

Two studies have explored children's beginning awareness of sex differences in toys and possessions. In one, Thompson (1975) showed boys and girls from 2 to 3 years of age 18 assorted pictures of toys, tools, appliances, pieces of clothing, and other articles that adult consensus defines as sex stereotyped. Even the 2-year-olds seemed to sort these pictures methodically, getting 61 percent of the 18 pictures correctly sorted according to sex-role stereotypes. By 2½ years of age, 79 percent of the children sorted items according to adult sex-role stereotypes.

In another more recent study, we saw 71 children between 26 and 36 months of age in the Infant Behavior Laboratory at Temple University. We asked the children to sort three categories of pictures — pictures of adult occupations and household tasks, pictures of adult clothing and possessions, and pictures of children's toys — into a "male" box or a "female" box. All items used in the pictures were validated on an adult sample. The number of pictures correctly sorted according to the adult stereotype was the score for awareness of sex differences in each category.

We found that as young as 26 months of age a significant number of children could demonstrate reliably knowledge of sex differences in adult possessions. Pictures of a three-piece suit, a shirt and tie, a shaving set, and men's hats were considered "male"; pictures of a dress, frilly blouses, pocketbooks, and a set of makeup were considered "female." Appropriate sorting behavior increased over age. Twenty-one percent of the 26-month-old children, 33 percent of those 31 months old, and 70 percent of those 36 months old were able to sort seven out of eight adult possessions in accordance with adult stereotypes (Weinraub, Brown, Sockloff, Ethridge, & Gracely, 1981).

However, in the area of children's awareness of sex differences regarding children's toys — that is, knowing that trucks are "for boys" and dolls "for girls" — the results were surprisingly different. The male pictures were of a dump truck, a cement mixer, a racing car, and a tool set.

The female pictures were of a baby doll, a teenaged doll, a feeding set, and a doll crib. Only at 36 months of age did we find that children were aware of sex-role stereotypes in toys. Although children may be aware of sex differences in adult possessions prior to 3 years of age, toys are toys. To the very young child, any toy the child wants to play with is considered appropriate to that child's sex. Not until 3 years of age do children appear to categorize toys into stereotypical female and male categories.

Similar studies with children from approximately 3 to 5 years of age chronicle the growth of knowledge of sex-role stereotypes across a number of areas. Vener and his colleagues (Vener & Weese, 1965; Vener & Snyder, 1966) tested children's knowledge of feminine task items that included an iron, a dustpan, a pot, a wooden spoon, a rolling pin, and an egg beater; and masculine task items that included a screwdriver, a wrench, pliers, a flashlight, a paintbrush, a clamp, and a tool box. They also asked about female possessions such as a brassiere, lipstick, hose, panties, a scarf, a blouse, a beach hat, and sunglasses; and male items including a necktie, a bowtie, a shirt, socks, shorts, a cap, a belt, and a razor. Even the youngest children (30–40 months) performed differently from chance and showed considerable knowledge of sex-role stereotypes.

Preschool children also have a good grasp of adult-validated sex-stereotyped beliefs about children's behavior. When asked in an interview-like situation which of two paper dolls — "Michael" or "Lisa" — would like to do certain activities in nursery school, end up in certain future roles, and have certain character traits, children 2½ to 3½ years old showed an impressive depth of knowledge (Kuhn, Nash, & Brucken, 1978). Children believe that girls like to play with dolls, help mother, cook dinner, clean house, talk a lot, never hit, and say "I need some help"; they also believe that boys like to play with cars, help father, build things, and say "I can hit you." Interestingly, the male stereotype was more thoroughly understood than the female stereotype by both girls and boys. However, both girls and boys attribute more positive characteristics to their own sex and more negative characteristics to the other sex.

Studies reveal an emerging cognizance of sex differences in children's toys. Using a projective test, (the IT Scale for Children; (Brown, 1957), Schell & Silber (1968) examined stereotyping in 3 and 4-year old children. Although 4 year olds show greater awareness than 3 year olds, even 3-year-old children differentially associate certain toys with girls and boys in agreement with adult stereotypes.

By the time they enter kindergarten, children's notions of what items are associated with each sex are very similar to those of adults. Masters & Wilkerson (1976) asked 4 year olds, 7-to-8 year olds, and adults to indicate the sex appropriateness of 52 toys arranged on a table. Of the 52 toys, only 12 failed to reach a minimum criterion for moderate stereotyping in the eyes of adults and older children. While there was almost perfect agreement between older children's and adults' ratings (r = .94), the forced choices of the 4-year-old children showed relatively high agreement with adult ratings (r = .71) and older children's ratings (r = .77).

There is no doubt that by elementary-school age, children differentially associate toys with females and males in accordance with adult stereotypes (Houde & Lester, 1976). Children from 5 to 9 years of age, were asked to choose with which of two toys a pictured child of the same sex as the subject would like to play. They matched adult judgments of sex differences on such items an erector set, a plane, a racing car, a football, a wheelbarrow, a jump rope, a dish cabinet, a doll wardrobe, a cleaning set (DeLucia, 1963). Other examples of activities that 5-to-8 year olds categorize by sex with increasing accuracy include owning a train set, playing football, boxing, smoking a pipe, hunting tigers, pushing a doll buggy, dressing a doll, giving a tea party, using perfume and lipstick, and making pastry (Nadelman, 1970, 1974).

Thus, children can demonstrate as early as the third year of life rudimentary understanding of sex differences in adult possessions and activities. In the fourth year of life, they are beginning to differentiate children's toys and children's behavior by sex. Kindergarten children arrive at school with fundamental knowledge of sex differences in these areas; they continue to refine this knowledge in interaction with new adults and peers. Certainly, by 7 or 8 years of age, children are in almost perfect agreement with adults about the sex typing of children's toys and adults' and children's activities.

Awareness of Sex Differences in Personality Characteristics

Adults associate some personality characteristics with men, others with women. For example, in Broverman et al.'s well-known study (1972), both women and men attribute the characteristics of dominance, aggression, and competition to men; and warmth, verbal ability, and emotionality to women. When do children begin to show evidence of having acquired similar notions?

Attempts to discover the extent of stereotyping of personality characteristics in children under 5 years of age have been hindered by the children's limited understanding of language. In a study of children from 2½ to 3½ years of age, it was found that by age 3½ both girls and boys identify girls as talking a lot, saying "I need help," and never hitting; they identify boys as saying "I can hit you" (Kuhn et al., 1978). Thus, certain traits that are easily defined behaviorally ("Who says I can hit you?" "Who cries sometimes?") are stereotypically assigned to boys and girls, respectively. More abstract qualities are not differentiated as easily. For instance, most of the items on which the children in Kuhn's study failed to stereotype concerned personality traits such as fearfulness, laziness, leadership, and tenacity ("Who is not scared?" "Who does not like to work?" "Who is the leader?" "Who has not given up?").

Just as children attribute certain valued activities to their own sex regardless of societal stereotypes (Kuhn et al., 1978), so boys and girls both attribute more negative personality traits to the other sex and more positive traits to their own sex. Thus, girls, but not boys, believe that girls look nice, give kisses, and say "I can do it best"; and that boys like to fight, are mean, are weak, and say "I did it wrong." Boys, but not girls, think girls cry sometimes, are slow, say "you hurt my feelings," and say "you're not letting me have a turn." Boys also think boys work hard, are loud, and are naughty.

Studies of knowledge of sex typing of emotions in children from 3 to 5 years of age suggest that children as young as 3 often associate anger with males and happiness and fear with females (Chemelski & Birnbaum, 1979; Birnbaum, Nosanchuk, & Croll, 1980). However, analyses of the reasons given for their choices and different judgments about the same emotions in different situations suggest that stereotyping of emotions in young children may be situation specific.

Flerx, Fidler & Rogers (1976) measured several different aspects of children's sex-role stereotypes, including intelligence, play activities, occupation, and affect expressiveness. Children at 4-, 5-, and 6 years of age were presented with a doll family and asked to point to the doll who would show particular characteristics and perform certain activities and roles. Two reliable stereotypical views were shown to increase with age: the view that boys are smarter than girls and the sex typing of certain children's work activities, such as raking leaves and setting the table. In an early study (Taddenham, 1952), 6-, 8- and 10-year-old children from the Berkeley Child Guidance Study were asked to rate "typical" boys and girls. Typical girls were rated as quiet, popular, full of fun, not quarrelsome, good-looking, good sports, not "show-offs," tidy, and friendly. Typical boys were considered wigglesome, quarrelsome, bossy, show-offish, good at games, and not bashful. More recently, investigators have chosen adult-validated, sex-stereotyped characteristics and asked children to state whether such characteristics are associated with males or females. Silver (1972) found that 3- to 4-year-old children did not attribute certain characteristics to one sex more than the other; however, in children 5 to 8 years of age, aggressiveness was considered more characteristic of males and nurturance of females. Also, with increasing age, these two characteristics became increasingly sex differentiated.

In another look at the developmental aspects of awareness of sex differences in personality traits, Williams, and colleagues (1975) read 24 short, adult-validated, sex-stereotyped personality descriptions to kindergarten, second-grade, and fourth-grade children. Each of the 24 stories was paired with pictures of a male and female adult. An example of one of their items is "One of these people is emotional. They cry when something good happens as well as when everything goes wrong. Which is the emotional person?" Williams and his colleagues report that kindergarten children show rather extensive knowledge of sex-role stereotypes; this knowledge increases with age. Traits on which kindergarten children score greater than chance agreement with adult stereotypes include aggression, strength, adventurousness, coarseness, independence, loudness, appreciation, dominance, emotionality, sophistication, ambition, and softheartedness.

In summary, children's knowledge of sex-role stereotypes in the area of personality characteristics has been demonstrated with consistency only in children aged 5 and above. Although this is an interesting area to explore, attempts to demonstrate knowledge of sex stereotypes regarding personality characteristics are necessarily limited by the fact that many younger children are not aware of the meaning of the verbal labels for the personality characteristics described.

Awareness of Sex Differences in Adult Occupations

The belief that certain occupations should be performed by one sex rather than the other continues to pervade our society. When do children first categorize jobs by sex, and how well do their categorizations match those of adults? Do their perceptions match the realities of the employment figures?

Kuhn and her colleagues (Kuhn et al., 1978) have found that children as young as 30 months know that girls will grow up to clean the house, be a nurse, or be a teacher, and boys will grow up to "be boss." Three-year-old boys (but not girls) believe boys (rather than girls) will grow up to be a governor, a doctor, or a pilot. In our study of 26- to 36-month-old children (Weinraub et al., 1981), we found that as early as 26 months, some children believe certain household and occupational tasks — such as truck driving, fire fighting, mail delivery, and car repairing — are jobs for men, while other tasks — such as cooking, cleaning, sewing, and washing clothes — are jobs for women. By 36 months of age, the majority of children are able to classify stereotypically at least 7 out of 8 household and occupational tasks.

By school entry, children have definite notions about sex stereotyping of adult occupations. Barclay (1974), using 20 pictures of vocational situations with one-sentence descriptions of jobs, asked middle-class kindergarten children to point to the picture of the person, woman or man, who would do the job. Although some jobs were seen as neutral (musician, lab worker), the majority were assigned to the man (doctor, carpenter, firefighter, police officer, gas station attendant) and only three were reserved for the woman (nurse, teacher, and secretary). Schlosberg & Goodman (1975) showed lower-class and upper-middle-class kindergarteners and sixth-grade children pictures of 12 work environments. Children were more likely to exclude women from male occupations than to exclude men from female occupations. Although most of the children said men could be nurses, secretaries, housekeepers, teachers, and waitresses, most of the children felt women could not fix televisions, radios, or cars. No age differences were found in children's responses.

Older children show similar views of the occupational world. Scherensky (1976) showed a large sample of 6, 8, and 10 year olds from both rural, suburban, and inner-city populations a number of photographs showing various occupations. She asked the children to indicate whether a man or a woman would do the job. She found that children consider the occupations of firefighter, truck driver, garbage collector, and minister the province of the male, while nurse and homemaker are seen to be the province of the female. Interestingly, girls are less likely than boys to view the role of executive and doctor as exclusively male occupations.

Although Scheresky did not observe developmental trends, other researchers have. Garrett and her colleagues (1977) asked 6-, 8-, and 10-year-old children from a middle-class suburban school to rate whether men, women, or both men and women could do each of 40 occupations. Many of the jobs were seen as exclusively masculine. Most predominantly masculine were football coach, ship captain, firefighter, plumber, train engineer, airplane pilot, and carpenter. Fifteen of the jobs, including writer and teacher, were seen as neutral; seven were seen as feminine. Feminine occupations included nurse, flight attendant, secretary, hotel maid, sewing-machine operator, model, and librarian. It is of interest that, although older children are more likely to be cognizant of culturally defined roles in a broader range of occupations, they also are more willing than younger children to permit both women and men to perform similar jobs.

With age, children's knowledge of sex differences in occupations becomes more congruent with census data on the percentage of men in those jobs (Garrett et al., 1977; O'Bryant, Durrett, & Pennebaker, 1980; Tremaine, Schau, & Busch, 1978; Cummings & Taebel, 1980). Thus, children's knowledge reflects reality in this area. Whether we like it or not, children seem to be attuned to what "is"!

The results of these studies show that by the time children reach kindergarten they associate a wide range of occupations with men. Male-associated occupations include those that are exciting and powerful. Children associate only a small number of occupations with women, and these tend to be low-paying, less skilled and less-powerful positions. In some cases, children specifically exclude women from more skilled, traditionally male occupations.

Summary of Children's Awareness
of Sex-Role Streotypes

Our review suggests that elementary-school children have considerable knowledge of sex-role stereotypes in the areas of personality characteristics, occupations, and toys and possessions. Sex-role stereotypes also have been demonstrated in preschool children in the categories of toys and possessions. Children 3 years of age or younger show some understanding of elementary sex differences in personality characteristics and occupations as well. The next question to direct our attention to this is: When do children begin to show sex-typed interests and preferences in conformity to societal sex-role stereotypes?

THE DEVELOPMENT OF SEX-TYPED PREFERENCES

Sex-typed behavior in children refers to "role behavior appropriate to a child's ascribed gender" (Sears, Maccoby, & Levin, 1957, p. 171). Sex-typed behaviors are those behaviors that "typically elicit different rewards for one sex than the other" (Mischel, 1966, p. 56). Although some behaviors may be defined as sex-typed, that is, as leading to differential consequences for one sex than for the other, it is not necessarily the case that there are empirical sex differences in that variable. An example of such sex-typed behavior is dependency. Although dependency is seen as a feminine characteristic (Broverman et al., 1972), it has not been demonstrated that females are in general more dependent than males (Maccoby & Jacklin, 1974).

In this discussion two sex-typed behaviors on which boys and girls *do* differ — toy preference and occupational preference — will be considered. These sex-typed behaviors are chosen because they form an important and readily observable component of a child's sex-role identification and they may have implications for the later sex-typed interests. Particular attention will be devoted to establishing how early such sex-typed behavior preferences can be observed and to understanding the developmental course of these preferences. Sex-typed preferences for toys and occupations will be examined in preschool and elementary-school children.

Toys and Activities

The existence of sex-typed toy preferences in children under 2 years of age is equivocal. Although none of the studies of children 1½ years of age and younger have yielded sex differences on clearly sex-typed toys, such as dolls and trucks, other less clearly sex-typed differences have been reported. For instance, studies of 1-year-old opposite-sexed twins done by Lewis and his colleagues (Brooks & Lewis, 1974) and with lower-class children (Messer & Lewis, 1972) have failed to find sex differences on any of a number of toys. On the other hand, Goldberg & Lewis (1969), studying 13-month-old children, found that girls prefer to play with stuffed animals while boys spend more time manipulating such nontoy objects as doorknobs, floor tile, and electrical outlets. Similarly, Bronson (1971) found that 15-month-old girls spend more time than boys playing with stuffed animals. However, when Jacklin, Maccoby, & Dick (1973) presented 13 month olds with toys differing on the dimension of *faceness*, softness, and manipulability, the only sex difference in toy preference that emerged was a preference for robots by boys. Finally, a study by Benjamin (1932) has been cited as demonstrating sex-typed toy preferences in children 1 to 6 years of age, but the extremely small sample sizes in his youngest age groups — 14 to 22 months and 22 to 29 months — preclude conclusions regarding sex-typed toy preferences within these ages.

Sex differences on sex-typed toys do appear to emerge around 2 years of age. When observed in the home, boys spend more time than girls with blocks and transportation toys and in manipulating objects, while girls spend more time with soft toys and dolls and in dressing up and dancing (Fagot, 1974, 1977b). In a similar home study of 24 20-month-old children (Fein, Johnson, Kosson, Stork, & Wasserman, 1976) girls spent significantly more time playing with adult-validated girls' toys (bead bracelet, doll, iron) than boys' toys (hammer, truck, gun), while boys preferred to play with boys' toys. In particular, the bracelet, doll, and hammer yielded significant sex-typed differences.

In our laboratory, we have observed strong sex differences in sex-typed play behavior as early as 26 months of age using a simple 6-minute, standardized toy play situation. We presented boys and girls from 26 to 36 months of age with a group of adult-validated toys, including a large dump truck, a small cement mixer, a tool set, and a race car for the male toys and a baby doll, teenaged doll, a doll crib, and a feeding set for the female toys. Even in our youngest group of children, boys preferred to play with the boys' toys over the girls' toys and girls preferred to play with girls' toys over boys' toys. No age differences were observed (Weinraub et al., 1981).

From the age of 3 years on, sex-typed toy preferences emerge consistently in the literature. Observations of preschoolers reveal that boys spend more time than girls in play with transportation toys (Clark, Wyon, & Richards, 1969; Fagot & Patterson, 1969; Harper & Sanders, 1975; Partin, 1933; Sears, Rau, & Alpert, 1965), with blocks (Clark et al., 1969; Fagot & Patterson, 1969; Partin, 1933), and in the sandbox (Fagot & Patterson, 1969; Harper & Sanders, 1975; while girls spend more time with dolls and arts and crafts activities (Barry & Barry, 1976; Clark et al., 1969; Fagot & Patterson, 1969; Harper & Sanders, 1975; Partin, 1933; Sears et al., 1965).

42 : : *Introduction*

Projective techniques using the IT Scale (Brown, 1956) also show sex-typed toy preferences in the preschool child (Fling & Manosevitz, 1972; Hartup & Zook 1969). Although there are various methodological difficulties with the test (see, for example, Fling & Manosevitz, 1972), children 4 years old and up have been known to make definite sex-typed toy preferences (Brown, 1956; Fling & Manosevitz, 1972; Laosa & Brophy, 1972; Ward, 1969).

Sex-typed toy preferences continue to develop and expand as children grow older. Five and 8 year olds indicate that sex-stereotyped toys are their favorites (Nadelman, 1970, 1974). Kindergarten children also prefer pictures of children engaged in same-sex-typed activities over those engaged in opposite-sex-typed activities (Fauls & Smith, 1956). Among older children 8 to 11 years of age, boys prefer complex team games, games with forceful physical contact, and games involving propulsion of objects through space; girls prefer games with one central character, noncompetitive ritualistic games, and verbal, choral-rhythmic games (Rosenberg & Sutton-Smith, 1964).

Not only do children choose same-sex-typed activities, but they also will actively avoid opposite-sex-typed activities (Hartup, Moore, & Sager, 1963). From 5 years old on, children will spend more time with unattractive neutral toys rather than more attractive opposite-sex-typed toys. In addition, there is some evidence that simply labeling activities as sex appropriate affects the attraction value of these activities for elementary-school children (Helper & Quinlivan, 1973; Liebert, McCall, & Hanratty, 1971; Montemayor, 1974; Stein, Pohly, & Mueller, 1971). Even in 2½-year-old children, Thompson (1975) found that neutral items were differently preferred when they were labeled for boys or for girls.

Awareness of Sex-Role Stereotypes and Conformity to Them. Children's attraction to and rejection of certain activities appear to be dependent upon the sex appropriateness of the activity. One might expect, then, that the extent of the child's knowledge about what is and is not sex appropriate would affect directly the child's behavior and attitudes. Do children modify their everyday activities to conform to their understanding of what is sex appropriate? Very few studies have addressed this question.

In our study of 26-to-36 month olds (Weinraub et al., 1981), we measured children's preference for sex-typed toys and their awareness of societal expectations about sex appropriateness in the area of children's toys, adult possessions, and adult occupations and tasks. We found that children's preferences for certain toys are not related to the extent of their knowledge of sex differences in these toys or to their awareness of sex differences in adult possessions and tasks. Children who know about the culturally defined appropriateness of certain toys do not necessarily play in conformity to these notions when presented with a choice of both masculine and feminine toys.

Using a slightly older group of children, Edelbrock and Sugawara (1978) found that boys' scores on the IT Scale for Children (Brown, 1956) are related to their knowledge of sex differences in adult and child activities and possessions. Girls' preferences, however, are not related to their awareness of these sex differences. In a study of elementary-school children, Hartley (1964) found that beliefs about sex-role-appropriate behavior and sex-typed preferences are correlated in 8 and 12 year olds. Although the evidence is tentative, it would appear that children's personal preferences in toys and activities become more congruent with their knowledge of societal expectations for the sexes as they grow older.

Summary. Preference for toys that adults consider sex appropriate is not found with any consistency in children under 1½ years of age. When children are about 2 years of age, sex differences in the kinds of toys they prefer to play with begin to emerge and are established clearly by the age of 3. The range of toys and preferred play activities expands to fit the developing interests of boys and girls, but sex-typed preferences remain strong and consistent into elementary school. Children also avoid opposite-sex-typed activities and modify their interest in neutral activities when they are labeled sex appropriate or sex inappropriate. In addition, there is some evidence that the extent of children's understanding of sex-role stereotypes affects their preferences for toys and activities that are sex-typed by our society.

Occupational Preference

Occupational preference refers to the vocational aspirations children have for themselves as they project themselves into future adult roles. We will trace the developmental course of occupational preference in children 3 to 18 years of age. The relationship between awareness of sex-role stereotypes in occupations and personal choice of future occupations has not been researched extensively. A few suggestive findings in this area will be presented.

Children 3 to 6 years of age, when asked what they want to be when they grow up, respond with specific adult occupations more frequently as they grow older (Vondracek & Kirchner, 1974). Although their ability to project themselves into adult roles does not differ between the sexes, the occupations preferred do. Even preschool children express future aspirations along sex-stereotyped lines. Both preschool and elementary-school girls choose a parenting role significantly more often than boys (Looft, 1971; Vondracek & Kirchner, 1974). In addition, the range of occupational choice is more restricted for girls, with nurse and teacher being the most popular answers (Vondracek and Kirchner, 1974; Beuf, 1974). Boys' choices include more action oriented occupations (police officer, sports superstar) and more prestigious careers (doctor, public servant, pilot).

Taking the question one step further, Beuf (1974) asked children 3 to 6 years of age what they would do if they were of the other sex. Approximately 70 percent of the children replied with a job considered appropriate for the imagined sex. More interestingly, boys frequently imagined themselves as nurses and girls imagined themselves as doctors when asked, "What if you were a girl (boy)?" Several girls confided that they really would prefer to be doctors rather than nurses when they grew up, but couldn't because they were girls. This suggests that, as we said earlier, children know vocational sex-role stereotypes for both sexes at a very young age and that they may modify their personal ambitions to conform to the stereotype.

Considering the fact that children have clear sex-role stereotypes in the elementary-school years, it is not surprising that children also have clearly developed sex-typed occupational preferences during this period. Asked, "What would you like to be when you grow up?" over 70 percent of children from kindergarten to sixth grade choose occupations traditionally reserved for their sex (Looft, 1971; Scholsberg & Goodman, 1975; Siegel, 1973). Boys choose a wide variety of occupations, from football player to police officer to astronaut to priest, while girls choose from a more limited repertoire, including teacher, nurse, housewife, mother, flight attendant, and salesclerk. In most studies, typically female aspirations include being a nurse and a teacher.

Although the majority of children choose to aspire to traditional sex-typed adult occupations, several girls in these studies, but very few boys, indicate an interest in jobs generally considered the domain of the other sex (Vondracek & Kirchner, 1974; Beuf, 1974). As they grow older, girls continue to make more nontraditional choices than boys (Tremaine et al., 1978), although the range of girls' occupational choices in general remains more restricted than boys'. Current investigations indicate sex appropriateness remains a significant influence on job preference from kindergarten to twelfth grade (O'Connor, 1980); however, it is likely that the effects of sex typing on personal career choice diminish with age (Umstot, 1980; Cummings & Taebel, 1980).

FACTORS INFLUENCING CHILDREN'S SEX-ROLE DEVELOPMENT

Television

Television programming frequently is cited as one of the influences on children's sex-role development. Certainly, more male than female characters are portrayed and the males engage in active roles while the females passively look on (Sternglanz & Servin, 1974). Correlational studies show that children who watch many hours of television each week hold more sex-stereotyped views of the world than infrequent television viewers (Freuh & McGhee, 1975; Beuf, 1974).

In an interesting study exploring the effects on preschool children deliberately exposed to counterstereotyped cartoons, stereotyped, or neutral cartoon (Davidson, Yasuna, & Tower, 1979), girls exposed to an overtly counterstereotyped cartoon showed less stereotyping immediately after viewing than girls who watched either stereotyped or neutral cartoons. However, 5 and 6 year olds who saw counterstereotyped films of female doctors and male nurses reported afterwards that they had seen films of male doctors and female nurses, thus relabeling reality to fit the sex-role stereotypes (Cordua, McGraw, & Drabman, 1979).

The evidence so far is suggestive that television may contribute to the development of sex-role stereotypes. It is possible, however, that TV programming simply perpetuates existing sex-role stereotypes in society. Further studies concerning the effects of counterstereotyped portrayals on the development of sex-role stereotypes is warranted.

Teachers and Peers

As we have shown, children arrive at kindergarten and even nursery school with rudimentary understanding of sex-role stereotypes and definite sex-typed preferences. In their school interactions with teachers and peers, children receive further reinforcement for sex-typed behavior.

Although teachers in general reinforce certain "feminine" behaviors — also seen as task-oriented behaviors — in both girls and boys (Etaugh, Collins & Gerson, 1975; Fagot & Patterson, 1969; Fagot, 1977a, 1977b), they also give boys positive reinforcement for male behaviors, as do preschoolers' peers. Peer reinforcement in particular is considered a highly significant factor in encouraging masculine sex-typed behavior in boys (Fagot, 1977b). Girls also are reinforced for sex-appropriate behaviors and criticized for sex-inappropriate behavior by both teacher and peers (Fagot, 1977a, 1977b).

Appropriate sex-typed preferences can be elicited in preschool children by the mere presence of an other-sexed peer, without overt reinforcement being delivered (Serbin, Connor,, Burchardt, & Cirton, 1979), suggesting that children learn very early that they may be rewarded or punished by peers for their conformity or lack of conformity to sex-role stereotypes. Serbin and her colleagues speculate that sex-typed behaviors may be the result of a pattern of strong stimulus control whereby "permission" for performing certain behaviors may be granted or denied by teachers' and peers' modeling, labeling, and reinforcing selected behaviors (Fagot & Patterson, 1969; Perdue & Connor, 1978; Serbin & Connor, 1979; Serbin, Tonick, & Sternglanz, 1977).

Numerous questions concerning the effects of the school environment remain unanswered. For instance, there is speculation that the "feminine" reinforcement patterns boys are subjected to by teachers may result in their defining school achievement as inappropriate behavior for their sex. Also, whether cross-sex play groups are more desirable than single-sex play groups is at this point only conjecture, since no one has investigated exactly what children learn about sex roles from either type of play group. Similarly, the effects of male teachers (in an often female-dominated profession) on preschool and elementary-school children's sex-role development may be to perpetuate rather than overcome sex-role stereotypes. While it is obvious that the school environment is a major influence on sex typing and sex-role stereotyping (Minuchin, Biber, Shapiro, & Zimiles, 1969), the effects of particular school circumstances on sex-role development remain to be explored (for a review, see Minu-chin & Shapiro, in press).

Development of Sex-Typed Behaviors and Interests

Popular accounts of the development of sex-typed preferences in activities and interests point to sex-differential treatment of females and males throughout the life cycle. Parents have been shown to hold sex-role stereotypes concerning their children prior to their children's birth, and they respond to neonates sex differentially (Rubin, Provenzano, & Luria, 1974; see Lewis & Weinraub, 1979, for a review). As children grow older, parents continue their differential treatment of the sexes, giving their toddler girls more praise and more criticism than boys and playing with boys more than they play with girls (Fagot, 1974).

However, it remains to be shown whether the differential treatment *causes* sex differences or whether children *elicit* sex-differential responses (for a more detailed discussion, see Lewis & Weinraub, 1979). For instance, are infant girls more attentive to auditory signals because of some biological differences (Buffrey & Gray, 1972; Watson, 1969), or are they more interested in auditory stimuli because their mothers talk to them more (Lewis & Freedle, 1973)? Similarly, do mothers verbalize more to their daughters because it is more rewarding to talk to someone who is better equipped to respond, or is it because it is "expected" that girls are more verbally responsive than boys? The answer may lie, not in a linear cause–effect relationship, but in a reciprocal system of interactions among the biological differences in the child, the differences in treatment,the expectations from the child and adults, and the child's outcome behaviors.

Development of Sex-Role Stereotypes

Sex-role stereotypes are definitely not inborn or biologically determined. Children learn from the people around them what it means to be masculine or feminine. The results of our recent study (Weinraub et al., 1981) indicate that children's knowledge of sex differences in adult activities and adult possessions is affected by what they see their parents doing. Children whose fathers perform more feminine sex-typed tasks in the home, such as washing dishes, grocery shopping, cooking, making beds, cleaning house, and feeding small children, and children whose mothers work outside the home have less traditional notions of sex differences than children whose parents divide household responsibilities along more traditional lines. Not surprisingly, children's understanding of adult sex roles does *not* seem to be affected by their parents' attitudes about sex roles. Children learn from what they see, not from attitudes parents profess.

Other influences on children's sex-role stereotypes, as we noted earlier, include the models presented on children's television programs and the reinforcement patterns they are subject to from parents, teachers and peers. Differential modeling and reinforcement of sex-typed behavior also may serve a second function: to clarify and emphasize culturally defined sex-role differences, providing information from which children *actively construct* their own understanding of both sex roles and the consequences of failing to conform to appropriate sex-role behavior. Thus, it is not surprising to find that children's I.Q. is an important predictor of preschoolers' knowledge about sex roles (Weinraub et al., 1981).

Working from a cognitive developmental approach, Kohlberg (1966) argues that children's social cognitions — their gender identity and awareness of sex-role stereotypes — play a crucial role in the development of sex-typed behaviors. According to the cognitive developmental position, children first become aware of their own gender label and of differential behavior, attitudes, and preferences common to that sex and then find rewarding the opportunity to do like-sexed behaviors. This developmental view often is contrasted with Mischel's social learning explanation (1966), in which the child wants rewards, finds he or she is rewarded for like-sexed activities, and therefore assumes he or she is a boy or a girl. Although there are some major differences between the two positions (see Lewis & Weinraub, 1979), common to both approaches is the child's awareness of the culture's division of people, behavior, and attitudes into two different categories based on gender. In addition, according to both approaches, the child is aware that behaving in congruence with one of these categories is more likely to be rewarded than behaving in congruence with the other.

Thus, children are building their sense of self through these processes, trying on adult roles and taking pride in acting grown up. However, the extent to which children's understanding of sex roles limits their aspirations, restricts their role playing, and results in the suppression of individual strengths and abilities is a measure of the potential lost to our society. Narrowly defining possible outlets for individual talents can lead to feelings of inadequacy and possible depression. What can be done to insure that the socialization process results in individuals able to choose activities that provide personal satisfaction and develop individual capacities to the fullest?

KEEPING SEX-ROLE STEREOTYPES IN THEIR PLACE

In our laboratory, we have seen parents attempting to counteract sex-role stereotypes using one or both of two strategies. In the first strategy, we see parents buying their children toys considered appropriate for children of the other sex — dolls for their sons or trucks for their daughters. Parents are often dismayed, however, to find that their children seldom play with these toys. Parents have commented that, try as they might, they cannot interest their sons in doll play or their daughters in trains. Thus, sex-role stereotypes about children's toys seem to be confirmed and parents are left puzzled as to the origins of their children's toy preference. As one mother gulped, "Could it really be . . . innate?"

The second strategy used by parents consists of pointing out to children that role reversals are possible and that all roles are open to them. However, we believe that the now-familiar "You can be anything, and everything, you want to be" may be misleading, unfair, and potentially dangerous. Children by age 2 have begun to construct internal notions of their sex-role and gender identity based on their assimilation of reality. When well-meaning parents and teachers point out that some women are doctors and some men are nurses, children may become confused and could even begin to distrust their own perceptions. It may begin to erode a parent's credibility to tell a child "There are women doctors and men nurses" if the child rarely, if ever, sees such sex-role reversals. Moreover, children who have been told that they can be anything they want to be may be unprepared for the crushing realities of sex-differentiated play on the playground and the stereotyped attitudes of their peers. Without adequate preparations, these children can become confused and disillusioned later on by sex typing and discrimination in the social, educational, and corporate worlds.

Recent interviews with young women indicate that current pressures to combine career, marriage, and motherhood in a perfect "superwoman" role lead to conflict and resentment in some women (Kleiman,

1980). With only a few vague hints of *how* this difficult task can be accomplished, some young women today feel confronted with an either/or decision: either a strong marital relationship and devoted mothering or a successful professional life. The net effect of presenting young women with confused or weak role models while making unrealistic demands upon them may be to produce a new generation of conflicted and self-doubting women, unsure of what is expected of them.

We believe there are at least four different child-rearing techniques that parents and other adults can use to combat the negative effects of sex-role stereotypes on children's interests and aspirations. First, parents can call children's attention to sex-role reversals when they occur and model such behaviors themselves. Fathers who share in child-rearing and household tasks will model these behaviors for their sons, just as mothers who accept responsibilities outside the home will model these behaviors for their daughters. Parents who are aware of and comfortable with their own sexuality will enable children to express their developing sexuality in healthy and appropriate ways. Second, parents can distinguish between the existence of sex-role stereotypes and personal conformity to them. By distinguishing between cultural sex-role expectations and personal expectations, parents offer children options suitable for meeting individual needs. In this way, parents teach children that everyone has a number of choices and the options that are best to choose are those that allow the individual the expression of her or his own unique talents, skills, and interests.

Third, children can be helped to place sex-role stereotypic models of men and women in a sociohistorical framework. Knowledge of the circumstances under which sex-role-related lifestyle decisions were made in the past by parents and grandparents may keep children from disparaging such decisions and their consequences. Mothers or grandmothers should not be belittled for staying home to raise a family; fathers or grandfathers should not be held in contempt for failure to change diapers 20 years ago.

Finally, children can be helped to deal more directly with sex-role stereotyping and to develop skills that will aid them in transcending such stereotypes. What does a parent do when her daughter comes home from school angry that the boys in the neighborhood won't let her play stickball with them? Or when, more seriously, she complains that even though the coach has let her join the neighborhood baseball team, the boys make fun of her and say they don't want a girl on their team? Nearly all children have had the experience of being excluded from groups or teams they want to be part of. Often it happens within single-sex groups as a result of other children's cruelties and insensitivities. Are the methods children learn to cope with exclusion and discrimination any different when exclusion occurs along the lines of sex-role stereotypes? The skills children learn to cope with these problems in childhood and adolescence will be helpful in dealing with more subtle but more dangerous types of discrimination later on in the professional world.

In addition, children should be forewarned gently of the obstacles they may face should they choose life roles divergent from traditional sex-typed ones. The little girl who has her heart set on becoming a physician or a pilot or a police officer already knows that few women in today's world hold these positions. Though she should be encouraged strongly to pursue her goals, she also should be let in on the fact that in seeking to attain these goals, she may face problems along the way. Better to acquaint her with the facts of sex discrimination early so she can learn adaptive coping skills than to force her to learn later when she has fewer familial and peer supports and more competing demands. Experience in single-sex groups may help young girls to develop important leadership skills; experience in mixed-sex groups may enable girls to practice and diversify these skills.

Only by recognizing and challenging social reality in our daily lives, educating our children, and preparing the educational and political way so theirs will be an easier course can we make inroads in overcoming sexual inequality in society. Gradually, by our refusal to conform to those aspects of sex roles and sex-role stereotypes that stifle individual potential and by the development of strategies to confront sex stereotypes and discrimination in our everyday lives, sex roles will evolve to a higher level of individual expression. Our best hope for the future lies in raising healthy and creative children, confident of and knowledgeable about their talents and abilities, able to accept limitations in themselves and others, competent in getting along with others, and dedicated to pursuing humanistic goals; children prepared to confront the difficulties that lie ahead.

REFERENCES

Barclay, L. K. The emergence of vocational expectations in preschool children. *Journal of Vocational Behavior*, 1974, *4*, 1–14.
Barry, R., & Barry, A. Stereotyping of sex roles in preschool kindergarten chil-

dren. *Psychological Reports,* 1976, *38,* 948–950.

Bem, S. Beyond androgyny: Some presumptuous prescriptions for a liberated sexual identity. In J. Sherman & F. Denmark (Eds.), *Psychology of women: Future directions of research.* New York: Psychological Dimensions, in press.

Benjamin, H. Age and sex differences in the toy preferences of young children. *Journal of Genetic Psychology,* 1932, *41,* 101–129.

Beuf, A. Doctor, lawyer, household drudge. *Journal of Communication,* 1974, *24,* 142–145.

Biller, H. B. The father and personality development: Parental deprivation and sex role development. In M. F. Lamb (Ed.), *Role of the father in child development.* New York: John Wiley, 1976.

Birnbaum, D. W., Nosanchuk, T. A., & Croll, W. L. Children's stereotypes about sex differences in emotionality. *Sex Roles: A Journal of Research,* 1980, *6,* 435–443.

Bronson, W. Exploratory behavior of 15-month-old infants in a novel situation. Paper presented at the meetings of the Society for Research in Child Development, Minneapolis, April 1971.

Brooks, J., & Lewis, M. Attachment behavior in thirteen-month-old, opposite-sex twins. *Child Development,* 1974, *45,* 243–247.

Broverman, I., Broverman, D., Clarkson, F., Rosenkrantz, D., & Vogel, S. Sex-role stereotypes: A current appraisal. *Journal of Social Issues,* 1972, *28,* 59–78.

Brown, D. G. Masculinity-femininity development in children. *Journal of Consultants Psychology,* 1957, *21,* 197–202.

Buffrey, A., & Gray, J. Sex differences in the development of spatial and linguistic skills. In C. Ounsted & D. C. Taylor (Eds.), *Gender differences: Their ontogeny and significance.* Baltimore: Williams and Wilkins, 1972.

Chemelski, B., & Birnbaum, D. Preschooler's stereotypes about sex differences in emotionality: A metacognitive approach. Paper presented at the Annual Meeting of the Society of the Eastern Psychological Association, Philadelphia, April 1979.

Clark, A., Wyon, S., & Richards, M. Freeplay in nursery school children. *Journal of Child Psychology and Psychiatry,* 1969, *10,* 205–216.

Cordua, G. D., McGraw, K. O., & Drabman, R. S. Doctor or nurse: Children's perception of sex-typed occupations. *Child Development,* 1979, *50,* 590–593.

Cummings, S., & Taebel, D. Sexual inequality and the reproduction of consciousness: An analysis of sex-role stereotyping among children. *Sex Roles: A Journal of Research,* 1980, *6,* 631–644.

Davidson E., Yasuna, A., & Tower, A. The effects of television cartoons on sex-role stereotyping in young girls. *Child Development,* 1979, *50,* 597–600.

Deaux, K. Sex: A perspective on the attribution process. In J. H. Harvey, W. J. Ickes, and R. F. Kidd (Eds.), *New directions in attribution research*, vol. I. Hillsdale, N.J.: Lawrence Erlbaum, 1976.

DeLucia, L. A. Toy preference test: A measure of sex-role identification. *Child Development*, 1963, *34*, 107–117.

Edelbrock, C., & Sugawara, A. Acquisition of sex-typed preference in preschool-aged children. *Developmental Psychology*, 1978, *14*, 614–623.

Etaugh, C., Collins, G., & Gerson, A. Reinforcement of sex-typed behaviors of two-year-old children in a nursery school setting. *Developmental Psychology*, 1975, *11*, 255.

Fagot, B. Sex-related stereotyping of toddlers' behaviors. *Developmental Psychology*, 1973, *9*, 429.

Fagot, B. Sex differences in toddler's behavior and parental reaction. *Developmental Psychology*, 1974, *10*, 554–558.

Fagot, B. Consequences of moderate cross-gender behavior in preschool children. *Child Development*, 1977, *48*, 902–907. (a)

Fagot, B. Sex determined parental reinforcing contingencies in toddler children. Paper presented to the Society for Research in Child Development, biennial meeting, New Orleans, March 1977. (b)

Fagot, B. Children elicit differential responses. Paper presented at Society for Research in Child Development, biennial conference, San Francisco, March 1979.

Fagot, B., & Patterson, C. An in vivo analysis of reinforcing contingencies for sex-role behaviors in the preschool child. *Developmental Psychology*, 1969, *1*, 563–568.

Fauls, L., & Smith, W. Sex-role learning of five-year-olds. *Journal of Genetic Psychology*, 1956, *89*, 105–117.

Fein, G., Johnson, D., Kosson, N., Stork, L., & Wasserman, L. Sex stereotypes and preferences in the toy choices of 20-month-old boys and girls. *Developmental Psychology*, 1976, *14*, 527–528.

Flerx, V., Fidler, D., & Rogers, R. Sex role stereotypes: Developmental aspects and early intervention. *Child Development*, 1976, *47*, 998–1007.

Fling, S., & Manosevitz, M. Sex typing in nursery school children's play interests. *Developmental Psychology*, 1972, *7*, 146–152.

Freuh, T., & McGhee, P. Traditional sex role development and amount of time spent watching television. *Developmental Psychology*, 1975, *11*, 109.

Garrett, C., Ein, P., & Tremaine, L. The development of gender stereotyping of adult occupations in elementary school children. *Child Development*, 1977, *48*, 507–512.

Goldberg, S., & Lewis, M. Play behavior in the year old infant: Early sex differences. *Child Development*, 1969, *40*, 21–31.

Harper, L., & Sanders, K. Preschool children's use of space: Sex differences. *De-*

velopmental Psychology, 1975, *11*, 119.

Hartley, R. E. Children's concepts of male and female roles. *Merrill-Palmer Quarterly*, 1960, *6*, 83–91.

Hartley, R. E. A developmental view of female sex-role differences and identity. *Merrill-Palmer Quarterly*, 1964, *10*, 3–16.

Hartup, W., Moore, S., & Sager, G. Avoidance of inappropriate sex-typing by young children. *Journal of Consulting Psychology*, 1963, *27*, 467–473.

Hartup, W., & Zook, E. Sex-role preferences in three- and four-year-old children. *Journal of Counseling Psychology*, 1960, *24*, 420–426.

Helper, M., & Quinlivan, M. Age and reinforcement value of sex-role labels in girls, *Developmental Psychology*, 1973, *8*, 142.

Houde, C. R., & Lester, L. F. The development of sex-role perceptions in children. Paper presented at the Eastern Psychological Association meeting, New York, April 1976.

Jacklin, C., Maccoby, E., & Dick, A. Barrier behavior and toy preference: Sex differences (and their absence) in the year-old child. *Child Development*, 1973, *44*, 196–200.

Kleiman, D. Many young women now say they'd pick family over career. *The New York Times*, Sunday, December 28, 1980, pp. 1, 24.

Kohlberg, L. A. A cognitive-development analysis of children's sex-role concepts and attitudes. In E. E. Maccoby (Ed.), *The development of sex differences*. Stanford, Calif.: Stanford University Press, 1966.

Kuhn, D., Nash, S. C., & Brucken, L. Sex role concepts of two- and three-year olds. *Child Development*, 1978, *49*, 445–451.

Lambert, W., Yackley, A., & Hein, R. Child training values of English Canadian and French Canadian parents. *Canadian Journal of Behavioral Science*, 1971, *3*, 217–236.

Laosa, L., & Brophy, J. Effects of sex and birth order on sex-role development and intelligence among kindergarten children. *Developmental Psychology*, 1972, *6*, 409–415.

Lewis, M. Parents and children: Sex-role development. *School Review*, 1972, *80(2)*, 229–240.(a)

Lewis, M. State as an infant–environment interaction: An analysis of mother–infant interaction as a function of sex. *Merrill-Palmer Quarterly*, 1972, *18*, 95–121.(b)

Lewis, M., & Cherry, L. Social behavior and language acquisition. In M. Lewis and L. Rosenblum (Eds.), *Interaction, conversation and the development of language: The origins of behavior*, vol. 2. New York: John Wiley, 1977.

Lewis, M., & Freedle, R. Mother–infant dyad: The cradle of meaning. In P. Pliner, L. Krames, and T. Alloway (Eds.), *Communication and affect: Language and thought*. New York: Academic Press, 1973.

Lewis, M., & Goldberg, S. Perceptual-cognitive development in infancy: A generalized expectancy model as a function of the mother–infant interaction. *Merrill-Palmer Quarterly*, 1969, *15*, 81–100.

Lewis, M., & Weinraub, M. The father's role in the child's social network. In M. E. Lamb (Ed.), *Role of the father in child development*. New York: John Wiley, 1976.

Lewis, M., & Weinraub, M. Origins of early sex role development. *Sex Roles*, 1979, *5*, 135–153.

Liebert, R., McCall, R., & Hanratty, M. Effects of sex-typed information on children's toy preferences. *Journal of Genetic Psychology*, 1971, *119*, 133–136.

Looft, W. R. Sex differences in the expression of vocational aspirations by elementary school children. *Developmental Psychology*, 1971, *5*, 366.

Lott, B. Sex role ideology and the observed social behavior of children. Paper presented at the Eastern Psychological Association, symposium on *Measuring sex roles: Methodologies and problems*, Boston, April 1977.

Lynn, D. *Parental identification and sex role*. Berkeley, Calif.: McCutchan, 1969.

MacBrayer, C. Differences in perception of the opposite sex by males and females. *Journal of Social Psychology*, 1960, *52*, 309–314.

Maccoby, E., & Jacklin, C. *The psychology of sex differences*. Stanford, Calif.: Stanford University Press, 1974.

Masters, J. C., & Wilkerson, A. Consensual and discriminative stereotypy of sex-type judgments by parents and children. *Child Development*, 1976, *47*, 208–217.

Messer, S., & Lewis, M. Social class and sex differences in the attachment and play behavior of the year old infant. *Merrill-Palmer Quarterly*, 1972, *18*, 295–306.

Minuchin, P., Biber, B., Shapiro, E., & Zimiles, H. *The psychological impact of school experience*. New York: Basic Books, 1969.

Minuchin, P., & Shapiro, E. The school as a context for social development. In P. Mussen (Ed.), *Handbook of child psychology*, 4th ed. Volume on Social development, E. M. Hetherington (Ed.). New York: John Wiley, in press.

Mischel, W. A social-learning view of sex differences in behavior. In E. Maccoby (Ed.), *The development of sex differences*. Stanford, Calif.: Stanford University Press, 1966.

Montemayor, R. Children's performance in a game and their attention to it as a function of sex-typed labels. *Child Development*, 1974, *45*, 156.

Moss, H. Sex, age and state as determinants of mother–infant interaction. *Merrill-Palmer Quarterly*, 1967, *13*, 19–36.

Nadelman, L. Sex identity in London children: Memory, knowledge and preference tests. *Developmental Psychology*, 1970, *13*, 28–42.

Nadelman, L. Sex identity in American children: Memory, knowledge and preference tests. *Development Psychology*, 1974, *10*, 413–417.

O'Bryant, S., Durrett, M., & Pennebaker, J. Sex differences in knowledge of occupational dimensions across four age levels. *Sex roles: A Journal of Research*, 1980, *6*, 331–337.

O'Connor, P. The role of sex-stereotyping in children's occupational selection. Paper presented at the annual meeting of the Eastern Psychological Association, Hartford, Conn., April 1980.

O'Leary, V. *Toward understanding women*. Monterey, Calif.: Brooks/Cole 1977.

Parke, R., & O'Leary, S. Father–mother–infant interaction in the newborn period: Some findings, some observations, and unresolved issues. In K. Riegel and J. Meachan (Eds.), *The developing individual in a changing world*. Vol. II, Social and environmental issues. The Hague: Mouton, 1975.

Partin, M. Social play among preschool children. *Journal of Abnormal and Social Psychology*, 1933, *28*, 136–147.

Perdue, V., & Connor, J. Patterns of touching between preschool children and male and female teachers. *Child Development*, 1978, *49*, 1258–1262.

Rosenberg, B., & Sutton-Smith, B. The measurement of masculinity–femininity in children. *Child Development*, 1959, *30*, 373–380.

Rosenberg, B., & Sutton-Smith, B. The measurement of masculinity–femininity in children: An extension and revalidation. *Journal of Genetic Psychology*, 1964, *104*, 256–264.

Rosenkrantz, P., Vogel, S., Bee, H., Broverman, I., & Broverman, D. Sex role stereotypes and self-concepts in college students. *Journal of Consulting and Clinical Psychology*, 1968, *32*, 287–295.

Rubin, J., Provenzano, F., & Luria, Z. The eye of the beholder: Parents' views on sex of newborns. *American Journal of Orthopsychiatry*, 1974, *44*, 512–519.

Schaffer, D., & Wegley, C. Success orientation and sex-role congruence as determinants of the attractiveness of competent women. *Journal of Personality*, 1974, *42*, 586–600.

Schau, C., Cherry, F., Kahn, L., & Diepold, J. The relationship of parental expectations and preschool children's verbal sex-typing to their sex-typing toy play behavior. Paper presented at the annual meeting of the American Psychological Association, San Francisco, August 1977.

Schell, R., & Silber, J. Sex-role discrimination among young children. *Perceptual Motor Skills*, 1968, *27*, 379–389.

Scherensky, R. The gender factor in six- to ten-year-old children's views of occupational roles. *Psychological Reports*, 1976, *38*, 1207–1210.

Scholsberg, N., & Goodman, J. A woman's place: Children's sex stereotyping of occupations. *Vocational Guidance Quarterly*, 1975, *20*, 266–270.

Sears, R. R., Maccoby, E. E., & Levin, H. *Patterns of child rearing.* Evanston, Ill.: Row Peterson, 1957.

Sears, R., Rau, L., & Alpert, R. *Identification and child-rearing.* Stanford, Calif.: Stanford University Press, 1965.

Serbin, L., & Connor, J. Environmental control of sex related behaviors in the preschool. Paper presented at the Biennial meeting of the Society for Research in Child Development, San Francisco, March 1979.

Serbin, L. A., Connor, J. A., & Citron, C. C. Effects of peer presence on sex-typing of children's play behavior. *Journal of Experimental Child Psychology,* 1979, *27,* 303–309.

Siegel, C. Sex differences in the conceptual choices of second graders. *Journal of Vocational Behavior,* 1973, *3,* 15–19.

Silver, D. S. The normative development of psychological variables in gender identification in 3–8 year old children. *Dissertation Abstracts International,* 1972, *33,* 5525–5526.

Spence, J., & Heimreich, R. The attitudes toward women scale: An objective instrument to measure attitudes towards the rights and roles of women in contemporary society. *Catalog of Selected Documents in Psychology,* 1972, *2,* 66–67.

Stein, A., Pohly, S., & Mueller, E. The influence of masculine, feminine and neutral tasks on children's achievement behavior, expectancies of success, and attainment values. *Child Development,* 1971, *42,* 195–207.

Sternglanz, S., & Serbin, L. Sex role stereotyping in children's television programs. *Developmental Psychology,* 1974, *10,* 710–715.

Taddenham, R. D. Studies in reputation: Sex and grade differences in school children's evaluations of their peers. *Psychology Monographs,* 1952, *133,* 1–39.

Thompson, S. Gender labels and early sex role development. *Child Development,* 1975, *46,* 339–347.

Tremain, L., Schau, C., & Busch, J. A multidimensional view of children's sex-typing of occupations. Paper presented at the annual meeting of the American Psychological Association, Toronto, Canada, August 1978.

Umstot, M. Occupational sex-role liberality of third, fifth and seventh-grade females. *Sex roles: A Journal of Research,* 1980, *6,* 611–617.

Vener, A., & Snyder, C. The preschool child's awareness and anticipation of adult sex roles. *Sociometry,* 1966, *29,* 159–168.

Vener, A. M., & Weese, A. The preschool child's perceptions of adult sex-linked cultural objects. *Journal of Home Economics,* 1965, *57,* 49–54.

Vondracek, S. I., & Kirchner, E. P. Vocational development in early childhood: An examination of young children's expressions of vocational aspirations. *Journal of Vocational Behavior,* 1974, *195,* 251–260.

Watson, J. Operant conditioning of visual fixation in infants under visual and auditory reinforcement. *Developmental Psychology*, 1969, *1*, 408–416.

Weinraub, M., Brown, L., Sockloff, A., Ethridge, T., & Gracely, E. The development of sex role stereotypes in preschoolers: Relationship to gender knowledge, gender identity, sex-typed toy preference, and family characteristics. Unpublished manuscript, 1981.

Weinraub, M., & Lewis, M. The determinants of children's responses to separation. *Monographs of the Society for Research in Child Development*, 1977, *42*, (4, Serial No. 172).

Williams, J., Bennett, S., & Best, D. Awareness and expression of sex stereotypes in young children. *Developmental Psychology*, 1975, *11*, 635–642.

■ 4
Sex Roles and Language Use: Implications for Mental Health

BARBARA KIRSH

INTRODUCTION

Both scholars and common speakers of language long have been convinced that men and women speak differently. The stereotypes of "men's" and "women's" language differences reflect many other stereotypes related to sex differences. This article examines what these stereotypes of language are, how they are similar to stereotypes of psychological sex differences, and what research reveals about the validity of these stereotypes. Implications for mental health and changing sex roles are discussed both in light of these beliefs about language differences and in view of actual language patterns.

Folk wisdom abundantly documents the contrasting ways in which women and men use language. Recent studies have examined what these stereotypes are and whether they reflect social reality. Why should we concern ourselves with comparing beliefs with actual behavior? The belief that women and men speak differently conditions people to expect differences that are indicative of an individual's "appropriate" sex role; we are labeled and evaluated according to whether we live up to the stereotypes. The reality of language use, however, may paint a more complex picture, one in which social situations and statuses are very important in generating contrasts in speech; that is, sex stereotypes of how people speak may correspond to power differences in society, and actual usage of differential speech may portray status more accurately than gender. As women's social status changes, language use may be an area manifesting substantial conflict.

Language is a particularly vital tool we use in everyday life, both to communicate information and to present what we think and feel about ourselves. What we say and how we say it constitute much of the material others use to assess us and to classify us as one sort of person or another. Gender and its accompanying indicators are salient status characteristics that people take into account in coordinating interaction and in labeling and assessing individuals.

The old stereotypes of the rational male and the emotional female surface in the following beliefs about language use: women's vocabulary is smaller than men's, although women talk far more than their male peers; male language is more useful, constructive, and abstract, containing more complex and embedded forms; female language is best adapted to trivial subjects and is used in highly emotional ways with unnecessary exaggerations (Key, 1975). We can compare these stereotypes of male and female speech with the personality stereotypes presented in the oft-quoted article by Broverman, Vogel, Broverman, Clarkson, & Rosenkrantz (1972). With language, as with other manifestations of sex roles, a woman can choose to act "like an adult" and be considered masculine or to conform to a feminine standard and not be taken seriously.

As clinicians and lay people concerned about sex-role change became aware of this double bind, it could be overcome to some extent by more flexible sex-role norms and ideals. This has been particularly the case for obvious role conflicts, such as those dealing with the dual careers of occupation and motherhood, or obvious personality traits such as passivity–assertiveness, dependence–independence and rationality–emotionality. However, the basics of individual interaction are so routine and taken for granted, it is difficult to bring to full consciousness what we actually do when we converse with various other people and what we communicate along with our words. These patterns are fairly difficult to change because of their ingrained, reflexive nature. Our relationships with others and, indeed, with ourselves, are built on a foundation of how we act and how others see us (the "looking-glass self"). From this stems the interrelatedness of concerns for language use, sex roles, and mental health.

Language patterns and sex roles are related directly to mental health in several ways. First, as children develop self-concepts and notions of sex roles, they incorporate their perceptions of how their gender is evaluated by society. Certain usages in English convey the impression that women gain their identity through association with men and never attain full adulthood themselves. Examples of this type of usage are calling a woman by her husband's name (Mrs. John Doe); asymmetrical naming (the man is Mr. Jones, the woman is Camille); the journalistic practice still used by *The New York Times* of referring to a man by his last name but retaining "Miss" or "Mrs." before a woman's last name, both to indicate that women need gentler, protective treatment and to communicate the woman's marital state; and calling mature women "girls," thus denying them respect and the assumptions of competence due to adults. Children pick up these social indicators of women's status and incorporate them into self-concepts and expectations.

Connotations of words also can be detrimental to an individual's feelings of worth. For example, generations of young women have studied textbooks concerned with the problems of "man's origins" or "political man" and read generalizations of "man's potential." Texts present "caveman" who invented fire, art, and hunting, while the few illustrations that include women generally present them hovering around the cave with their children, waiting for the men to appear with food. Being so completely excluded from history and from serious educational study can communicate that women are not expected to contribute to society, aside from procreation related roles. This problem is continued and reinforced by such language use as considering "man" inclusive of all people and "he" sufficient for both "he" and "she."

Another way in which language and sex roles are related to mental health is by the linguistic and paralinguistic patterns used in everyday interaction, especially those between men and women. These typified patterns prevail both in personal and impersonal contacts; however, in English, generalizations about language use by sex are not rigid and categorical but rather statistical probabilities or higher frequencies of occurrence for men or women. These patterns and what they communicate about relationships between the sexes and individual competencies, self-concepts, and expectations are the main concern of this chapter.

Many individuals are caught in conflict situations in these days of rapid sex-role change. Parts of identities, self-concepts, and feelings of worth are tied to older traditions of what it means to be masculine or feminine, and yet other parts are striving for more modern, androgynous definitions. Much of the conflict prevails in speech between men and women; some specific indicators of sex-role conditioning are patterns of silence and interruptions, affirming or ignoring another's speech, topic change, tone and volume of voice, word choice, hedging or overqualifying one's meaning, using hypercorrect grammar, and pure quantity of speech. Breaking the semiconscious verbal taboos for each sex can result in embarrassing discomfort; however, women's conforming to norms for female speech also can reinforce a negative self-image and feelings of incompetence, passivity, and emotionality.

The following sections will present the stereotypes of language use, research of sex-role indicators in language, and the implications of both for mental health concerns and sex-role conflicts.

BELIEFS ABOUT SEX DIFFERENCES

Quantity of Speech

In "The Sex of the Speaker as a Sociolinguistic Variable" (1975), Swacker notes that many languages and cultures have popular sayings to the effect that women talk more than men and that women's speech is centered on trivial topics and is in nonstandard (i.e., nonmale) form. In England, China, Spain, and many other geographically disparate places, variations exist on this theme. Linguists Otto Jespersen (1922) and Theodor Reik (1954) agreed with folk wisdom that "women talk and talk and talk while men are the strong, silent type" (Swacker, 1975, p. 77). While people believe women talk more than men, they also think that women should try to refrain from verbosity and encourage men to talk. Kramer notes a 1972 *New Yorker* ad for a *Seventeen* publication that quotes teenage boys: "I like a girl who talks — but not a whole lot," and "I like girls who listen to me without interrupting and who pay attention" (Kramer, 1975, p. 47).

Kramer compiled studies of actual male–female differences in language use, as well as what people believe these differences are. She found that people confuse what they believe to be the facts of language differences with what they think these differences should be, like the teenage boys in the above-mentioned ad. Kramer wonders whether a "talkative" woman is one who speaks with the same frequency and length of utterance as the "average" man.

Kramer, Thorne, & Henley (1978) caution that the same behavior by men and women can be defined in wildly different ways; for example, where men are assertive, women are judged aggressive and bitchy. So a small amount of female speech is heard as too much and of inconsequential content, while male speech is deemed necessary, important, and just sufficient. Men may feel more social pressure for successful verbal performance, while women receive tacit support for silence or supportive head-nodding behavior while men speak. There is speculation among speech therapists that this pressure on boys surfaces in the high percentage of stutterers who are male.

Folk beliefs about sex differences in verbosity have been proven wrong in studies observing both sexes, both in group situations and alone. Men talk far more than women in most of these studies. In Swacker's work (1975), she found great variation in verbosity between college men and women when they were asked to describe a series of Albrecht Durer drawings. Seventeen women and 17 men individually spoke into a tape recorder and described the prints with as much detail as they wanted. Three of the men spoke for the full 30 minutes, until the tape cassettes finished; these subjects considerably raised the male average for speaking time. The descriptions of the three pictures averaged 780 seconds for men and 222 seconds for women; the average description for the middle picture was 333 seconds for men and 96 seconds for women.

Eakins & Eakins (1978) taped seven faculty meetings at a university during an academic year, transcribed the tapes, and timed speaker turns. They report that, "with one exception, the males surpassed the females in number of verbal turns taken. The women with the fewest turns averaged 5.5 a meeting. The man with fewest turns not only had over twice as many as she, but he exceeded all the other women except one in number of turns" (p. 26). They continue,

> Except for the department chairman, who often could be present for only a portion of the meetings, the number of turns follow a hierarchy of power or status, according to rank, importance, or length of time in the department. The person with more power tended to take more turns. Of course, it could be argued that the more talkative person achieves more status and acquires more power in the group situation. The males, without exception, spoke longer per turn. The longest average turn for a male was 17.07 seconds. The longest average turn for a female was 10 seconds. But it was not quite so

long as the average shortest turn for a male, 10.66 seconds. Shortest average turn time for a female was three seconds. [Eakins & Eakins, 1978, p. 26]

Men also talked more than women in a study by Marion Wood (1966). Wood had 18 women and 18 men describe 12 photographs of a man's face. The expression was different on each picture and subjects were supposed to describe each picture so that someone else could select the right picture out of many others. The subjects were told whether their partner picked the correct picture; however, these results were fixed so that predetermined success or failure was reported to the subject, to study the effect of success and failure. The dyads were arranged in same-sex or mixed-sex pairs. The all-male dyads used more words per utterance than the all-female pairs. The men also spoke more with women partners, despite success or failure. Women spoke neither more nor less depending on the sequence of failure, success, or alternating failure and success. Men, however, spoke longer when they at first encountered alternating outcomes and then failure. Perhaps men are more concerned with communication failure than women, who don't expect to succeed. "If females accept the folk view that women's speech is unorganized or illogical or confused, they may view communication failure casually with a so-what-else-is-new attitude of resignation" (Eakins & Eakins, 1978, p. 27).

Fishman's study (1978) of verbal patterns among three heterosexual couples (each living together) presents a good example of what she calls "interactional shit-work." In over 50 hours of taped conversations from the three couples' homes, overwhelming evidence appeared that the women had to struggle constantly to receive any interest or affirmation for what they said. The men usually ignored the women's speech, interrupting or abruptly changing the topic. The women worked hard to converse, resorting to bids for attention such as "Guess what?" and "Ya know?" at the end of statements. The men also controlled the tape recorder, turning over and changing the tapes and sometimes turning the machine on when the women were unaware of it.

During a recent (April 1981) N.O.W. meeting at which the members split up into eight-person discussion groups, the author and one of the editors participated in a group with six women and two men. One of the men talked almost nonstop for the entire hour, controlling topics, interrupting others' speech, and presenting sidetracking questions. Several women pointed out to the group that this typical male dominance pattern was especially ironic and out of place at a feminist meeting, but the man merely incorporated this subject into his control of the conversation.

Spender's review (1980) of sex differences in speech frequency and quantity confirms that men generate far more than their share in conversations with women. Much of women's verbalizations in mixed-sex talk, particularly among couples, involves reinforcing the man's speech by asking him questions on his topic choices and affirming his opinions or interests.

Social Dialect Differences

Key presents several features of what she calls "social dialect differences" (1975, p. 36). She says women often listen silently while a group of men talk, although the reverse pattern is rare. Men use patronizing and familiar language ("dear") to women, but not women to men. Also, "Males are forever explaining things to women. It is rare that a male will have the patience or desire to listen to explanations from females. Males are the givers of information, not the receivers" (p. 37). This reinforces the stereotype of the competent male leader and the passive, uninformed female follower.

Robin Lakoff (1979) ventures so far as to propose that people have unified personality and speech styles and that substantial gender differences exist among English speakers. Lakoff dichotomizes mode of rapport and posits four styles of speaking, two of which are associated with males (clarity and distance) and two with females (deference and camaraderie). As Jessie Bernard notes (1979), this typology is exceedingly close to Parsons and colleagues' (1955) sex-role differentiation theory of males as instrumental and females as expressive.

Another stereotype of women's speech is that it lacks authority. Lakoff's typology (1975) characterizing women's language as deferent and socially facilitating suggests more specific indicators of what constitutes a nonauthoritative speech style. For example, Lakoff claims that women use more "empty" adjectives and intensifiers (so, very, really, such) than men. This usage focuses attention on the intensified words rather than on the content of the sentence.

Kramer (1975) suggests that women ask more questions than men, for example, by ending declarative sentences with a question (a tag question). With this form, a woman weakens the content of the statement by seeking affirmation or reassurance from the listener. "It looks like rain today, doesn't it?" is an example of this practice. Lakoff mentions a rise in intonation at the end of information as a female speech form: Husband: "When is dinner?" Wife: "Around six o'clock?"

According to Kramer, women qualify their opinions so they can be changed easily. Examples she presents are "I kinda like that house" and "That dress is rather pretty." We can add "It's sort of gloomy here" and the use of "just" to abridge the importance of an activity or belief, as in, "I'm just making a phone call" or "It's just an idea I had."

One stereotype of women's speech is that it trivializes ideas and activities, conveying the speaker's lack of self-confidence. This appears to be a chicken-or-the-egg problem, since women's self-confidence may be decreased by other people not taking them seriously; and yet speech can confirm or justify a lack of being owed respect. Whittaker & Meade (1967) were among the first to find that women are believed less often than men when presenting information. The Goldberg study (1972) confirmed this finding: Women college students rated identical written material more favorably when the author had a male name than when the author had a female name.

Another stereotype about women's speech is the pitch of their voices, often characterized as a cackle. Kramer (1975) mentions that etiquette books warn women to avoid loud, high-pitched speech. Television networks justified the nonexistence (until recently) of women newscasters on the pretext that high-pitched voices did not command attention or carry the necessary authority to present serious news. Even so, the women now on news programs usually present the human-interest stories, while the prime-time "important" news is presented by fatherly male announcers. Most voices in television advertisements are male, particularly the background "voice over" that conveys authority and assures the reliability of any product, from the latest car model to dish detergent.

The question of authority in speech patterns has been examined in studies of small-group interaction. For example, a 1977 study by McMillan, Clifton, McGrath, & Gale videotaped single-sex and mixed-sex groups as they tried to solve a hypothetical murder. The speech then was coded for four speech events reputed to occur more often in women's speech than in men's speech. These four speech events were intensifiers (just, so vastly), modal constructions that indicate insecurity (might, could, would), tag questions (didn't I, don't you think?), and question directives (Will you please close the door?). Overall, the results showed that women used intensifiers six times as often as men, modal constructions and tag questions twice as often, and question directives three times as often as men. It was predicted that the mixed-sex groups would elicit more sex-stereotyped speech; indeed, this was the case for three of the four speech events. Only intensifiers appeared more often in women-only groups than in mixed-sex groups; otherwise, women used more of the stereotyped speech forms when men were present.

Men's speech was not significantly different in mixed- or single-sex group discussions; however, both men and women interrupted women far more often than men, and most of the interruptions were made by men to women.

Kekelis' study, "Comparisons of the Linguistic Styles of Men and Women" (1976), attempted to quantify verbal interaction differences between men and women. Following Lakoff's distinction of status displayed as instrumental communication by males and social-expressive communication by females, Kekelis looked for differential use of tag questions, hedge words, questions, agreement words, personal pronouns, and mm'h'mms.

Same-sex and mixed-sex pairs of college students were taped during discussions of two issues, marriage and future goals. Transcripts of these discussions were judged for frequencies of the study variables.

The clearest findings were that mixed-sex pairs produced more mm'h'mms than same-sex pairs, and dyads of two women used twice as many mm'h'mms as did the male dyads. Male dyads used the most agreement words, nearly twice as many as in male–female pairs. Female dyads fell in between mixed-sex and male pairs in frequency of agreement words. In same-sex interaction, women used more mm'h'mms serving as supportive verbalizations, and men preferred agreement forms that were more assertive (e.g., "Maybe you're right," "Yeah, I know what you mean"). Both women and men used fewer typified agreements in mixed-sex interaction; that is, women used fewer mm'h'mms with male partners and men used fewer "assertive" agreements with female partners. Only one tag question occurred in the tapes, and hedge words and questions were infrequent and not found differentially in conversations of same-sex and mixed-sex dyads. Kekelis suggests the short duration (5 minutes) and the contrived situation account for there being no data on these measures.

STATUS AND CONVERSATION

Don Zimmerman and Candace West, in "Sex Roles, Interruptions and Silences in Conversation" (1975), propose that unequal power distribution in society also is manifested in daily interaction, such as conversation between women and men. They investigated inattentiveness, pauses, and interruptions occurring in conversations and found asymmetry of male–female power. They recorded conversations in public places, such as coffee shops and drug stores, and in private homes. There were equal numbers of recorded conversations among male–male, female–female, and male–female partners.

In the same-sex conversations, approximately equal numbers of overlaps and interruptions were produced by each speaker. In male–female conversations, 98 percent of the interruptions ($n = 48$) and all of the overlaps ($n = 9$) were produced by the male speaker. These intrusions were spread uniformly among all mixed-sex conversations; in contrast, only seven interruptions occurred in the 20 same-sex conversations, and all of these seven were within three dyads. Five of the 11 male–female tapes contained the nine overlaps, and ten of the 20 same-sex tapes produced the 22 overlaps. When the conversations were analyzed for patterns of silence, women in the cross-sex pairs were silent most often. In same-sex conversations, silence was distributed more equally. Zimmerman & West (1975) note that 62 percent of all female silences in cross-sex situations occurred after (1) a male delayed "minimal response," (2) a male overlap, or (3) a male interruption. The person interrupting changes the topic and denies the other person's determining the topic. The men in cross-sex conversations assert their right to topic control, and women do not penalize them but become silent, yielding the speech turn. These conversational dynamics parallel male–female power asymmetry in other societal institutions, according to Zimmerman & West.

Another stereotype of women's speech is that of talking "like a lady," which includes using correct grammar and nonslang pronunciations and aspiring to upper-class modulations rather than working-class patterns. In fact, one of the clearest differences in English to be documented so far is that women use more "correct" or prestige forms of pronunciation than men of comparable demographic characteristics. Women also use fuller pitch range and change intonation more than men, and men speak louder and are less "fluent" (don't use "fancy" words), although they speak far more in mixed-sex conversations. One way in which men can be castigated for breaking sex-role stereotypes is to use hypercorrect grammar, tone fluctuations, and big words; this pattern is acceptable in upper-class settings, but otherwise is stereotyped as "affected" or "sissyish" in American speech.

In American English dialects, women tend to use standard forms more often than men. A common example is female use of "ing" rather than the male use of "in" at the end of words. Males also use the non-standard "ain't" more than women. Labov (1972) found that lower-middle-class women in New York City tend to display more hypercorrect usage than men of their class. Trudgill (1972) offers two possible explanations for his findings that British women use more standard, correct language forms than British men: (1) women hold lower social statuses than men and have to use every means for presenting higher status, and (2) men attain social status or respect by structural positions but women are judged by daily performance and appearance. Also, working-class occupations and their cultural concomitants are stereotyped as "masculine." Another possible explanation is that women are expected to present themselves as sexually purer than men, and coarse language implies coarser sexual tendencies. Thus, the sexual double standard may appear in daily life as a linguistic double standard that requires women to use more refined, ladylike speech.

CHILDREN AND LANGUAGE PATTERNS

Some people might suppose that these stereotypes and the women and men who fulfill them are a vanishing breed and that cultural changes that have affected sex roles in the past decade will phase out female and male speech patterns. These optimistic people might predict that one avenue of change would be children's speech; certainly changes in sex-role socialization should encourage children to speak alike and not embody older stereotypes. Recent studies on children and language, however, do not validate this optimistic point of view.

Although very young children seem not to articulate stereotypes of male and female speech, by third grade, children approximate adult knowledge of sex typing in language. Carole Edelsky (1977) studied male and female English speakers' conceptions of stereotyped male and female speech, including such slightly different versions as, "Oh dear, the TV set broke" and "Damn it, the TV set broke," and "Close the door" or "Won't you please close the door?" First graders had least agreement with themselves and with adults as to sex stereotypes; third and sixth graders approximated adults' judgments more closely. Edelsky commented, "Despite the fact that adults sometimes disclaimed a personal belief in the justice or validity of the sex assignment of language variables, with near unanimity, they admitted to knowing the linguistic stereotype" (1977, p. 52).

One pervasive myth about sex differences in children's language is that girls speak much more than boys and are more verbally aggressive. This notion does not bear up under careful study, however, although girls are more aggressive in verbal than physical encounters. According to the comprehensive review by Maccoby & Jacklin (1974), many studies have indicated that boys are more aggressive than girls, both verbally and physically. Girls seem to begin speaking earlier than boys and to show greater aptitude for verbal tasks after the age of 11. Girls and boys between these ages, though, have similar verbal abilities, although most studies show that boys (like men) talk more than their female peers in mixed-sex groups.

A recent study of preschool children (Kirsh, 1980) explored the problem of whether the status of gender or the status of peer-group popularity most influences the use of verbal directives. It was hoped to compare the ascribed status (gender) with the effects of an achieved status (popularity) on interpersonal power in the preschool setting. Directives are verbal attempts to induce another person to behave in a desired manner; their form and content are thought to reflect social hierarchies.

Videotaped speech of two preschool classes was coded by directive type: permission, need, imperative, embedded imperative, question, hint, and suggestion. Each of the 32 white, middle-class children had an equal amount of time to wear a small wireless microphone in the pocket of a denim vest. In addition, each child was administered a sociometric interview individually and asked to name classmates who were (for example) his or her best friend, fun to play with, good to invite to a birthday party, and so on.

From the literature on directive use, particularly the work of Ervin-Tripp (1977), certain predictions were made as to how children would exhibit social status in using directives; that is, some directive forms were expected to be spoken by people with higher status to those of lower status, and the reverse. Past work suggested that need statements, permission requests, hints, and question directives would appear most often when people of lower status spoke to people of higher status. Imperatives, embedded imperatives, and suggestions were expected to be directed downward in status.

Analysis of the videotapes yielded several results based on the two statuses. The clearest result was that boys spoke much more than girls and therefore produced more directives of each type. However, gender and popularity both influenced the relative frequency of the type of directives that were spoken and heard by each sex. Girls talked least to each other but used a much higher percentage of imperatives, while boys talked most to other boys and used a higher percentage of indirect requests. Boys were spoken to more by both sexes and were directed more need statements and permission requests. Very popular children of both sexes spoke and were spoken to more than moderately popular or unpopular peers. These most popular boys and girls used more indirect than blunt requests, in contrast with the unpopular children who followed the girls' pattern of lower general speech frequency with a high percentage of imperatives. Popular girls spoke more like popular boys than like their unpopular female classmates.

Lower status children — girls and unpopular preschoolers — spoke less but chose the most aggressive directives, in contrast to the higher status children. We could say that the children who feel it is legitimate to make demands make them more often and more smoothly, with less social disruption. Children less confident of their ability to obtain what they want resort to stronger verbal tactics but use them less frequently. This recalls the women's movement's discussions of the fine line between assertiveness and aggressiveness: Women are supposedly less accustomed to making requests of others, to being assertive, so they can overreact easily to situations in an inappropriately aggressive manner. In the directive study, it is possible to imagine the higher status children ignoring their lower status peers until the latter feel compelled to shriek out an imperative: "Give me that block!"

A study by Jacklin & Maccoby (1978) found that children of 2 years and 9 months of age directed more behavior, both positive and negative, to same-sex peers. Boys ignored or frustrated girls' demands and girls became passive, seeking their mothers in the presence of male peers. Both sexes spoke the same amount in same-sex dyads. So, beginning very early in life, interaction patterns between the sexes present frustrating messages to girls; the boys ignore mild female requests, setting the stage for sharper demands or physical intervention, and girls often respond by withdrawing. Jacklin & Maccoby speculated that boys dislike strong male prohibitions and try to prevent their encounters from becoming physically aggressive by using "smoother," less confrontational requests. This would confirm and explain the findings from the directive study (Kirsh, 1980) in which the girls — who spoke least — used the most confrontational demands, while the boys — who talked most often — chose the most sophisticated, least disruptive directives.

Haas (1979) reports a search for sex differences in mixed-sex dyadic interaction with children ages 4, 8, and 12. The main sex-related findings were that boys gave more information and the girls were more compliant. In mixed-sex dyads, girls laughed more than boys (noted as a deferential response); boys made more requests to girls than girls made to boys; and again, girls were more compliant with boys' wishes. Girls also spoke more about their personal needs and wishes than did the boys. Haas summed up her results by stating, "Some evidence was found . . . for an increase in gender-associated speech in girls between the ages of four and twelve. Boys by age four already seemed to use male-associated spoken language" (1979, p. 108).

CHANGING SEX ROLES AND LANGUAGE

The evidence, sparse though it is, points to very young children both knowing the linguistic stereotypes for males and females and also mirroring adult verbal patterns according to sex. What implications does this have on efforts to maximize life opportunities and mental health by expanding sex roles?

It should be of some concern that language patterns and their paralinguistic accompaniments reflect so accurately the social power of men and women, or at least are widely believed to do so. However, growing consciousness of language patterns and stereotypes can mobilize concerted social efforts to change them. The mass media spread ideas rapidly, and popular language is highly susceptible to change. Within the past decade, several changes in English have gained widespread use and acceptance, reflecting the conscious efforts of the women's movement to modify concepts about women.

Using "Ms" as an alternative to "Miss" and "Mrs." is an example of a remarkably successful politically motivated effort to change language. Many nouns have new gender-neutral forms; for example, chairman now is chairperson, mailman now is mail carrier, fireman now is firefighter, and manpower has been changed to workforce. The term "man" as generic for all people often is replaced by "humanity." "He" is no longer the only grammatically correct single-person article; writers and speakers can use "she or he" or switch both the subject and verb to plural "they." The word "woman" has been recommended strongly as a replacement for "girl"; the implication of greater respect and maturity for adult females counteracts the notion that all women want to be young and incompetent, perpetual children.

The increasing publicity given to conversation patterns in mixed-sex groups is exemplified in the May 1981 issue of *Ms Magazine*, with its cover story, "The Politics of Talking." General discussion in the media of sex-typed language patterns is one way of surmounting the belief that each couple has "problems communicating," and perhaps this awareness of how pervasive the patterns are will mobilize individual and group change.

It is probably easier to change individual word usage than whole speaking patterns, but both issues are amenable to conscious alteration to some extent. The experience women have had in rap groups during the past decade indicates that they can, indeed, speak to groups, that it is possible to introduce and sustain a topic, and that people can reaffirm the importance of another person's ideas by head nods or mm'h'mms rather than a lack of acknowledgment or untimely interruptions. Men in single-sex groups grow adept at making a clear point and taking the time to elaborate their ideas, learn to have the courage to tell jokes or narrate stories, and receive reinforcement for voicing ideas and getting them implemented. The difficulty at this point is in bringing women and men together to share the best of both speaking styles, without either sex resorting to the old, more comfortable routines. As sex roles continue to change, with most women acquiring occupational roles and many men venturing into wider household and child-care roles, language patterns also can be expected to change.

The language patterns that have been discussed in this chapter generally appear among hierarchical groups where certain members have greater or less prestige. Kramer (1975) wonders whether the so-called "female" speech patterns concomitant with lower power positions do, in fact, change when women reach higher positions of power:

If . . . women learn to control their speech to convey an impression that they are living in the background, does the woman who has obtained a position of some power alongside or over men have these techniques perfected? Or, alternatively, has she other characteristics of speaking which have aided her in obtaining a position of power? [p. 50]

This is an important question for further research and for consideration by mental health practitioners. Do powerful women, or women trying to expand their roles, need to prove their femininity by using stereotypically female speech to be accepted by men, thus stabilizing their own self-images; or must they prove their competence by speaking and acting "like a man" in order to resolve the stereotypical double bind in which being feminine and competent are incompatible?

IMPLICATIONS FOR MENTAL HEALTH

This chapter has discussed the stereotypes of sex differences in language and reviewed some of the research on actual sex-differential patterns in speech. While there are some indications that change is occurring in word use pertaining to gender, pervasive linguistic and paralinguistic patterns are more difficult to change because of their nearly unconscious nature. These language patterns still are tied intricately to notions of sex roles, and efforts to expand women's and men's roles must consider seriously the messages people give and receive when interacting.

The traditional stereotypes of the female role include passivity, emotionality, and incompetence, and these characteristics are perpetuated in some of the typical female speech patterns, or at least in the beliefs about how women speak. The beliefs that women talk too much and talk about insignificant subjects function to keep women quieter than they might be and to allow men to monopolize social conversations and work groups. The expectation that whatever a woman says is trivial and unimportant creates insecurity, timidity in presenting ideas, and lower feelings of self-esteem.

Current language patterns contribute to the dissonance between women's aspirations for themselves on the one hand and the social expectation that they display the behavior of a "real" woman on the other. The lack of authority attached to female speech patterns lowers a woman's chances for success in many fields and can reinforce the belief that women should stick to the traditional careers of mother and home-maker. This dissonance between aspirations and achievement is liable to be manifested in anxiety and depression. At the least, many women feel ambivalence toward their interaction patterns, worrying about appearing too aggressive by making requests or voicing ideas and yet feeling disgust and self-hatred when they repress their suggestions or make their needs clear to others.

The study examining directives (Kirsh, 1980) found that the children lowest in status resorted to the most aggressive verbal demands when they finally voiced their needs; the line between assertiveness and aggression seems to be problematic for people who do not feel they can legitimately make demands of others, and anxiety and guilt often accompany this dilemma. Perceiving that one's own gender is socially powerless can have negative effects on both girls and women. Many studies of minority groups show the emotional problems attached to being labeled as "the other" in comparison to the socially powerful group; common traits are deference and dependence accompanied by distrust of both the majority group and one's own group. Powerless people often identify with those who do have power, just as wives are expected to lose their own names and assume their husbands' names, vicariously enjoying the men's social class and professional associates. Until the past decade, when the women's movement made it acceptable for women to socialize with one another, women were expected to see others of their gender as their competitors for men and to shun the company of women as "boring." This dislike of one's gender must carry over into one's own self-concept, reinforcing the stereotype of women's ideas and speech as trivial, flighty, and irrational.

The attitudes people develop toward their gender are shaped partly by language used to describe women and men and by the connotations of those words. Different connotations exist, for example, for bachelor and spinster: The unmarried male is a dashing and enviable figure, while the unmarried female is the object of pity for her unloved and unattached status. A bachelor is assumed to be active in determining his life and is seen as sexual and competent, while a spinster is assumed to fall into her status passively, because no man wants her, and is seen as asexual and a failure at performing the feminine role of nurturance. Many women would recoil in horror from the label "spinster" and follow traditional sex-role norms to avoid that status; labels that connote negative stereotypes function as social control mechanisms to perpetuate the sexual status quo, in which women are defined only in relationship to men. As the connotations for "bachelor" indicate, men aspire to the least possible relationship with women (at least in cultural mythology). These firmly embedded notions reinforce the norms by which women work at relationships and interaction, while men concentrate their time and efforts at "instrumental," nonemotional tasks. An outcome of these norms is that many women can respect themselves and feel worthwhile only if they are loved by a man and have a secure identity in relationship to him. The high divorce rate and the probability of widowhood — since men often die younger than women — means that many women will need their own internal source of self-esteem and definition.

Epidemiological studies, however, have shown that mental illness is highest among married women and single men. This may appear to contradict the notion that women are happiest in a relationship. This norm, however, is mostly romantic myth; more likely is that interaction patterns within many married couples systematically strip away the wife's self-confidence, leaving her an impaired sense of her intellectual ability and a fundamental belief in her incompetence.

Some possible results of the sexual struggle in language patterns are the various forms of sexual inequality, some subtle and others blatant. The fact that men "win" much of the interaction by speaking more, interrupting more, ignoring what women say, and changing topics from female-initiated ones, while women do the verbal support work by reinforcing and affirming what men say, perpetuates the occupational structure whereby men hold higher status and women do "menial" support work. The job of secretary epitomizes the pattern of women's work supporting the male superior; the secretary (nearly always a woman) does much of the actual work and carries out the daily necessities of running an organization, while the boss (most frequently a man) claims all the glory and a higher salary. He is secure in his feelings of self-worth and competence because the secretary gets the work done and affirms his abilities through subtle forms of flattery: He is Mr. Smith; she is his "girl," called by her first name. He can touch her affectionately to assert his superiority.

With all the supposed change in sex roles during the past decade, the differential salaries of men and women have remained the same. Women who work full time still make approximately 60 percent of what men take home in salary. Language patterns and the stereotypes that accompany them make it more difficult for women to choose jobs with higher salaries and status. Being poor and unable to support one's self and family does little to enhance a person's mental health.

Feelings of incompetence and lack of an intact sense of worth contribute to various behaviors more typical in women than in men. Fear of driving or of being alone is fairly common in women, and agoraphobia very likely is a more severe manifestation of the belief in one's own incompetence and inability to succeed in complex interactions. People are socialized to believe that men are competent and women are emotional, and daily interaction patterns reinforce these beliefs; it is no wonder that disabling behaviors result in some women who have been systematically exposed to these beliefs.

SUMMARY

Traditional sex roles are maintained both by stereotypes of language use and by actual linguistic and paralinguistic patterns. Disturbances in women centering around low self-image, insecurity, depression, anxiety, and role conflict may be connected to general notions of what it means to be a woman and also to specific relationships in which sex roles create belief in a woman's incompetence, passivity, and dependence. Mental health practitioners should be alert to the ways in which interaction damages individual self-concepts, and they should look for ways of pointing out and changing self-defeating verbal and paralinguistic patterns in themselves and the clientele they serve.

REFERENCES

Bernard, J. Discussion. *Annals of the New York Academy of Sciences*, 1979, 327, 115.

Broverman, I. K., Vogel, S. R., Broverman, D. M., Clarkson, F. E., & Rosenkrantz, P. S. Sex role stereotypes: A current appraisal. *Journal of Social Issues*, 1972, 28, 59–78.

Eakins, B. W., & Eakins, R. G. *Sex differences in human communication.* Boston: Houghton Mifflin, 1978.

Edelsky, C. Acquisition of an aspect of communicative competence: Learning what it means to talk like a lady. In S. Ervin-Tripp & C. Mitchell-Kernan (Eds.), *Child discourse.* New York: Academic Press, 1977.

Ervin-Tripp, S. Wait for me, roller skate! In S. Ervin-Tripp & C. Mitchell-

Kernan, (Eds.), *Child discourse*. New York: Academic Press: 1977.

Fishman, P. Interaction: The work women do. *Social Problems*, 1978, *25*, 397–406.

Goldberg, P. Are women prejudiced against women? In C. Safilios-Rothschild (Ed.), *Toward a sociology of women*. Lexington, Mass.: Xerox, 1972.

Haas, A. The acquisition of genderlect. *Annals of the New York Academy of Sciences*, 1979, *327*, 101–114.

Jacklin, C. N., & Maccoby, E. E. Social behavior at thirty-three months in same-sex and mixed-sex dyads. *Child Development*, 1978, *49*, 557–569.

Jespersen, O. The women. In D. Jespersen (Ed.), *Language: Its nature, development and origin*, chapter XIII. London: Allen and Unwin, 1922.

Kekelis, L. S. *Comparison of the linguistic styles of men and women*. Unpublished manuscript. San Francisco, Calif.: San Francisco State University, 1976.

Key, M. R. *Male/female language*. Metuchen, N.J.: Scarecrow Press, 1975.

Kirsh, B. Status and verbal power assertion: Does gender or popularity better predict directive use? Unpublished dissertation. New Brunswick, N.J.: Rutgers University, 1980.

Kramer, C. Women's speech: Separate but unequal? In B. Thorne & N. Henley (Eds.), *Language and sex: Difference and dominance*. Rowley, Mass.: Newbury House, 1975.

Kramer, C., Thorne, B., & Henley, N. Perspectives on language and communication. *Signs*, 1978, *3*, 638–651.

Labov, W. *Sociolinguistic patterns*. Philadelphia: University of Pennsylvania Press, 1972.

Lakoff, R. *Language and woman's place*. New York: Harper & Row, 1975.

Lakoff, R. Stylistic strategies within a grammar of style. *Annals of the New York Academy of Sciences*, 1979, *327*, 53–80.

Maccoby, E. E., & Jacklin, C. N. *The psychology of sex differences*. Stanford, Calif.: Stanford University Press, 1974.

McMillan, J. R., Clifton, A. K., McGrath, D., & Gale, W. S. Women's language: Uncertainty or interpersonal sensitivity and emotionality? *Sex Roles*, 1977, *3*, 545–559.

Parsons, T., Bales, R. F., Olds, J., Zelditch, M., & Slater, P. E. *Family, socialization and interaction process*. New York: The Free Press, 1955.

Reik, T. Men and women speak different languages. *Psychoanalysis*, 1954, *2*, 3–15.

Spender, D. *Man made language*. London and Boston: Routledge and Kegan Paul, 1980.

Steinem, G. The politics of talking—in groups: How to win the game and change the rules. *Ms Magazine*, 1981, *9*, 43–45 & 84–89.

Swacker, M. The sex of the speaker as a sociolinguistic variable. In B. Thorne &

N. Henley (Eds.), *Language and sex: Difference and dominance.* Rowley, Mass.: Newbury House, 1975.

Trudgill, P. Sex, covert prestige and linguistic change in the urban British English of Norwich. *Language in Society,* 1972, *1,* 179–195.

Whittaker, J. O., & Meade, R. D. Sex of the communicator as a variable in source credibility. *Journal of Social Psychology,* 1967, *72,* 27–34.

Wood, M. M. The influence of sex and knowledge of communication effectiveness on spontaneous speech. *Word,* 1966, *22,* 112–137.

Zimmerman, D., & West, C. Sex roles, interruptions and silences in conversation. In B. Thorne & N. Henley (Eds.), *Language and sex: Difference and dominance.* Rowley, Mass.: Newbury House, 1975.

■ two
TRADITIONAL CATEGORIES OF PSYCHOPATHOLOGY

■ 5
Sex-Role Stereotypes and Depression in Women

ESTHER D. ROTHBLUM

Dear Ann Landers: How does a person know if he is depressed? I realize it isn't possible to be happy all the time, yet I fear my bout with "the blahs" or "the blues" is more intense than what the average person experiences.

Please describe the symptoms of depression so I can have a better understanding of what goes on with me. I feel isolated and inadequate. — OK Today But Worried About Tomorrow.

Dear Worried: Between six and eight million Americans suffer from severe depression, according to the National Institute of Mental Health, so if you are severely depressed, you are not alone.

Clinical depression is one of the most widespread psychiatric disorders existing today. In addition, most people sometimes feel down, "blue," or depressed as the result of common stresses of living, so what constitutes a "clinical" depression must be differentiated from a temporary

Portions of this manuscript were supported by NIMH Training Grant MH 14235 and by the Yale Mental Health Clinical Research Center (MHCRC) NIMH Grant MH 30929. The author would like to thank Myrna M. Weissman, Ph.D., for her helpful comments. Requests for reprints should be sent to Esther D. Rothblum, Ph.D., Department of Psychology, John Dewey Hall, University of Vermont, Burlington, VT 05405.

sad mood. This chapter will begin by describing the problems encountered with the definition and assessment of depression. Next, due to the fact that women consistently are found to have higher rates of depression than men — usually at a ratio of two to one (Weissman & Klerman, 1977) — we will discuss some hypotheses regarding the effects of sex-role stereotypes on the difference in depression rates between women and men. Then the chapter will examine the available research evidence as it provides information on how specific areas of functioning, (e.g., social, marital, parental, and occupational roles) affect depression among women.

The next decade will see continuing changes in the marriage and divorce rates, the structure of the family, and the job market for women. The final section of this chapter will present some implications for future research and treatment of depression in women.

DEFINITION AND PREVALENCE

Depression can be considered a mood, a series of symptoms, or a syndrome. The *Diagnostic and Statistical Manual of Mental Health Disorders* (DSM-III) (APA, 1980) defines a major depressive episode as consisting of these following three criteria:

1. A dysphoric mood or loss of interest and pleasure is present and relatively persistent.
2. At least four of the eight symptoms of poor appetite or weight loss, insomnia or increased sleep, psychomotor agitation or retardation, loss of interest in usual activities, loss of energy or fatigue, feelings of worthlessness, diminished concentration, and suicidal ideation are present every day for at least two weeks.
3. There is no evidence of mania, psychosis, organic mental disorder, or normal bereavement.

The Research Diagnostic Criteria (RDC) for a depressive syndrome (Spitzer, Endicott, & Robins 1978) include a dysphoric mood, at least five symptoms of depression, persistence for at least two weeks, absence of psychosis, and either impairment of functioning or seeking of treatment. While some studies use DSM III or RDC criteria for selecting depressed individuals for clinical or community research, others use cutoff scores on symptom scales. Popular inventories for depression include the MMPI

Depression Scale, the Beck Depression Inventory, Zung Depression Scale, and the Hamilton Rating Scale. Levitt & Lubin (1975) reviewed 16 inventories of depression and found a total of 54 separate items that were listed in at least two of the inventories. Thus, in addition to those listed in *DSM-III*, symptoms of depression include behaviors such as crying, inability to do ordinary work, and neglect of personal appearance; affect such as sadness, hopelessness, irritability, and guilt; cognitions such as self-devaluation, sense of failure, indecisiveness, dullness, and worry; and interpersonal items such as dependence, distrustfulness, and lack of eye contact (Rothblum & Green, 1979).

Two problems must be kept in mind about the diagnosis and assessment of depression. First, although authors of depression inventories often provide norms that correspond with clinical depression, not all researchers adhere to these norms. The MMPI has a definite cut-off score for depression, and scores below this are "within normal limits." On the other hand, whereas Beck & Beamesdorfer (1974) consider a score of 21 to represent "pure depression," studies using the Beck Depression Inventory with college students often use a cut-off score of seven. The second problem in depression research is that most symptoms of depression, including the dysphoric mood, are difficult if not impossible to assess directly, so that the diagnosis of depression is primarily made on the basis of patient self-report.

The point prevalence (defined as the proportion of the population that has a specific disorder at a specific point in time) for depression based on symptom scales ranges from 9 percent to 22 percent (Boyd & Weissman, in press). Point prevalence rates for men range from 6 percent to 19 percent; for women from 11 percent to 34 percent. Without exception, the rates for women exceed those for men in every survey cited by Boyd and Weissman. Point prevalence rates based on the depressive syndrome using RDC, *DSM-III*, or similar international criteria are much lower, ranging from 3.7 percent to 4.7 percent in U.S. surveys, with women's rates exceeding those of men (Boyd & Weissman, in press). Finally, lifetime risk of developing depression ranged from 2 percent to 12 percent for men and from 5 percent to 26 percent for women (Boyd & Weissman, in press).

The two-to-one ratio of depression in women versus men is evident in different regions of the United States, as well as in other parts of the world, for people under treatment for depression (Weissman & Klerman, 1977). Eleven studies that review sex ratios for treated depressed individuals in the United States and 26 studies that review similar sex ratios from other countries consistently indicate twice as many depressed women as men, over time. Exceptions are studies that focus on manic-depression, where the sex ratio is a fairly balanced 1.2:1 of women to men; and studies of developing countries (such as India, Iraq, New Guinea, and Rhodesia), where there are more depressed men than women (Weissman & Klerman, 1977).

It could be argued that women seek treatment for depression more than men and that these statistics do not reflect actual rates of depression in the community. However, Weissman & Klerman (1977) have collected similar data from community surveys. These surveys utilized large samples of nonpatients drawn randomly from the general population in both urban (cf. Hogarty & Katz, 1971) and rural (cf. Schwab, McGinnis, & Warheit, 1973) areas. Methods of gaining information included home interviews (Schwab et al., 1973), self-report questionnaires (Benfari, Beiser, Leighton, & Mertens, 1972), and interviewing one family member about the rest of the family (Siassi, Crocetti, & Spiro, 1974). Again, women generally preponderate in all countries surveyed and over all time periods.

An argument for biological susceptibility also has been put forth. If depression is not an artifact of women's preponderance to seek treatment, what about the possibility of biological factors? Can they account for the sex differences in depression? In the most complete review to date, Weissman and Klerman (1977) have investigated the evidence for possible genetic transmission and for female endocrine physiological processes. The evidence they cite concerning the relationship between depression and endocrinological factors is inconsistent. There is very good evidence that depression increases during the postpartum period. The evidence for premenstrual tension and depression as the result of oral contraceptives is inconsistent. Finally, there is very good evidence that menopause does not result in higher depression.

CONTRIBUTION OF SEX-ROLE STEREOTYPES TO DEPRESSION IN WOMEN

Sex-role stereotypes refer to beliefs concerning the nature of men and women. When asked what men and women are like, most people describe men in terms of competency, rationality, and assertion, and women in terms of warmth and expressiveness (Deaux, 1976). Although research about sex-role stereotypes has focused mainly on traits (Brover-man, Broverman, Clarkson, Rosenkrantz, & Vogel, 1970; McKee & Sherriffs, 1957), any commonly held belief about the characteristics of women or men, such as "women want to stay home and raise a family," can be considered a sex-role stereotype.

Sex-role stereotypes can be hypothesized to contribute to depression among women in three ways. First, the definition and symptoms of depression may be more similar to sex-role stereotypes of women than of men, resulting in differential diagnosis. Second, stereotypes about women and men may account for more restricted roles for women. Thirdly, women may be socialized to behave more passively and there-fore may not take action when under stress. Each of these hypotheses now will be described.

Sex Differences in the Diagnosis of Depression

Although the criteria for the diagnosis of depression are identical for men and women, it could be argued that some of the symptoms of de-pression either coincide with stereotypic descriptions of women or would be more acceptable if displayed by women. Table 5–1 lists de-pressive symptoms from Levitt and Lubin's survey (1975) of depression inventory symptoms that have a corresponding or similar item in Bro-verman's Sex-Role Stereotype Questionnaire (Broverman et al., 1970). Six symptoms of depression are similar to nine sex-role stereotypes for females, whereas only three depressive symptoms are similar to four sex-role stereotypes for men. Thus there is a slight tendency for the symp-toms of depression to coincide more with sex-role stereotypes of women than those of men. It should be noted, however, that depression inven-tories may not include all (or even any) of these symptoms and that the majority of depression symptoms are neutral with regard to sex-role stereotypes. Furthermore, *DSM-III* and RDC criteria for the diagnosis of depression are not based on any symptoms that are related to sex-role stereotypes as listed by Broverman.

Other critics have claimed that men are not diagnosed to be de-pressed as often as women, even when they report similar symptoms. Women tend to present more psychological and expressive problems, whereas men more often present physiological problems (Phillips & Segal, 1969). Men also predominate among alcohol and drug abusers (Weissman & Klerman, 1977). It is possible that men drink alcohol when they are depressed and that society discourages drinking in women.

TABLE 5-1. Comparison of depression inventory symptoms and items from Broverman's sex-role stereotype questionnaire

Depression Symptoms	*Sex-Role Stereotype: Female*
Crying	Cries very easily
Dependence	Very dependent
	Not at all independent
	Very submissive
Self-devaluation	Not at all self-confident
Indecisiveness	Has difficulty making decisions
Lack of anger (possibly)	Not at all aggressive
Social withdrawal (possibly)	Very uncomfortable about being aggressive
	Very home oriented

Depression Symptoms	*Sex-Role Stereotype: Male*
Lack of emotion	Not at all emotional
Irritability and anger (possibly)	Very aggressive
	Not at all uncomfortable about being aggressive
Neglect of personal appearance (possibly)	Not at all interested in own appearance

Lack of Reinforcement

Societal–environmental hypotheses for the two-to-one sex ratio for depressed women and men would need to include speculations about actual discrimination against women. Lewinsohn (1974) defines depression as a low rate of response-contingent positive reinforcement. Depression results when there are few available reinforcers in the environment or when individuals do not possess the skills necessary to elicit reinforcement for themselves. It could be argued that women's efforts to succeed have not been reinforced to the extent that men's have. In addition, women's roles may be more restricted and allow for less reinforcement.

Learned Helplessness

One could argue that, rather than there being actual social and economic discrimination against women, women are socialized to be unassertive, dependent, passive, or helpless, all of which behaviors lead to depression rather than action under stress. Beck (1967) considers depression to be mainly a cognitive disorder. According to him, the attitudes that individuals have about themselves, their environment, and their future are the result of distorted or irrational cognitions. Some of the cognitive distortions include overgeneralization, arbitrary inference (drawing a conclusion without sufficient evidence), selective abstraction (ignoring all but a few details in a situation), personalization (relating external events to oneself when there is no basis for such a relation), and magnification or minification (gross errors in evaluation). Perhaps rising expectations of women's roles with little opportunity to meet these expectations could result in distorted cognitions on the part of women. However, this model places undue focus on how the individual views the world rather than on how these cognitions concerning incompetency and hopelessness may be related to men's and women's roles in the environment.

Seligman's model (1975) considers depression to be the result of learned helplessness, or the belief that responding will not bring about reinforcement. This helplessness can be brought about through continuous response–reinforcement independence. Women who are trained to be submissive, dependent, or passive will not feel they have much control over their environment, so that the perception of no relationship between their efforts and any significant results in their lives would result in the feeling of helplessness.

REVIEW OF RESEARCH ON WOMEN AND DEPRESSION

This section will review available research on depression among women in an attempt to investigate evidence for the preceding hypotheses regarding the influence, on depression, of sex-role stereotypes about women's roles in society. Specifically, research on social, marital, parental, and occupational factors will be reviewed, as well as research on women in traditional and nontraditional roles and research on others' perceptions of depressed men and women.

Symptoms of Depression

Sex-role stereotypes permit women to be passive, emotional and expressive. Given this fact, are there sex differences in the ways women and men show depression? Preliminary research has focused on symptom differences on self-report depression inventories. Stein, DelGaudio, and Ansley (1976) found no sex differences on mood and symptom scales between male and female depressed outpatients. Hammen and Padesky (1977) found depressed college men to exceed depressed college women on the following items of the depression scale of the MMPI: memory not all right, not a good mixer, feel like smashing things, can't get going, hard to concentrate, fitful sleep, difficulty starting task, and cannot work under tension. Women exceeded men on only three items: low self-confidence, apathy, and criticism hurts terribly. On the Beck Depression Inventory (Beck & Beamesdorfer, 1974), depressed college men exceeded depressed college women on these items: inability to cry, social withdrawal, somatic preoccupation, sense of failure, weight loss, and sleep disturbance (Hammen & Padesky, 1977). Women exceeded men on two items: indecisiveness and self-dislike. Funabiki, Bologna, Pepping, and FitzGerald (1980) found female college students to exceed males on increased food intake, self-deprecation, unable to express feelings, verbal hostility, seeking personal supports and social support. Depressed females exceeded depressed males on increased food intake, adaptive responses, seeking personal support, self-deprecation and social withdrawal. Depressed males were higher only on self-preoccupation.

The results indicate some sex differences in the expression of depressed symptoms, with a tendency for women to report more expressive, social symptoms. It must be cautioned, however, that primarily college students were used who were not patients, that the results are by no means clear cut, and that further research should use more direct measures of symptoms than self-report inventories, such as direct ratings by observers.

Social Interpersonal Factors

Since sex-role stereotypes about women focus on warmth and expressiveness, will lack of an intimate relationship lead to depression? Several studies have focused on the correlation between depression and social or interpersonal deficiencies.

Among studies comparing depressed and nondepressed women, Brown, Bhrolchain, and Harris (1975) found women who were involved in an intimate relationship to be lower on depression than low-intimacy women. Weissman and colleagues (Weissman, Paykel, Siegel, & Klerman, 1971) found depressed women to be significantly more impaired than nondepressed women on the majority of expressive roles, including marital and parental roles, relations with the nuclear and extended family, and social participation in the community.

In a community survey (Pearlin & Johnson, 1977), unmarried subjects were found to experience more social isolation than married subjects. Altman and Wittenborn (1980) found six factors to distinguish depressed from nondepressed women: low self-esteem, preoccupation with failure, unhappy, pessimistic outlook, "narcissistic vulnerability," and a lack of a sense of competence. However, these studies did not look at sex differences.

Other research has investigated differences between women and men on interpersonal factors. Chevron, Quinlan, and Blatt (1978), using Broverman's Sex-Role Stereotype Questionnaire, found men higher than women on competency and women higher than men on warmth–expressiveness. Similarly, depression in men was associated with less competency and in women with less warmth and expressiveness. Furthermore, depressed men reported negative experiences centered around self-criticism; depressed women reported negative experiences associated with dependency. Miller and Ingham (1976) found that women who reported the lack of an intimate confidant had more physical and psychological symptoms than other women, including tiredness, anxiety, and depression. The same trends were true of men, but were not significant. Finally, Parker (1980) found women more likely than men to report depression in response to rejection or distance in a relationship and after experiencing a loss of self-esteem.

It is evident that negative social or interpersonal experiences and deficiencies are a major risk factor for depression. The absence of significant others increases isolation and one's vulnerability to depression. Furthermore, women seem to be affected by expressive–interpersonal factors to a greater degree than men.

Marital Status

Depression rates for married and never-married individuals show differences according to sex. Married men are less depressed than never-married men, whereas married women are more depressed than those who were never married (Gove, 1972; Radloff, 1975; Radloff & Rae, 1979). In Radloff's study (1975) of marital status and depression, depression rates for women and men who were never married are nearly equal.

The large sex difference in depression rates is accounted for by the low depression rates (using the Center for Epidemiologic Studies Depression Scale) among married men.

Not only are married women more depressed than married men, but depressed women have more marital problems than nondepressed married women. Some research has focused on social and interpersonal functioning of wives (Bullock, Siegel, Weissman, & Paykel, 1972). In this study, five areas of social functioning within the marriage were assessed by means of structured interviews of 40 depressed women and 40 matched nondepressed controls. Specifically, married women were questioned about interpersonal communication, submissiveness–dependency, sexual relations, feelings toward their spouse, and interpersonal friction. Depressed wives showed greater impairment than control wives on all variables that composed the five marital areas, with the sole exception of "domineering behavior." Women's records that indicated adaptive, stable, and supportive marriages before the onset of depression showed significantly less "submissive" behavior than in women whose records indicated maladaptive marriages before depression. Women in the former category of adaptive marriages reported being more "assertive and communicative" to their spouses, tended to withdraw from the husband during their depression in order to protect him from its consequences, and reported their husbands to be "protective and maternal" during the depression. Women in the category of maladaptive marriages blamed their husbands for contributing to the depression and " . . . used the symptoms to obtain attention, communicate needs, or exploit the spouse's feelings of guilt."

Controlling for age, education, and income of currently married individuals does not change the significant sex difference in depression (Radloff, 1975). The only exception was that unemployed married men in Radloff's sample were more depressed than comparable women, presumably because of sex-role expectations for men to be breadwinners.

Much speculation has focused on specific components of the married woman's role, in an attempt to account for the high depression rates. A popular theory is that the role of homemaker is boring and unrewarding and thus results in depression. Gove (1972) views married women without jobs as occupying only one social role, and one that in modern society requires few skills and is a position of low prestige. Brown and Harris (1978) isolated four factors that predispose women to depression: (1) a lack of confiding intimacy with her husband, (2) having lost her own mother before age 11, (3) having three or more children under 14 living at home, and (4) a lack of paid employment. This last factor becomes apparent only when the other factors have been taken into account and thus can be viewed as serving a protective effect.

Weissman and her colleagues (Weissman, Pincus, Radding, Lawrence, & Siegel, 1973) investigated the characteristics of depressed women who were highly mobile as a result of their husbands' careers. Frequent transitions were reported as the primary reason for inability to find employment that was satisfactory. Nearly all women in this sample had enjoyed being employed and missed the experience.

Weissman et al. (1971) found differences in the work performance between depressed housewives and depressed employed women, although they did not include employed men in their sample. Housewives were

> unable to carry out their usual houshold tasks for at least one to two weeks, they experienced impaired performance, needed assistance in household chores, experienced friction with several people, felt considerable distress while doing their housework, were minimally interested in what they were doing and frequently felt inadequate about their performance. [p. 395]

Employed women, on the other hand, did not stay home from work or experience friction with others on the job, displayed less depressed affect, and seemed more satisfied with their jobs. Both depressed housewives and employed wives felt considerable dissatisfaction with their relationships with their husbands and children. Marriages were "characterized by friction, poor communication, decreased affection and diminished sexual satisfaction" (p. 401). Thus, a housewife's role places her in more direct contact with her husband and children and increases her marital friction, decreases her work satisfaction, and increases depression.

A second theory to explain sex differences in depression rates of married individuals concerns the "superwoman" role of employed wives. Even when wives are employed outside the home, the burden of housework and child care usually is still theirs, so that employed wives in effect have two full-time jobs: career woman and homemaker. In order to investigate this theory, Radloff (1975) analyzed the amount of housework that married men and women engaged in. Her results indicate that 23 percent of husbands "work around the house or yard every day," compared with 69 percent of employed wives and 80 percent of housewives. Thus, employed wives engage in nearly as much housework as housewives do, indicating a dual load of work.

The research findings by Gove (1972) and by Radloff (1975) may seem contradictory. What they indicate, however, is a conflict in fulfilling the role of a married woman. Lack of employment may be boring, unstructured, and unrewarding, whereas combining housework with a job outside the home leads to depression through overload and stress.

Marital Disruption

Depression rates are highest for separated and divorced women, followed by the group of single, widowed, and divorced men, and by the group of single and widowed women (Hirschfeld & Cross, 1981). The divorce rate in the United States has approached 50 percent of all marriages. Less is known about marital separation rates, although a 1971 U.S. Bureau of the Census survey indicates that women are separated for longer periods of time than men (Bloom, Asher, & White, 1978). Furthermore, women represent the majority of single parents. Women are also more likely than men to become widowed, given the longer life span and the fact that husbands are generally older than wives. Thus, marital disruption is a significant risk factor for depression in women.

Briscoe and Smith (1973) interviewed 139 divorced individuals for the presence of primary affective disorders before, during, and after their divorces. Thirty-two percent of their sample met the *DSM-III* criteria of unipolar depression; the male-to-female ratio was 1:2. In general, individuals who had been depressed before the divorce were significantly more likely to be depressed following the divorce. Depressed divorced women were indistinguishable from nondepressed divorcees on all demographic and "domestic" variables with the single exception of inlaws disapproving of the marriage more often in the case of depressed women. On the other hand, depressed divorced men differed from nondepressed divorced men on a number of variables. The depressed men were older at the time of their first date, were less likely to have engaged in sexual intercourse with their ex-wives before marriage, were less than 30 years old when married, and were married longer than the nondepressed men. Furthermore, depressed men were more likely to have seen a marital counselor and to have had sexual problems within the marriage.

An analysis of the course of depression among divorced males and females (Briscoe & Smith, 1973) indicated that women were more depressed during the marriage, whereas men became depressed at the time of the marital separation. More women than men had depressive symptoms that were associated temporally with specific precipitating events, such as being informed of the spouse's adultery or the spouse's request for a divorce. Interestingly, the depressive symptoms of 17 of the 45 divorced individuals in this study were considered by the interviewing psychiatrist to have contributed to the marital disruption rather than to have been the result of the divorce.

Briscoe and Smith's study (1973) thus indicates that depressed divorced women and men constitute different samples. Women are more likely than men to become depressed in a disrupted marriage, often as the result of specific events contributing to the marital friction. Few demographic variables distinguish depressed women from their nondepressed counterparts, suggesting that it is the events leading to divorce that also result in depression. Divorced men, on the other hand, have a history of precipitating interpersonal and sexual factors that is not present among nondepressed divorced men. This suggests that among men, the incapacitating symptoms of depression may result in divorce.

Marital disruption similarly places individuals at risk for suicide. Separated and divorced persons are twice as likely to commit suicide as the general population (Bloom et al., 1978). Although suicide rates for women are lower than those of men, suicide rates for white females are highest for the divorced than any other marital-status category. Among nonwhite females, the divorced are twice as likely as the married to commit suicide, but the highest category of completed suicides is among the widowed (Bloom et al., 1978).

One of the specific problems affecting newly single women is raising children alone. The 1970 U.S. Census reports that over 85 percent of single parents are women (Brandwein, Brown, & Fox, 1974). Single mothers are faced with difficulties that range from financial problems and problems with childrearing to loneliness and the stress of socialization. Ilgenfritz (1961) identified fear of loneliness, loss of self-esteem, practical problems of living, and specific concerns for children as the major stresses facing single mothers attending a parent education program. Brandwein and colleagues (1974) focused specifically on the social situation of divorced mothers. Single motherhood usually implies downward economic mobility, since women earn lower incomes than men and mothers with young children often work only part time. Divorced mothers are shown little respect, and social attitudes are negative. Brandwein and colleagues (1974) state:

> Stigmatization is multifaceted. Stigma is ascribed to divorced and separated women for their presumed inability to keep their men. The social myth of the gay divorcee out to seduce other women's husbands leads to social ostracism of the divorced woman and her family. There are expectations of neighbors, schools, and courts that children from broken homes will not be properly disciplined, will have sex role confusion, and will be more likely to get into trouble. The mothers themselves may incorporate society's attitudes, feeling insecure and guilt-ridden regarding their childrearing abilities. They may seek solutions in attempting the "superwoman" role, or in fleeing to remarriage. [p. 499]

Furthermore, divorced mothers have no clearly defined social status and in fact often are blamed for a variety of social problems, such as the need for welfare (Brandwein et al., 1974). They are isolated and have few social supports, yet socialization with others and dating present difficulties given the multiple roles and stresses with which a single mother is confronted. Additionally, the remarriage rate for divorced women is lower than that for divorced men (Bloom et al., 1978), so that the role of single parent for women is likely to be longlasting. However, women who have left their spouses and who do not become reinvolved report better social adjustment than those who resume relationships with men (Rounsaville, Prusoff, & Weissman, 1980).

Finally, women constitute 85 percent of widowed persons (Abrahams, 1972). There is little research on social roles and problems of widows, even though much evidence exists that depression resulting from bereavement is long lasting. Abrahams (1972) reports that requests to a mutual-help program for widows stem primarily from loneliness, followed by requests for specific information for social and financial problems. Ninety percent of these requests came from women. Older women who expressed loneliness asked for a listener; younger women who were lonely wanted to meet new people.

Motherhood

In their review on mothers and depression, Shapiro, Parry, and Brewin (1979) stated that the presence of young children was the single most important factor related to conflict in mothers. It was mentioned earlier that Brown and Harris (1978) consider the presence of three or more children under age 14 living at home to be one of four major predisposing factors for depression. Brown et al. (1975) found a social-class difference in psychiatric disturbances among women who had a child less than six years old, with women exhibiting more disturbance in the lower class. Presumably, middle-class women have more avenues of child care.

Parental responsibility is regarded as a major life strain among unmarried individuals. Pearlin and Johnson (1977) found that the more children an unmarried person has, the more depressed he or she is. Because of the high frequency of single mothers compared to fathers, the results of this community survey indicated a large sex difference in the prevalence of depression as a function of parental role overloads. The presence of children has been related similarly to marital stress. Orden and Bradburn (1968) indicated that preschool children at home served to strain a marriage, based on marriage adjustment scale ratings by married individuals.

The studies on mothers of young children usually stress the burden of child care as an antecedent of depression. Weissman's research (Weissman et al., 1971; Weissman, Paykel, & Klerman, 1972), on the other hand, has examined impaired parental role performance as a consequence of depression. Specifically, depressed women were evaluated to be less involved in their children's lives, to have difficulty communicating with their children, as showing loss of affection for their children, and as exhibiting considerable friction, compared with nondepressed mothers (Weissman et al., 1971). Furthermore, depressed mothers were to have problems that varied as a function of the children's ages (Weissman et al., 1972). Weissman summarizes:

> Depressed mothers of infants were helpless in caring for the children, over concerned or directly hostile, laying the ground work for future problems with the child. Mothers of school age children were irritable, uninvolved and intolerant of the children's noise and activity. Most school age children, however, did not develop overt psychological symptoms. The most severe problems occurred with the adolescents who reacted to the mother's hostility and withdrawal with serious deviant behavior. While conflict existed between the depressed mothers and the children leaving home, most children were able to make the physical break from home. [p. 98]

It is not surprising that Radloff (1980) reports that, contrary to experiencing the "empty nest syndrome," mothers diminish in depression when their children grow up and leave home.

The evidence thus suggests that depression among mothers of young children is a highly significant problem, whether the depression is the result of the chronic stress of caring for young children or leads to child-rearing problems because of the mother's incapacitated state. Furthermore, the incidence for increased depression during the postpartum period additionally places the mothers of young infants at risk.

Employment

Traditional sex-role stereotypes for women stress housework and child care rather than employment outside the home. On the one hand, the role of housewife has become increasingly simple, requiring fewer skills and occupying a low-prestige position (Shapiro et al., 1979). On the other hand, Radloff's results (1975) showing that employed married women actually perform the majority of housework in addition to their career have been discussed. Does employment increase or decrease depression rates among women?

A study on career conflict and satisfaction among married women (Hall & Gordon, 1972) found full-time employed women to report significantly higher satisfaction than part-time employed women or housewives. However, housewives and part-time volunteers who indicated they preferred this role were more satisfied than those who did not prefer to be unemployed. Full-time employed women experienced the most time conflicts, yet time pressure contributed the least to role conflicts. Part-time employed women reported the most home-related conflicts and the greatest number of roles. Housewives reported low time pressures and a high incidence of self-related conflicts. Hall and Gordon (1972) found home pressures to be the most important contributors to role conflicts, which suggests that the part-time employed woman has the most difficult position.

Orden and Bradburn (1968) studied marriage happiness among employed women and housewives. They found both husband and wife to be lower in marriage happiness (using the Marriage Adjustment Balance Scale) if the wife was employed out of economic necessity than if she participated by choice. This finding was supported across the factors of age, educational level, and full-time or part-time employment. Interestingly, the authors found that marital strain among less-educated couples resulted from increased tension among husbands and a decline in sociability by wives. Among better-educated couples, both partners increased in tension and decreased in sociability.

Weissman and colleagues (1973) conducted structured interviews about depression on a sample of married women who had applied to a university career counseling center. Most had had multiple moves in the past few years, nearly all as the result of their husband's career. Eighty-seven percent of the women were unemployed and only 4.3 percent were working full time. Results showed 39 percent of the women to exhibit mild to moderate depression, with their social adjustment characterized by boredom, impairment in housework, and marital friction. When the depressed sample was reinterviewed four months later, all women but one were working or studying and there was considerable improvement on depression. The authors point out that the process of job seeking could have been stressful in itself; the study involved women who already had made the decision to apply to a career counseling center.

A study focusing on employed women and housewives in treatment for depression (Mostow & Newberry, 1975) found employed women to display significantly more depressed symptoms before treatment but to recover faster than housewives. Housewives were more impaired in social adjustment, had more economic problems, and displayed more boredom after treatment. Similarly, Brown and Harris (1978) found predisposing factors for depression in women to be less significant for women who were employed.

The evidence seems clear that employment generally has a protective effect for depression; however, one note of caution should be included: Welch and Booth (1977) found full-time mothers who return to paid employment to perceive their job as stressful and not to benefit physically or emotionally from the first year of their return to work.

Traditional Roles

Earlier research has described conflicts that women face between sex-role stereotypes about their household roles on the one hand and the pressures of employment on the other. Feminists point out that housewives once had a more prestigious role and that household duties required more skill. If that is the case, then women in more traditional societies should have lower depression rates. Gove and Tudor (1973) argue that, since women's position in society has undergone more changes than men's, the ratio of mental illness for women should be changing. The authors' review of community surveys indicates that prior to World War II most studies showed higher rates of mental illness for men, with a shift in the ratio in postwar years. Furthermore, communities that are under-

going a severe economic depression, with high unemployment rat
show higher rates of mental illness for men. Finally, communities
which women occupy more traditional roles show lower rates of men
illness than communities in which women's roles are changing rapid
(Gove & Lester, 1974). Specifically, Gove and Lester found depressi
rates for married women to increase as one progressed from southern to
northern cities in the United States. Rates for men from the more conservative South to the more liberal North show opposite trends. It must be
stressed however, that Gove's research has not been replicated, that he
did not include the diagnoses of alcohol and drug abuse in which men
predominate, and that cultures differ on too many variables to justify
any correlation with depression.

Nontraditional Roles

One may argue that women in the labor market occupy jobs with lower
salaries, status, and opportunities for upward mobility than men's. Now
that some women are beginning to obtain more highly paid and prestigious jobs, how has this affected their mental health?

There has been little research on professional or executive women.
Welner and colleagues (Welner, Martin, Wochnick, Davis, Fishman, &
Clayton, 1979) investigated psychiatric illness among community
women who were physicians or held Ph.D.s. Their results indicated that
51 percent of women physicians and 32 percent of women Ph.D.s had
primary affective disorder. There was little evidence of other forms of
psychiatric illness. The physicians, in addition to being significantly
more depressed than the Ph.D. sample, also were more severely depressed and had had more depressive episodes. Furthermore, 73 percent
of the depressed physicians were psychiatrists. The majority of women
reported prejudice in their training or employment, defined as " . . . her
income was lower than her male counterpart's or . . . she was strongly
discouraged or prohibited from pursuing her career." Sixty-seven percent of the depressed physicians and 70 percent of the depressed Ph.D
holders reported prejudice; the figures for nondepressed M.D.s and
Ph.D.s were 50 percent and 48 percent, respectively. Thus, prejudice
was reported significantly more often by the depressed women, although the authors did not ask whether prejudice was associated with
depression. Finally, career disruption was higher both in depressed
women and in nondepressed women with children.

Pitts, Schuller, Rich, and Pitts (1979) examined the American Medical Association records of deaths of physicians. They found the suicide rate for women doctors to be 6.56 percent, higher than that of male doctors and four times higher than the suicide rate for white American women of the same age. Although additional research is needed to corroborate these findings, it seems that professional women are at highly increased risk for depression and suicide.

Interactions with Depressed Individuals

Women and men generally exhibit similar patterns of depression. Recent research, however, points out that depressed women and men are perceived differently by others. Hammen and Peters (1977) presented college students with a written description of a male or female student who was undergoing academic and interpersonal problems. Symptoms of the hypothetical student were either those of depression, anxiety, or blunted affect. Results indicated that the male character was evaluated more negatively than the female on all ratings of severity, personal rejection, and perceived functioning. The depressed male was rejected more than the depressed female as a close friend, fellow student, and partner in an intimate relationship. There was no difference in ratings by male and female college students.

Coyne (1976) asked college women to interact with either depressed or nondepressed female patients and with nonpatients. He found depressed patients to be evaluated more negatively. Furthermore, the college women who spoke with depressed patients were more depressed, anxious, and hostile following the conversation. Hammen & Peters (1977) used both male and female college students as raters and both male and female confederates who played a standardized, depressed, or nondepressed role over the telephone. Results show that depressed persons of the opposite sex were rejected most strongly. Female raters made little distinction between depressed males and females on role impairment. Male raters, however, considered the depressed females more impaired. As in Coyne's study (1976), subjects were more depressed following an interaction with depressed actors. Finally, depressed actors of both sexes were viewed as scoring in the more feminine end of the Broverman categories of male- and female-valued traits.

The implications of these studies are provocative. Depressed individuals are "depressing" to have around and are evaluated negatively.

Depressed men are rated more severely and rejected in personal situations. They also are considered more "feminine." Thus, one could hypothesize that men may not express depression as readily as women.

What are the effects of long-term interactions with depressed individuals? Kreitman and colleagues (Kreitman, Collins, Nelson, & Troop, 1970; Nelson, Collins, Kreitman, & Troop, 1970) have investigated the effects on women of living with a neurotic husband in a marital relationship. Sixty male outpatients and their wives were interviewed and compared with 60 control couples (Kreitman et al., 1970). Wives of patients were five times as likely to be incapacitated as control wives on household roles, social activities, health, and child-rearing activities. Wives of patients were also twice as likely to have a psychiatric history than control wives. The longer the marriage, the less difference there was between patient and control husbands. The reverse was true for wives of patients: The longer the marriage, the more incapacitated wives of patients became compared with wives of controls.

When the same researchers interviewed couples regarding the types of activities they engaged in (Nelson et al., 1970) they found patient pairs to spend significantly more time together without others present than control couples did. Control wives spent significantly more time engaged in separate social activities than patient wives. Patient wives also scored lower than control wives on a scale of social integration. When the duration of marriage was taken into account, social activity increased over time for control wives and decreased over time for patient wives.

Kreitman et al. (1970) refute the theory of assortative mating in their study, since patient–spouse impairment increases with the duration of the marriage. Rather, they argue for a theory of "pathogenic interaction," where disability between spouses increases as a result of interacting in the marital relationship, with wives "modeling" the social activity of impaired husbands.

Coping Strategies and Supports

Certainly not all women become depressed, even under stressful conditions, yet most research focuses on factors that predispose an individual for depression rather than on protective measures. Weissman (1980) describes five factors that can serve to protect against depression: (1) a happy childhood, (2) no strong family history of depression, (3) a confidant, (4) social supports, (5) utilization of the health care system.

Pearlin and Schooler (1978) investigated coping measures that serve to aid people in avoiding harmful or stressful life events. A community survey was conducted to study coping mechanisms in four areas: marriage, parenting, household economics, and occupation. Coping mechanisms were most effective in bringing about change in the areas of marriage and parenting and least in the area of occupation. Men were found to make more effective use of coping mechanisms compared to women. Thus, women are not only at higher risk for depression but there is some evidence to imply that they are more poorly trained to cope with disruptive life events.

PRESENT IMPLICATIONS

The following conclusions can be made regarding the influences of societal factors and roles on depression among women.

1. Even though some symptoms of depression are more in accord with female sex-role stereotypes and although women tend to report more social–expressive symptoms than men do, the evidence for a sex difference in how depression is displayed is not compelling.
2. Lack of a social network or intimate relationship is a major risk factor for depression, and there is some evidence that women are more affected by absence of interpersonal relationships than men are.
3. Marriage serves a protective role for men but not for women. Housewives experience more marital friction and are less satisfied with their work than employed married women. Conversely, employed married women carry a dual load of work as they combine housework with their jobs.
4. Separated and divorced women constitute the category with the highest rate of depressed individuals. Women seem to become divorced as a result of specific precipitating events in the marriage; men who become divorced more often have a history of depression that may have contributed to the marital disruption.
5. Women constitute the majority of single parents and widows, with accompanying financial problems, loneliness, and difficulties in socializing.

6. The presence of young children in the home is the single most important factor contributing to depression among women. Additionally, depressed women have difficulties with child rearing, and the effect of their mother's depression on children, notably adolescents, is negative. Women become less depressed when grown children leave home.

7. Full-time employment has generally beneficial effects for women; however, recent research indicates that, as women enter nontraditional areas as a result of M.D. and Ph.D. degrees, depression and suicide rates rise dramatically, especially if they have experienced prejudice or career disruption in their work.

8. It is more acceptable for women than for men to express depression in society, but depressed individuals of either sex engender depression in others. Living with a depressed husband results in increased impairment and social isolation, over time, for wives.

9. There is some evidence that men make better use of coping strategies in the face of stressful life events.

What are the conclusions which may be drawn regarding sex-role stereoptypes and their effects on depression in women? Basically, the woman who hopes for marriage, a family, and a providing husband who will be the sole wage earner is dramatically increasing her chances of depression. On the other hand, the woman who enters graduate or medical school to pursue an advanced degree traditionally reserved for men is not immune from stress and depression; rather, she is likely to encounter prejudice and find that rates of depression and suicide among professional women are extremely high. Thus it is evident that depression among women is affected significantly by sex-role stereotypes about women regarding work, the marital relationship, and motherhood. In general, traditional sex-role stereotypes about the woman place her at greater risk for depression.

IMPLICATIONS FOR THE NEXT DECADE

Demographic Changes

The next decade will see several demographic changes in the composition of society. Some of the demographic trends listed by the President's Commission on Mental Health (1978) subpanel on the mental health of women will be discussed as they constitute either risk factors (−) or preventative factors (+) for depression among women.

+ 1. There will be an increase in the number of never-married women. Research has shown that this group is at low risk for depression.
+ 2. Women are marrying later and postponing childbirth. This will decrease the number of women with children, who constitute a high-risk population.
− 3. The number of separated, divorced, and widowed women will increase. This group is at high risk for depression.
− 4. The number of single parents will increase, resulting in increased depression.
− 5. Because of economic trends and differences in birth rates, the number of people in the lower socioeconomic group will increase.
− 6. Employment opportunities are not keeping up with needs. It is likely to be more difficult for women, because of a limited employment history, to achieve the jobs they want, compared with men.
+ 7. More women will work outside the home. Research shows that women who are employed full-time are generally less depressed.
− 8. The difference in income between men and women grows wider each year, resulting in more financial difficulties for women.

In summary, our expectations for the prevalence of depression in the next decade cannot be optimistic.

Research Recommendations

As the structure of certain groups in society changes, new populations and areas will emerge about which little is known. Research on women and depression in the next decade should include the following:

1. As the population increases in mean age, depression among the widowed and the elderly should be investigated.
2. Never-married women rarely have been the target of research, so little is known about their lifestyle.

3. The composition of the family is changing rapidly, so alternate styles of family composition should be studied, including couples who choose not to have children.
4. It is not clear why both housewives and employed wives are more depressed than never-married women. Research should focus on marital roles of both women and men.
5. Populations of women in blue-collar jobs as well as in managerial jobs have not been investigated. Similarly, research has not targeted men in traditional "female" jobs.
6. As any social changes are made, their effect on both men and women should be investigated.

Treatment Recommendations

The issues discussed previously regarding demographic variables and the research on societal factors that affect depression among women may leave one feeling hopeless about the role any therapist can play in changing depression. Thus, several aspects of therapy and mental health services should be investigated:

1. The immediate and long-term efficacy of any therapy should be assessed as it affects men's and women's depressed feelings, their relationships with significant others, and their functioning in the home and on the job. For example, a type of therapy may result in increased happiness and feelings of well-being for a woman but result in marital disruption and divorce. On the other hand, therapy could "stabilize" a woman's home environment but maintain her depression.
2. Research findings indicate possible sex differences in the importance of social networks and in the roles of marriage, divorce, employment, and parenthood. Therapists should be educated concerning the differential effects of these risk factors on male and female patients.
3. Since the interpersonal environment plays such an important role in depression, therapists may want to include the spouse, family, or significant others in therapy or to intervene more directly in the patient's environment.
4. As research points out at risk populations such as single mothers, divorced individuals and widows, special funding should target these populations in clinics, hospitals, and the community.

Social Change

Although the amount of research on women and depression has been increasing exponentially, it is too early to make far-reaching conclusions about major societal changes. For example, recommending funding for day-care centers as a specific solution for depression among women is impulsive, given our lack of knowledge of specific factors that lead to depression in mothers of young children. Similarly, it is unclear why married women are at risk for depression regardless of their employment status. Any large-scale changes first must isolate more contributing factors for a better understanding of depression in marital relationships.

The present chapter has attempted to review the research evidence and implications for societal factors corresponding with depression among women, particularly as these societal factors reflect the influence of sex-role stereotypes. Four hypotheses were presented initially to account for the two-to-one sex difference in depression rates: (1) biological susceptibility, (2) a sex difference in the diagnosis of depression, (3) negative reinforcement in the form of actual discrimination, and (4) learned helplessness. Evidence for the first two hypotheses is inconclusive. Research evidence for the latter two hypotheses combined is strong, often implying an interaction between both factors. Thus, the next decade will need to focus not only on research and social policy that targets such issues as economic or social discrimination for women, but also that investigates how women are socialized to be more passive and helpless under stress. Failure to do so, in light of the demographic changes facing our society, would not only maintain the high preponderance of depression in women, but significantly increase it.

REFERENCES

Abrahams, R. B. Mutual help for the widowed. *Social Work*, 1972, *17*, 54–61.

Altman, J. H., & Wittenborn, J. R. Depression-prone personality in women. *Journal of Abnormal Psychology*, 1980, 89, 303–308.

American Psychiatric Association. *Diagnostic and statistical manual of mental disorders*, 3rd edition. Washington, D.C.: American Psychiatric Association, 1980.

Beck, A. T. *Depression: Clinical, experimental and theoretical aspects*. New York: Harper & Row, 1967.

Beck, A. T., & Beamesdorfer, A. Assessment of depression: The depression inventory. *Modern Problems of Pharmacopsychiatry*, 1974, 7, 151–169.

108 : : *Traditional Categories of Psychopathology*

Benfari, R. C., Beiser, M., Leighton, A. H., & Mertens, C. Some dimensions of psychoneurotic behavior in an urban sample. *The Journal of Nervous and Mental Disease*, 1972, *155*, 77–90.

Bloom, B. L., Ashner, S. J., & White, S. W. Marital disruption as a stressor: A review of analyses. *Psychological Bulletin*, 1978, *85*, 867–894.

Boyd, J. H., & Weissman, M. M. The epidemiology of affective disorders. *Archives of General Psychiatry*, in press.

Brandwein, R. A., Brown, C. A., & Fox, E. M. Women and children last: The social situation of divorced mothers and their families. *Journal of Marriage and Family*, 1974, *36*, 498–514.

Briscoe, C. W., & Smith, J. B. Depression and marital turmoil. *Archives of General Psychiatry*, 1973, *29*, 811–817.

Broverman, I. H., Broverman, D. M., Clarkson, F. E., Rosenkrantz, P. S., & Vogel, S. R. Sex role stereotypes and clinical judgments of mental health. *Journal of Consulting and Clinical Psychology*, 1970, *34*, 1–7.

Brown, G. W., Bhrolchain, M. N., & Harris, T. Social class and psychiatric disturbance among women in an urban population. *Sociology*, 1975, *9*, 225–254.

Brown, G. W., & Harris, T. O. *Social origins of depression*. London: Tavistock, 1978.

Bullock, R. C., Siegel, R., Weissman, M., & Paykel, E. S. The weeping wife: Marital relations of depressed women. *Journal of Marriage and the Family*, August 1972, 488–495.

Chevron, E. S., Quinlan, D. M., & Blatt, S. J. Sex roles and gender differences in the experience of depression. *Journal of Abnormal Psychology*, 1978, *87*, 680–683.

Coyne, J. C. Depression and the response of others. *Journal of Abnormal Psychology*, 1976, *85*, 186–193.

Deaux, K. *The behavior of men and women*. Monterey, Calif.: Brooks/Cole, 1976.

Funabiki, D., Bologna, N. C., Pepping, M., & FitzGerald, K. C. Revisiting sex differences in the expression of depression. *Journal of Abnormal Psychology*, 1980, *89*, 194–202.

Gove, W. R., The relationship between sex roles, marital status and mental illness. *Social Forces*, 1972, *51*, 34–44.

Gove, W. R., & Lester, B. J. Social position and self-evaluation: A reanalysis of the Yancey, Rigsby and McCarthy data. *American Journal of Sociology*, 1974, *79*, 1308–1314.

Gove, W. R., & Tudor, J. F. Adult sex roles and mental illness. *American Journal of Sociology*, 1973, *78*, 812–835.

Hall, D. T., & Gordon, F. E. Career choices of married women: Effects on conflict role behaviour and satisfaction. *Journal of Applied Psychology*, 1972, *58*, 42–48.

Hammen, C. L., & Padesky, C. A. Sex differences in the expression of depression. Paper presented at the Annual Convention of the American Psychological Association, San Francisco, Calif., 1977.

Hammen, D. L., & Peters, S. D. Differential responses to male and female depressive reactions. *Journal of Consulting & Clinical Psychology*, 1977, *45*, 994–1001.

Hammen, D. L., & Peters, S. D. Interpersonal consequences of depression: Responses to men and women enacting a depressed role. *Journal of Abnormal Psychology*, 1978, *87*, 322–332.

Hirschfeld, R. M. A., & Cross, C. K. Psychosocial Risk Factors for Depression. In D. A. Regier, & G. Allen (Eds.), *Risk factor research in the major mental disorders*. National Institute of Mental Health. DHHS Pub. No. (ADM) 81–1068, Washington, D.C.: Supt. of Docs., U.S. Govt. Print. Off., 1981.

Hogarty, G. E., & Katz, M. M. Norms of adjustment and social behavior. *Archives of General Psychiatry*, 1971, *25*, 469–480.

Ilgenfritz, M. P. Mothers on their own: widows and divorcees. *Marriage and Family Living*, 1961, *23*, 38–41.

Kreitman, N., Collins, J., Nelson, B., & Troop, J. Neurosis and marital interaction: I. Personality and symptoms. *British Journal of Psychiatry*, 1970, *117*, 33–46.

Levitt, E. E., & Lubin, B. *Depression: Concept, controversies, and some new factors*. New York: Springer Publishing, 1975.

Lewinsohn, P. M. Clinical and theoretical aspects of depression. In K. S. Calhoun, H. E. Adams, & K. M. Metchell (Eds.), *Innovative treatment methods in psychopathology*. New York: John Wiley, 1974.

McKee, J. P., & Sherriffs, A. C. The differential evaluation of males and females. *Journal of Personality*, 1957, *25*, 356–371.

Miller, P. M., & Ingham, J. G. Friends, confidants and symptoms. *Social Psychiatry*, 1976, *11*, 51–58.

Mostow, E., & Newberry, P. Work role and depression in women: A comparison of workers and housewives in treatment. *American Journal of Orthopsychiatry*, 1975, *45*, 538–548.

Nelson, B., Collins, J., Kreitman, N., & Troop, J. Neurosis and marital interaction: II. Time sharing and social activity. *British Journal of Psychiatry*, 1970, *117*, 47–58.

Orden, S. R., & Bradburn, N. M. Working wives and marriage happiness. *American Journal of Sociology*, 1968, *74*, 392–407.

Parker, G. Vulnerability factors to normal depression. *Journal of Psychosomatic Research*, 1980, *24*, 67–74.

Pearlin, L. J., & Johnson, J. S. Marital status, life-strains and depression. *American Sociological Review*, 1977, *42*, 704–715.

Pearlin, L. J., & Schooler, C. The structure of coping. *Journal of Health and Social Behavior*, 1978, *19*, 2–21.

Phillips, D. L., & Segal, B. E. Sexual status and psychiatric symptoms. *American Sociological Review*, 1969, *34*, 58–72.

Pitts, F. N., Schuller, B., Rich, C. L., & Pitts, A. F. Suicide among U.S. women physicians, 1967–1972. *American Journal of Psychiatry*, 1979, *136*, 694–696.

President's Commission on Mental Health. Report of the special population subpanel on the mental health of women, February 1978, 1022–1116.

Radloff, L. Sex differences in depression: The effects of occupation and marital status. *Sex Roles*, 1975, *1*, 249–265.

Radloff, L. S. Depression and the empty nest. *Sex Roles*, 1980, *6*, 775–781.

Radloff, L. S., & Rae, D. S. Susceptibility and precipitating factors in depression: Sex differences and similarities. *Journal of Abnormal Psychology*, 1979, *88*, 174–181.

Rothblum, E. D., & Green, L. The multidimensional behavior rating scale: A symptom assessment device for depressed patients and significant others. Unpublished manuscript, 1979.

Rounsaville, B. J., Prusoff, B. A., & Weissman, M. M. The course of marital disputes in depressed women: A 48-month follow-up study. *Comprehensive Psychiatry*, 1980, *21*, 111–118.

Schwab, J. J., McGinnis, N. H., & Warheit, G. J. Social psychiatric impairment: Racial comparisons. *American Journal of Psychiatry*, 1973, *130*, 183–187.

Seligman, M. E. P. *Helplessness: On depression, development and death.* San Francisco: W. H. Freeman, 1975.

Shapiro, D. A., Perry, G., & Brewin, C. Stress, coping and psychotherapy: The foundations of a clinical approach. In T. Cox & C. Mackay (Eds.), *Psychophysiological response to occupational stress.* New York: International Publishing, 1979.

Siassi, I., Crocetti, G., & Spiro, H. R. Loneliness and dissatisfaction in a blue collar population. *Archives of General Psychiatry*, 1974, *30*, 261–265.

Spitzer, R. L., Endicott, J., & Robins, E. Research diagnostic criteria: Rationale and Reliability. *Archives of General Psychiatry*, 1978, *35*, 773–785.

Stein, L. S., DelGaudio, A. C., & Ansley, M. Y. A comparison of female and male neurotic depressives. *Journal of Clinical Psychology*, 1976, *32*, 19–21.

Weissman, M. M. Depression in women: Risks and protections. Paper presented at the Eighth Annual Friends Hospital Clinical Conference, Philadelphia, Penn., 1980.

Weissman, M. M., & Klerman, G. L. Sex differences and the epidemiology of depression. *Archives of General Psychiatry*, 1977, *34*, 98–111.

Weissman, M. M., Paykel, E. S., & Klerman, G. L. The depressed woman as a mother. *Social Psychiatry*, 1972, *7*, 98–108.

Weissman, M. M., Paykel, E. S., Siegel, R., & Klerman, G. L. The social role performance of depressed women: Comparisons with a normal group.

American Journal of Orthopsychiatry, 1971, *41*, 390–405.

Weissman, M. M., Pincus, C., Radding, C., Lawrence, R., & Siegel, R. The educated housewife: Mild depression and the search for work. *American Journal of Orthopsychiatry*, 1973, *43*, 565–573.

Welch, S., & Booth, A. Employment and health among married women with children. *Sex Roles*, 1977, *4*, 385–397.

Welner, A., Martin, S., Wochnick, W., Davis, M. A., Fishman, R., & Clayton, P. J. Psychiatric disorders among professional women. *Archives of General Psychiatry*, 1979, *36*, 169–172.

■ 6
Women and Agoraphobia: A Case for the Etiological Significance of the Feminine Sex-Role Stereotype

KATHLEEN A. BREHONY

> I would like to see us take hold of ourselves and cease being afraid. [Eleanor Roosevelt, 1954, cited in Roosevelt, 1978]

INTRODUCTION

Overview

The general model employed by most clinical psychologists and other mental health professionals has focused on the individual client as the locus of psychopathological behavior. Traditional psychodynamic think-

I would like to acknowledge my indebtedness to Iris Fodor, whose bold and pioneering vision into the problem of agoraphobia in women spawned my initial interest in the subject. Her wisdom and scholarship have provided a sound and empirical foundation for my thinking and professional contributions to this literature. I would like to recognize my coling, for example, has posited a personality theory that requires inner traits and dynamics leading to "abnormal" behavior. Even the more empirically inclined behavioral approaches focus on the individual's behavior as a response to certain specific antecedents and followed by specific consequences. Few theories of human behavior generated by psychologists have focused on the larger sociocultural context in anything but an ancillary way. Nowhere is this lack of cultural perspective more salient than in the theories that have evolved regarding the clinical syndrome of agoraphobia.

The term *agoraphobia* comes from two Greek words: *agora*, meaning marketplace, and *phobas*, meaning panic, dread, fear, or flight from. Thus, in its literal sense the word means fear of the marketplace and describes a serious clinical syndrome in which individuals may become literally housebound for long periods of time, frequently an entire lifetime.

Theories of etiology have spanned a wide range of ideas describing these fears and subsequent avoidance behavior. These theories range from defenses against the expression of unacceptable sexual or aggressive impulses to the classical conditioning of fear to a previously neutral stimulus (e.g., a shopping center). A growing number of feminist therapists and researchers are unconvinced that any of these theories successfully explains the tremendous sex differences noted for this syndrome (i.e., approximately 85 percent of all reported cases are women). Rather, etiological factors are thought to reside in the cultural and social context that defines women's roles and behavior. It is an understanding of the societal sex-role expectations for women that is viewed as holding the key to the complex puzzle of agoraphobia. This chapter reflects this new and compelling feminist viewpoint. A rationale for this view using both clinical descriptions and empirical evidence will be presented.

leagues in this endeavor, Esther Rothblum, Violet Franks, Laura Solomon, Charlene Muehlenhard, and Marilyn Zegman, for their contributions to my formulation of this chapter through a history of stimulating collaboration. I owe a great deal to my very good friend, Laura Solomon, for her incisive and scholarly contributions to the development of my ideas through long and provocating discussions. I would like to thank Margo Kiely for her gentle yet stubborn insistence that I demonstrate the courage to say what I believe. I also would like to acknowledge my appreciation to my colleagues at Arthur Young and Company, especially Winnie Pizzano, for their encouragement and support of my professional development as a social scientist and my personal growth as an individual.

Description

Agoraphobia is the most pervasive and serious phobic response seen by clinicians. In fact, this disorder accounts for approximately 50 percent to 60 percent of all phobic problems (Marks, 1969). While the term literally connotes fear of entering a marketplace or public place of assembly, in reality the syndrome is far more complex. For example, agoraphobics report not only fears of entering into public places but also a generalized fear and avoidance response to leaving a place of refuge (almost without exception the home) and entering into the outside world. Additionally, agoraphobic symptoms tend to be more diffuse than is the case with more discrete phobias (e.g., fear of snakes). Goldstein and Stein (1976) noted that "agoraphobics tend to be more generally anxious and, at times, may appear undifferentiable from such clinical syndromes as anxiety states, affective disorders, or obsessive neuroses" (p. 173). The phobic individual usually recognizes the irrationality of her/his avoidance behavior, yet continues to avoid fear-provoking situations that elicit anxiety and panic states. The concomitant physiological symptoms of anxiety (e.g., hyperventilation, tachycardia, tremor, sweating) usually accompany acute phobic reactions, although there is a great deal of individual variation as to which physiological symptoms predominate (Malmo & Shagass, 1949).

Marks (1970) noted that agoraphobic individuals have fears not only of going out into open spaces but also of being in closed spaces and of shopping, traveling, and entering social situations, especially when alone. There is much fear generalization to additional stimuli throughout the course of the disorder, and numerous other symptoms commonly are present, including panic, "fear of fear," fear of fainting, tension, dizziness, frequent depression, depersonalization, obsessions, and numerous stress-related physical complaints. Furthermore, it is observed often that once the syndrome has persisted for more than a year it tends to run a fluctuating course, with partial remissions and relapses over a long period of time. Brehony, Geller, Benson, and Solomon (1979) observed that the mean duration of symptoms was about 19 years. Individuals with these fears generally develop extreme dependence upon others to take care of them in phobic situations and report that they feel unhappy, frightened, and lacking in confidence in their own abilities to handle themselves in panic situations. It is interesting to notice the similarity of symptoms from person to person, and Marks (1970) has suggested that there is little doubt from clinical and statistical evidence that agoraphobia is a coherent clinical syndrome with a well-defined cluster of behaviors that persist together over a long period of time. In short, this is a constricting, serious psychological/behavioral problem that disrupts almost all areas of an individual's life for a very long period of time (sometimes an entire lifetime).

Sex Differences

The observation that most agoraphobics are female (cf. Marks & Herst, 1969; Marks, 1970; Roberts, 1964; Brehony et al., 1979) is extremely important. Fodor (1974) noted that, on the average, 85 percent of agoraphobics seen by clinicians are female (ranging 64 percent to 100 percent). The data depicted in Table 6-1 illustrate the marked predominance of females reported as demonstrating agoraphobic behaviors.

The majority of agoraphobic women are married; in fact, this epidemiological observation caused Roberts (1964) to refer to the disorder as "housebound housewives," since most agoraphobic women defined their roles as that of "housewife" or "homemaker." Interestingly, Marks and Herst (1969) observed that 60 percent of the respondents to their large survey ($N = 1200$) in Great Britain indicated that they would prefer to work outside the home. These authors identified this group as "discontented housewives" and noted that they reported more severe symptoms of agoraphobia than women who reported being content with working only in their homes. Specifically, this group of "discontented housewives" reported more severe phobias, more psychiatric symptoms,

TABLE 6-1.

Investigator	Year	Total N	Percent Female
Tucker	1956	100	89
Bignold	1960	10	100
Warburton	1963	53	89
Snaith	1963	27	63
Klein	1964	32	81
Roberts	1964	41	100
Marks & Gelder	1965	84	89
Marks & Herst	1969	1200	95
Brehony et al.	1979	72	89

more fears of being alone, greater need of help from other people to deal with fears, more depression, and more extreme agoraphobic behaviors (e.g., avoidance behaviors). It was surprising, however, that this same group (discontented housewives) described their personality and behavior prior to the onset of symptoms as significantly more sociable, less anxious, and more independent than did those women content with working only in the home.

More recently, Buglass and colleagues (Buglass, Clarke, Henderson, Kreitman, & Preseley, 1977) compared agoraphobic women with a matched control group on a number of measures and found that their agoraphobic subjects ($N = 30$) were not significantly different from a carefully screened control group, in terms of frequency of nonphobic psychiatric disorders since age 16. Additionally, physical illness requiring hospital treatment (both inpatient and outpatient) did not differ between agoraphobic women and matched controls. In short, these researchers could not find any variables on which the agoraphobic women differed from matched controls (e.g., age, sex, SES) except on the agoraphobic symptoms themselves.

The marked predominance of women among agoraphobics is startling in view of the absence of such clear sex differences in most other neurotic disorders (Hare, 1965; Marks & Gelder, 1965). The possibility that women admit more fears than men does exist (Katkin & Hoffman, 1976) but this does not explain adequately the differential sex rations for the various phobic disorders. Indeed, the data suggest that animal phobias and agoraphobia are the phobias of women, whereas other specific and social phobias appear more equally in men and women (Fodor, 1974; Marks, 1970). In searching for potential causes for these clinical observations one notices an interesting relationship by considering the concept of social learning of sex-role stereotypes for women.

RELATIONSHIP TO THE FEMININE SEX-ROLE STEREOTYPE

The agoraphobic individual frequently has been described as soft, passive, anxious, shy, dependent, fearful, and nonassertive (Marks, 1970; Terhune, 1949; Tucker, 1956; Roberts, 1964). The similarity of these agoraphobic characteristics to the feminine sex-role stereotype seems clear. For example, women are viewed (by both men and women) as relatively emotional, submissive, excitable, passive, house-oriented, non-adventurous, and desiring security and dependency (Bem, 1974; Broverman, Broverman, Clarkson, Rosenkrantz, & Vogel, 1970). Fodor (1974) suggested that phobic symptoms, particularly those of agoraphobia, are associated with extreme helplessness and dependency and appear related to the social expectations for women. Additionally, she noted that interpersonal "trapped-ness" — the feeling of being dominated with no outlet for assertive behavior — may enhance further the development of agoraphobia. She also suggested that the agoraphobic response is an extreme and exaggerated extension of the stereotypic feminine role. Additionally, it is far more acceptable for a woman to remain homebound than it is for a man. The role of the "housewife" in this culture not only accepts many hours spent in the home but also encourages this behavior. In short, the stereotypic feminine role is typified by qualities of dependency, submissiveness, passivity, fearfulness, and nonassertiveness. In contrast, the stereotypic masculine role includes such characteristics as aggressiveness, assertiveness, independence, and competency (Bem, 1974). In light of this information, the concluding comment in Andrews' extensive review of the phobia literature (1966) is extremely significant. He writes that he has never heard of a phobic who has been described as "self-assertive, independent, or fearless." Furthermore, the phobic individual not only is characterized by dependency relationships with others but appears to establish broad-based avoidance of activities that involve self-assertion and independence in coping with stressful situations.

Empirically derived evidence for the relationship between self-reports of fear and anxiety and adherence to a sex-role stereotype was presented by Benson and Brehony (1978). Subjects were 174 college students (87 females and 87 males) who completed a number of questionnaires, including the Bem Sex Role Inventory (BSRI), the Wolpe-Lange Fear Survey Schedule (FSS), the Endler S-R Inventory of Anxiousness (S-R) and the Agoraphobia Research Questionnaire (ARQ). The ARQ is a new questionnaire being developed by these researchers and designed to assess symptoms of agoraphobia. The ARQ was tested with this college population as a preliminary to its use in clinical settings. Reliability and validity data are forthcoming. Subject sex and sex-role category designations (as measured by the BSRI) were employed as independent variables, with the FSS, S-R, and ARQ scores serving as the dependent measures in an analysis-of-variance procedure. Additionally, subject sex and the separate masculinity and femininity mean scores were entered into a multiple-regression analysis using the same dependent measures.

Results indicated that the ARQ was highly correlated with both measures of fear and anxiety (FSS and S-R). Furthermore, the data indicated that females scored higher than males and that androgynous and feminine subjects scored higher than masculine subjects on the ARQ. These data suggest a rather powerful relationship between adherence to a particular sex-role stereotype and self-reports of agoraphobic symptoms. The ARQ currently is being evaluated with several clinical populations of agoraphobic individuals.

The empirical literature in support of the hypothesized relationship between sex-role stereotypes and symptoms of agoraphobia has not matured to the point of allowing for unequivocal conclusions. Nevertheless, logical inference from an understanding of the sex-role expectations for women's behavior and clinical observations of agoraphobics support the general view, initially voiced by Fodor (1974), that the cultural expectations for women's behavior and the symptoms of agoraphobia do not qualitatively differ.

Fodor (1974) noted:

> Many women have been trained for adulthood as child women. Under the realistic stresses of adult life and marriage these "stereotypic" emotional, passive, helpless women become anxious, wish to flee, dream of being more independent or of rescue or escape. For some the emotional stress is too great and phobia provides another solution. [p. 133]

In fact, Fodor suggests that adult women's options to obtaining autonomy in their lives and relationships are obedience, flight, or phobia. The immersion into this exaggerated stereotypically feminine role allows the individual to become totally dependent, avoid autonomy and responsibility, and circumvent the need for responsible assertive behavior. Fodor noted that "this route is available to women since their socialization experience has not prepared them to be mature adults" (1974, p. 133).

Clinicians working with agoraphobic women frequently are impressed by the unwillingness of these individuals to take responsibility for their own well-being and by their lack of confidence in themselves as competent, coping adults. For example, Fairbank, Brehony, Sanders, and Ethridge (1980) asked a female agoraphobic client to enter a crowded shopping mall as a pretreatment behavioral assessment of avoidance behavior. She returned much later and reported that she had experienced very little anxiety during the time spent in the mall. When asked to go back into the mall while the therapists left temporarily she refused to return to the mall "for even a minute." She reported that she felt "safe" as long as someone she trusted would be available to "take charge" in case she panicked and lost control over her behavior. This response might be conceptualized as one method of abdicating responsibility for her well-being to another person (the therapists) in the event of an overwhelming panic attack. This dependency on others to take care of them is reported consistently by agoraphobic patients and also is commensurate with sex-role expectations for women in our culture.

Thus, agoraphobia may be construed, as Fodor suggests, as a logical—albeit extreme—extension of the cultural sex-role stereotype for women. This relationship becomes clearer when we illuminate the mechanisms by which women are conditioned to behave in fearful, passive, dependent, and helpless ways; indeed, in agoraphobic ways.

MECHANISMS BY WHICH SEX-ROLE STEREOTYPIC BEHAVIORS MAY RESULT IN AGORAPHOBIC BEHAVIORS

The central thesis of this chapter is that women are socially conditioning and educated to behave in a manner that predisposes them to develop agoraphobic behaviors. The mechanisms through which this socialization process takes place include classical and operant conditioning, modeling, and the transmission of information.

It is certainly true that the traditional social sex role for women appears to reinforce homebound behavior. Charlotte Perkins Gilman, an American writer and poet at the turn of the century, noted:

> The original necessity for the ceaseless presence of the woman to maintain the altar fire—and it was an altar fire in very truth at one period—has passed with the means of prompt ignition; the matchbox has freed the housewife from that incessant service, but the *feeling* that women should stay at home is with us yet. [1978, p. 111]

The matchbox—indeed, self-cleaning ovens, frost-free refrigerators, dishwashers, and other technological advances—have seemingly freed women of many household responsibilities and yet the feeling that women should stay at home is almost as pervasive today as it was when Gilman wrote over 70 years ago. For example, Franzwa (1975) reported data analyzing women's roles in women's magazine fiction from 1940 to 1970. This study revealed that the role of housewife–mother, including total dependence on the husband and complete dedication to the family, was the only proper role portrayed for women. Williams (1977) noted that this role was validated by "contrasting it to the deviant roles of spinster, divorcee, career woman, or any childless woman" (p. 289). Similarly, Lopata (1971) conducted a study of 600 Chicago women and asked them to rank-order the most important roles for women. Most respondents referred only to the roles of mother, wife, and housewife. Only 20 percent even mentioned roles connected with work or community or social organizations. Finally, a study by Rheingold and Cook (1975) demonstrated, through cultural artifacts, the expectations of this society for the behavior of males and females. Using a particularly innovated methodology, these researchers canvassed the furnishings and toys of boys' and girls' rooms (the children were all under 6 years old). Results showed that boys were provided more vehicles, educational and art materials, sports equipment, toy animals, depots, machines, fauna, and military toys. Girls were provided more dolls, doll houses, and domestic toys.

These data suggest empirical support for the notion that females are more likely to be reinforced for homebound activities, a behavioral pattern descriptive of agoraphobia. Thus, social contingencies actively reward women for taking on the role of housewife in our culture. Additional anecdotal evidence suggests that women frequently report some social punishment by family and friends for not meeting the "homebound" expectations of others. One only needs to consider the rationales of the many employers who are reluctant to hire women for certain positions since it is expected that once they marry and have families they will adopt the role of housewife and leave their job, as if the entry into the world of paid employment is but a brief excursion between adolescence and the role of housewife.

A second line of evidence attesting to the socialization of women toward agoraphobic-like directions concerns observations of differential responses of adults to the behavior of female and male children. A number of researchers (e.g., Hoffman, 1972; Kagan & Moss, 1962) have documented parental behaviors toward both female and male infants and children. The results of the studies and a host of others are compelling. For example, it has been observed that male infants demonstrate a higher activity level than do female infants (Garai & Scheinfeld, 1968). Hoffman (1972) notes that from these data alone one could expect to observe greater exploratory behavior from male infants. However, another study (Moss, 1967) has found that mothers handle and stimulate male infants more than female infants. This differential treatment was observed even while infant activity level was experimentally controlled for. Rubenstein (1967) suggested that this type of maternal behavior facilitates exploratory behavior. Thus, even shortly after birth the male infant appears to be encouraged to demonstrate greater activity directed toward exploring his environment. This sex-role expectation of greater exploration of the environment is maintained for males when we consider the sociocultural expectations for adults. In fact, Zuckerman (1971) has developed a scale to measure "sensation seeking," a behavior which in many ways reflects the propensity toward self-confrontation of novel stimuli, something closely akin to exploratory behavior. He has referred to the nonsensation-seeking end of his continuum as "agoraphobia." Indeed, agoraphobic individuals consistently report fear and avoidance of novel stimuli and say that their increased arousal in novel situations is always perceived to be aversive. This lack of encouragement in exploring one's environment, a hallmark symptom of agoraphobia, is characterized as being, perhaps uniquely, part of the socialization of females and is learned very early in life.

The developmental literature clearly suggests that adults encourage greater independence in male children, whereas they tolerate and reinforce dependent and helpless behavior in female children (Kagen & Moss, 1962). Collard (1964) noted that parents were more protective of female children. For example, parents of male children reported allowing boys to cross busy streets alone earlier than did parents of female children. Crandall and Rabson (1960) observed that grade-school girls were more likely than their male cohorts to withdraw from threatening situations and to ask for help from adults and peers frequently. Escape from threat and reliance upon others for help characterize the agoraphobic syndrome. It appears that the observations of children's behavior in a free-play situation are not qualitatively different from the observations of behavioral patterns of agoraphobic women.

Hoffman (1972) sums up a vast array of developmental literature by concluding:

Since girls as compared to boys have less encouragement for independence, more parental protection, less pressure for establishing an identity separate from the mother, and less mother–child conflict which highlights this separation, they engage in less independent exploration of their environments. As a result they develop neither adequate skills nor confidence but continue to be dependent upon others. Thus, while boys learn effectiveness through mastery, the effectiveness of girls is contingent on eliciting the help of others. [p. 403]

Early conditioning appears to produce differential social learning histories for girls and boys. The experiences of girls provide a history of encouragement for dependent and oftentimes helpless behavior, fearfulness, and escape from threatening situations. These behaviors characterize the agoraphobic individual, and it is posited that this social learning history provides an experiential background upon which the more full-blown agoraphobic symptoms of avoidance and dependency upon others are developed.

In addition to the individualized learning history of each person, all members of a society are presented with cultural images through a variety of forms, such as literature, advertising, art, and other media. That individuals learn to internalize cultural expectations and specific behaviors by modeling after these images has been demonstrated by Bandura and Walters (1963).

Most theorists of sex-role development (including Freud, 1933; Mischel, 1966; Kohlberg, 1966) emphasize the importance of the observation of sex-appropriate behaviors exhibited by female and male role models. Bandura and Walters (1963) clearly demonstrated modeling to be a highly effective method for influencing the acquisition of specific behaviors. That fear responses, in particular, can be learned effectively via modeling is supported by a variety of sources in the behavioral literature. For example, Jones (1924) found social imitation to be an important cause of irrational fear in children. Hagman (1932) found a significant correlation between the kind and number of fears expressed by mother and child. Murphy, Miller, and Mirsky (1955) demonstrated the acquisition of a conditioned avoidance response in monkeys who had observed other monkeys receive shock but had not received shocks themselves.

Indeed, Solyom, Beck, Solyom, and Hugel (1974) argue that vicarious learning or modeling is the salient etiological factor in the development of agoraphobia. This argument is made on the basis of their observation that mothers of agoraphobic patients ($N = 47$) had a significantly higher incidence of phobic neuroses than mothers of control subjects (31 percent versus 14 percent). Unfortunately, methodological problems preclude firm conclusions regarding the relative contributions of modeling, reinforcement contingencies, or genetic factors as variables in the etiology of agoraphobia. However, the Solyom study, taken with the other data, suggests that the social learning histories of individuals are likely to be a major variable in the etiology of agoraphobia.

Similarly, Fodor (1974) hypothesized that modeling extreme sex-role behaviors (often via media models) is a critical etiological factor in agoraphobia. In fact, she concluded that agoraphobia appears to be a "natural outcome of sex-role socialization rather than an illness" (Fodor, 1978). She presents rather striking evidence of agoraphobic-like behaviors in female characters in children's readers (NOW Task Force, 1975). Similarly, Sternglanz and Serbin (1974) evaluated sex-role stereotyping in children's television programs and demonstrated that female characters compared to male characters were shown to be significantly less behaviorally active and more deferent.

In conclusion, data regarding sex-role stereotypes (Bem, 1974) clearly suggest that the feminine stereotype consists of characteristics such as dependency, fearfulness, passivity, and low assertiveness. As such, most available female role models (both live and media images) present role-consistent behaviors as well. Andrews (1966), among others, has used almost identical language to describe both the female sex-role stereotype and the phobic personality. The similarities between characteristics of agoraphobia and the female sex-role stereotype are striking. This hypothesized relationship is enhanced when one considers that approximately 85 percent of all diagnosed agoraphobics are female. While the acquisition of the female sex-role stereotype may not be a sufficient cause for the development of agoraphobia (i.e., not all women who accept the traditional sex-role stereotype are agoraphobic), this set of social expectations may set a powerful backdrop for the subsequent development of agoraphobic fears and behaviors. Social prescriptions as to what constitutes appropriate sex-role behavior are likely to interact with other variables (e.g., classical and operant conditioning histories) in the etiology of this serious psychological disorder, resulting in the disruption of healthy functioning for many women.

IMPLICATIONS FOR THE 1980s:
DIRECTIONS FOR CLINICAL
AND RESEARCH ACTIVITIES

For too long, agoraphobic women have been asked to view their fears and lack of courage in confronting these as personal weaknesses or neurotic personalities. They have come to accept the notion that they exist, in Elizabeth Janeway's words (1980), as "solitary freaks," unable to cope with the world or even simple tasks in any normal, productive fashion. This definition, reinforced by many therapists, has served to isolate these individuals further and has forced the focus of their attention inward instead of outward toward the larger social context that has provided the arena for their helplessness and fears to be played out. The blame in this scenario lies not within the individual's own inability to cope but in the archives of a culture that has accepted and encouraged half its population to view the world with fear, helplessness, and the need to elicit help from others in far too many circumstances. Perhaps the question is more pertinent "Why are not all women agoraphobic?" rather than, "Why are some women agoraphobic?"

Elizabeth Janeway (1980) suggested that agoraphobia "is a kind of retreat into paralysis for those whose mistrust of life is pervasive but who can find no support that will settle the question of what to mistrust — oneself or the surrounding circumstances" (p. 169). The successful therapist will struggle with the agoraphobic client to re-identify the problem, to view fears within the context of one's own learning history, and to explain beliefs and behaviors as being a consequence of the experiences of women in a culture that encourages their helplessness. In this regard, their experiences are not likely to be viewed as qualitatively different from their more functional, nonagoraphobic sisters. This point must be made clear.

One powerful therapeutic technique for the accomplishment of this consciousness raising is the bringing together of individuals sharing these devastating fears; flesh-and-blood evidence affirming their experiences. Solitary freak no longer, the agoraphobic individual confronted with the reality of others sharing similarly aversive fears can question the notion that her own inability to cope resides in the lack of courage she inherits by virtue of being female. This is not to say that the agoraphobic should abdicate responsibility for her own behavior. Rather, through group validation and support she must learn that her eventual recovery lies in her strengt'ı and ability to confront the cultural expectations for her behavior and, frequently, the individuals that have supported her symptoms and been repressive to her growth. As Janeway (1980) noted, "The powerful may find it odd that a shared experience of weakness can strengthen the weak: but out of the sharing comes an ability to trust those who have been caught in the same bind as oneself" (pp. 169–170). Clinical and research evidence attests to the potent therapeutic value of shared group experiences in the resolution of problem behaviors. Nowhere is this strategy more salient than in the case of agoraphobia.

Treatment also must incorporate a relearning process. Individuals must learn to confront fear-eliciting situations in spite of the aversive and oftentimes overpowering panic that will ensue in these circumstances. The literature clearly points to this kind of extinction procedure as the treatment of choice (Brehony & Geller, 1981; Emmelkamp, 1979; Marks, 1978). While *in vivo* flooding procedures have been demonstrated to be more successful than imaginal procedures (Stern & Marks 1973), there is good reason to believe that methodological difficulties have obscured the importance of the imaginal technique. This relearning or extinction procedure may take a variety of forms, but the critical variable appears to be the confrontation of fear-eliciting stimuli and the emitting of new, more courageous behaviors in the presence of these stimuli.

Research efforts must address the issue of the relationship between sex-role stereotypes and other cultural expectations for women as potentially significant etiological factors for a variety of emotional–behavioral problems that demonstrate strong sex differences (e.g., depression, obesity). While this is acknowledged to be a difficult and arduous task, it no doubt will provide information valuable and critical to the understanding of the complex and compelling question of agoraphobia.

REFERENCES

Andrews, J. D. Psychotherapy of phobias. *Psychological Bulletin*, 1966, *66*, 455–480.

Bandura, A., & Walters, R. H. *Social learning and personality development.* New York: Holt, Rinehart and Winston, 1963.

Bem, S. The measurement of psychological androgyny. *Journal of Consulting and Clinical Psychology*, 1974, *42*, (2), 155–162.

Benson, B. A., & Brehony, K. A. *Sex-role stereotypes and self-reports of fear and anxiety*. Paper presented at the Psychonomic Society meeting, San Antonio, Texas, 1978.

Bignold, B. C. Agoraphobia: A review of ten cases. *Medical Journal of Australia*, 1960, *2*, 332–333.

Brehony, K. A., Geller, E. S., Benson, B., & Solomon, L. J. *Epidemiological data about agoraphobia: An American sample*. Unpublished manuscript, 1979.

Brehony, K. A., & Geller, E. S. Agoraphobia: Appraisal of research and a proposal for an integrative model. In M. Hersen, R. M. Eisler, & P. M. Miller (Eds.), *Progress in behavior modification, vol. 12*. New York: Academic Press, 1979.

Broverman, I. K., Broverman, D. M., Clarkson, F. W., Rosenkrantz, P., & Vogel, S. R. Sex-role stereotypes and clinical judgments of mental health. *Journal of Consulting Psychology*, 1970, *34*, 1–7.

Buglass, D., Clarke, J., Henderson, A. S., Kreitman, N., & Presely, A. S. A study of agoraphobic housewives. *Psychological Medicine*, 1977, *7*, 73–86.

Collard, E. D. *Achievement motive in the four-year-old child and its relationship to achievement expectancies of the mother*. Unpublished doctoral dissertation, University of Michigan, 1964.

Crandall, V. J., & Rabson, A. Children's repetition choices in an intellectual achievement situation following success and failure. *Journal of Genetic Psychology*, 1960, *97*, 61–165.

Emmelkamp, P. The behavioral study of clinical phobias. In M. Hersen, R. M. Eisler, & P. M. Miller (Eds.), *Progress in behavior modification, vol. 8*. New York: Academic Press, 1979.

Fairbank, J. A., Brehony, K. A., Sanders, S. H., & Ethridge, R. *Headache pain reduction as a function of intervention for a collateral behavior problem of longstanding agoraphobia*. Unpublished manuscript, University of Mississippi Medical Center, 1980.

Fodor, I. G. The phobic syndome in women: Implications for treatment. In V. Franks & V. Burtle (Eds.), *Women in therapy*. New York: Brunner/Mazel, 1974.

Fodor, I. Phobias in women: Therapeutic approaches. From BMA audio-cassette program; *Helping women change: A guide for professional counseling*. Guilford Publications, 1978.

Franzwa, H. H. Female roles in women's magazine fiction. In R. K. Unger, & F. L. Denmark (Eds.), *Women: Dependent or independent variable*. New York: Psychological Dimensions, 1975.

Freud, S. *New introductory lectures in psychoanalysis*. New York: W. W. Norton, 1933.

Garai, J. E., & Scheinfeld, A. Sex differences in mental and behavioral traits. *Genetic Psychology Monographs*, 1968, *77*, 169–299.

Gilman, Charlotte Perkins. Cited in Elaine Partnow (Ed.), *The quotable woman*. New York: Doubleday, 1978.

Goldstein, A. P., & Stein, N. *Prescriptive psychotherapies*. New York: Pergamon Press, 1976.

Hagman, C. A study of fear in pre-school children. *Journal of Experimental Psychology*, 1932, *1*, 110–130.

Hare, E. H. *Triennial statistical report, 1961–63*. London: Bethlem Royal and Maudsley Hospital, 1965.

Hoffman, L. W. Early childhood experience and women's achievement motives. *Journal of Social Issues*, 1972, *28*, 129–155.

Janeway, E. *Powers of the weak*. New York: Alfred Knopf, 1980.

Jones, M. C. The elimination of children's fears. *Journal of Experimental Psychology*, 1924, 7, 383–390.

Kagan, J., & Moss, H. A. *Birth to maturity*. New York: John Wiley, 1962.

Katkin, E. S., & Hoffman, L. S. Sex differences in self-report of fear: A psychophysiological assessment. *Journal of Abnormal Psychology*, 1976, *85* (6), 607–610.

Klein, D. F. Delineation of two drug-responsive anxiety syndromes. *Psychopharmacologia*, 1964, *5*, 397–408.

Kohlberg, L. A cognitive–developmental analysis of children's sex-role concepts and attitudes. In E. Maccoby (Ed.), *The development of sex differences*. Stanford, Calif.: Stanford University Press, 1966.

Lopata, H. Z. *Occupation: Housewife*. New York: Oxford University Press, 1971.

Malmo, R. B., & Shagass, C. Physiological study of symptom mechanisms in psychiatric patients under stress. *Psychosomatic Medicine*, 1949, *11*, 25–29.

Marks, I. M. *Fears and phobias*. New York: Academic Press, 1969.

Marks, I. M. Agoraphobic syndrome: Phobic anxiety state. *Archives of General Psychiatry*, 1970, *23*, 538–553.

Marks, I. Behavioral psychotherapy of adult neurosis. In S. L. Garfield & A. E. Bergin (Eds.), *Handbook of psychotherapy and behavior change: An empirical analysis. 2nd ed.* New York: John Wiley, 1978.

Marks, I. M., & Gelder, M. G. A controlled retrospective study of behavior therapy in phobic patients. *British Journal of Psychiatry*, 1965, *111*, 561–573.

Marks, I. M., & Herst, E. R. A survey of 1,200 agoraphobics in Britain: Features associated with treatment and ability to work. *Social Psychiatry*, 1969, *5*, (1), 16–24.

Mischel, W. A social-learning view of sex differences in behavior. In E. Maccoby (Ed.), *The development of sex differences*. Stanford, Calif.: Stanford University Press, 1966.

Moss, H. A. Sex, age, and state as determinants of mother–infant interactions.

Merrill-Palmer Quarterly, 1967, *13*, 19–36.

Murphy, J. V., Miller, R. F., & Mirsky, I. A. Inter-animal conditioning in the monkey. *Journal of Comparative Physiological Psychology*, 1955, *48*, 211–214.

NOW Task Force: Women on Words and Images. *Dick and Jane as victims: Sex-role stereotyping in children's readers*. Princeton, N.J.: National Organization for Women, 1975.

Rheingold, H. L., & Cook, K. V. The Content of boys' and girls' rooms as an index of parents' behavior. *Child Development*, 1975, *46*, 459–463.

Roberts, A. H. Housebound housewives—A follow-up of phobic anxiety states. *British Journal of Psychiatry*, 1964, *110*, 191–197.

Roosevelt, E. Cited in Elaine Partnow (Ed.), *The quotable woman*. New York: Doubleday, 1978.

Rubenstein, J. Maternal attentiveness and subsequent exploratory behavior in the infant. *Child Development*, 1967, *38*, 1089–1100.

Snaith, R. P. A clinical investigation of phobias. *British Journal of Psychiatric*, 1968, *114*, 673–698.

Solyom, L., Beck, P., Solyom, C., & Hugel, R. Some etiological factors in phobic neurosis. *Canadian Psychiatric Association Journal*, 1974, *19*, 69–78.

Stern, R. S., & Marks, I. M. Brief and prolonged flooding: A comparison in agoraphobic patients. *Archives of General Psychology*, 1973, *28*, 270–276.

Sternglanz, S. H., & Serbin, L. A. Sex role stereotyping in children's television programs. *Developmental Psychology*, 1974, *10*, 710–715.

Terhune, H. A study of 86 patients with phobic reactions. *Archives of Neurological Psychiatry*, 1949, *62*, 162–172.

Tucker, W. I. Diagnosis and treatment of the phobic reaction. *American Journal of Psychiatry*, 1956, *112*, 825–830.

Warburton, J. W. *Some Observations on the Aetiology of Phobic Anxiety*. Unpublished manuscript, 1963.

Williams, J. H. *Psychology of women: Behavior in a biosocial context*. New York: W. W. Norton, 1977.

Zuckerman, M. Dimensions of sensation seeking. *Journal of Consulting and Clinical Psychology*, 1971, *36*, 45–52.

■ 7
Sex-Role Stereotypes and Female Sexual Dysfunction

HELEN E. TEVLIN and SANDRA R. LEIBLUM

While in recent years traditional sex-role stereotypes have been widely challenged, the influence of such cultural norms on sexual behavior remains largely unchanged. Despite increasing appearance of androgynous behavior in political, professional, and social life, sexual relationships often continue to be characterized by traditional sex-role behavior, attitudes, and expectations. Adherence to such outmoded sex-role standards not only limits sexual pleasure but in most cases leads to the development of sexual problems. The purpose of the present chapter is to provide an explanation of the relationship between sex-role behavior and sexual dysfunction and, specifically, to show how culturally prescribed and reinforced sex-typed behaviors and expectations interfere with optimal female sexual functioning.

Although popular mythology suggests that sex is "perfectly natural," common experience shows us that sex is not naturally perfect. Responses from a variety of large surveys (Bell & Weinberg, 1978; Frank, Anderson, & Rubinstein, 1978; Hunt, 1974; Kinsey, Pomeroy, Martin, & Gebhard, 1953) indicate that a significant proportion of women ex-

The authors wish to thank Kenneth P. Morganstern, Ph.D., for his careful reading and helpful suggestions in the preparation of this manuscript.

perience a number of sexual difficulties and dissatisfactions (see Table 7-1). For example, in a recent study of happily married couples, Frank et al. (1978) found that 48 percent of the women reported difficulty becoming sexually excited, and 33 percent said they experienced difficulty in maintaining their arousal. Fifteen percent of the women reported that, regardless of the method of genital stimulation, they were consistently unable to experience orgasm. Twenty-eight percent said they were "turned off" to a variety of sexual activities, and 35 percent reported sexual disinterest. These results are consistent with the earlier report of Masters and Johnson (1970) that suggested that 50 percent of couples experience some kind of sexual dysfunction.

TABLE 7-1. Female sexual dysfunctions

Sexual Dysfunction	Definition
Inhibited sexual desire	Persistent and pervasive inhibition of sexual desire. May be primary, secondary, or situational.
Sexual aversion	Phobic, aversive reaction to the anticipation or actuality of sexual activity.
Arousal dysfunction	Little or no erotic pleasure; low levels (if any) of physiological components of arousal (lubrication and genital congestion)
Orgasmic dysfunction	
Primary orgasmic dysfunction	No experience of orgasm, despite genital stimulation
Secondary orgasmic dysfunction	Currently does not experience orgasm, despite past experiences of orgasm
Situational orgasmic dysfunction	Dissatisfaction with either frequency of orgasm, method of stimulation, or situation required for orgasm. Experience of orgasm in some situations
Dyspareunia	Painful intercourse
Vaginismus	Spasms of the muscles surrounding vaginal entrance when intromission is attempted; inability to engage in intercourse

In this, the age of the "sexual revolution" (in which sexual attitudes and behavior are supposed to have become liberalized), it is important to examine why so many women continue to experience a wide range of sexual difficulties. While a precise relationship between a given sexual dysfunction and the enactment of a particular stereotype role behavior is not as yet known, it is the major contention of the present chapter that partners' rigid adherence to a set of learned "feminine" and "masculine" role expectations during sexual encounters mediate and maintain the widespread prevalence of female sexual dysfunction.

SEX-ROLE STEREOTYPES

A variety of sex-typed traits assumed to characterize "masculine" and "feminine" behavior have been described (Bem, 1974; Eakins & Eakins, 1978; Frieze, 1978; Gross, 1978). Four of these prominent female sex roles are described here. It will be shown how the cognitive acceptance and behavioral enactment of any or all of these roles may interfere with optimal female sexual expression.

Women Are Asexual; Men Are Sexual

While cultural expectations and standards for appropriate sexual conduct of women currently are undergoing major changes, the majority of women today grew up with a consistent message: Women are inherently asexual (Leiblum, 1980). In contrast to males (who typically were described as experiencing strong and frequent sexual interest and need), females traditionally were characterized as "innocent" and having a natural disinterest in sex. Until quite recently, the widespread acceptance of sex-role stereotypes reflected the belief that a normal female experienced no natural curiosity about sexual functioning, experienced no physical sexual drive or desire, and was neither interested in, nor capable of, experiencing erotic pleasure. Instead of sex, feminine fulfillment was supposedly achieved through the gentle affection and verbal intimacies of "romantic love" and the eventual roles of wife and mother.

Since women were considered asexual, the expression of sexual desire by a female was considered unnatural, psychologically aberrant, a sign of masculinity, and immoral (LoPiccolo & Heiman, 1977). The sex-role stereotype of asexuality reflected the popular belief that only "bad" girls enjoyed, initiated, desired, or enthusiastically participated in sex. In contrast, "good" girls were modest, morally (and sometimes proudly) nonsexual, and "Madonna-like" in their virginal purity and sexual naiveté. The "good" girl avoided "fast" boys, set limits on her boyfriend's advances, and staunchly and virtuously maintained her virginity until marriage. After marriage she was expected to become the decorous wife and mother, dutifully sexually compliant, perhaps, but never sexually aggressive or expressive of autonomous sexual needs. While intercourse might be necessary for procreation (or an obligation to satisfy her husband's needs), a woman's admission of sexual interest was considered, even for a married woman, an indication of a "defective" character and was taboo (Leiblum & Pervin, 1980).

One simply needs to look at the usage of words that describe sexuality to understand the cultural attitude toward women's sexual expression and the obvious moral denigration of female sexual behavior. While a sexually active male is positively labeled a "lady's man," "Cassanova," or "stud," a woman who engages in sexual activity often bears the pejorative labels of "temptress," "whore," "tramp," and "slut." Even in the recent third edition of the *Diagnostic and Statistical Manual of Mental Disorders (DSM-III)* of the American Psychiatric Association (1980), sexual overactivity is classified as "Don Juanism" for men and "promiscuity" for women.

Females in this culture have learned little about sex that is not prohibitive. Until recent social changes, a girl learned that by "going too far" she most likely would suffer a variety of negative consequences. She risked losing not only her moral reputation but also the precious opportunity to marry a "good" man who would want a virgin bride. Moreover, having experienced sexuality, she was threatened with the prospect of becoming unfemininely and uncontrollably oversexed. Before easier access to birth-control methods, sexual activity also put a single woman at risk for the lifelong stigma and responsibility of unwed motherhood. Finally, popular mythology promised that females would find the sexual act itself (i.e., intercourse) painful, degrading, and emotionally disturbing.

As a result of both the sexual revolution and the women's movement, many of the stereotypic expectations of women have changed. Sexual pleasure and expression no longer are considered by the culture (at least in the middle classes) as distinctly a male prerogative. For the "liberated" couple today, *mutual* sexual satisfaction is the expected goal.

Women, in fact, now are *expected* to be sexual; they are expected to experience sexual desire, arousal, and orgasm, even multiple orgasms (Leiblum & Pervin, 1980).

Many women, however, have found it difficult to live up to the new cultural prescription of sexual expression, even though they may strongly desire such change. Despite recent changes in popular attitudes, women's overlearned model of asexuality (and the associated prohibitions of female sexual behavior) continues to interfere with current sexual functioning. The following sections illustrate how early sexual learning still may mediate current female sexual behavior.

Inhibition of Arousal. A frequent comment of sex therapists is that the most important sex organ is not located below the waist but rather between the ears. That is, how we think and feel about sex is at least as important in sexual functioning as physical technique. Negative thoughts or emotions may interfere with sexual responsiveness by inhibiting sexual arousal on a physiological level. Both sexual arousal (clitoral enlargement and vaginal distention) and orgasm are predominantly parasympathetic functions of the autonomic nervous system and are inhibited or diminished by sympathetic neural responses associated with negative emotions. Thus, fear, guilt, shame, doubt, anger, or frustration experienced during sexual encounters may decrease sexual arousal and preclude orgasm (Kaplan, 1974). Similarly, through higher-order conditioning, sexual words, thoughts, symbols, and images, if given negative connotations, can become powerful conditioned stimuli with the potential to elicit sympathetic autonomic responses and inhibit sexual arousal (Mischel, 1966).

Since female sexual behavior traditionally has been negatively evaluated and punished, it is little wonder that so many women have learned to associate sex with fear, shame, guilt and to experience these inhibiting emotions during sexual encounters (Barbach, 1980; Dinnerstein, 1976; Fisher, 1973; Friday, 1977; Frieze, 1978; Hunt, 1974; Kaplan, 1974; LoPiccolo & Heiman, 1977). Thus, while a woman currently may *want* to enjoy sex, her arousal and responsiveness may be inhibited by *overlearned* negative attitudes toward her own sexuality and the conflicts inherent in trying to integrate changing cultural sex-role expectations.

It is not unusual, for example, for women to describe sexual encounters as "tense" rather than pleasurable. In fact, in the sample of happily married women studied by Frank et al. (1978), 47 percent of the wives (as opposed to only 12 percent of the husbands) reported an inability to relax during sex. These findings support earlier research indicating that women are more likely to report sexual anxiety than men (Hunt, 1974) and that women who experience difficulty reaching orgasm are more likely to be anxious about sex (and particularly fearful of losing their partner's love) than women who are regularly orgasmic (Fisher, 1973; Shope, 1975).

The extent of anxiety during sex also is evident from the frequent reports of female clients in sex therapy. For example, such women often feel *guilt* about focusing on her own pleasure ("I shouldn't be taking so long to climax; he must be getting tired of stimulating me; I'd better start stimulating him instead"); *shame* about their own bodies ("I look too fat in this position; I shouldn't ask my partner for oral sex or to touch my 'dirty' genitals; I don't smell good"); *fear* of disapproval ("He'll get angry if I suggest this position or if I ask for more/lighter/lower stimulation"); and the *fear* of pregnancy or penetration.

Even for the woman who begins the sexual encounter by being aroused from kissing, hugging, and caressing (behaviors more consistent with a "romantic" script) an internal monologue of fear, shame, and guilt, especially about "sexual" (i.e., genital) behavior can diminish or terminate her arousal, precluding orgasm. For other women, inhibition of arousal may begin even before overt sexual behavior. The *idea* of sex may produce such heightened anxiety that arousal either is terminated quickly or in fact is never experienced. Generalized anxiety about sex may even lead to an avoidance of situations that have the *potential* of becoming sexual, such as dating and emotional intimacy. Even private sexual thoughts and fantasies may be squelched quickly. Noteworthy in this respect are the clinical histories of women with low sexual interest, which often reveal long-standing anxieties about sex, absence of sexual curiosity, and phobic avoidance of erotic contact (Kaplan, 1979).

Practice Deficit. Rather than being an instinctive response triggered by biologically determined drives, sexual behavior in humans is influenced largely by learning (Ford & Beach, 1951; Gagnon & Simon, 1973; Gagnon, 1977). Like any other learned behavior, sexual responsiveness (including arousal and orgasm) is dependent on, and enhanced by, practice and experience. Women who adopt the stereotype of asexuality and accept the cultural taboos against premarital sexual behavior are likely to approach adulthood with little or no direct sexual experience. Large national surveys report, in fact, that far fewer girls and women engage in masturbation or premarital intercourse than their male peers; among those who do, masturbation takes place far less often and there are fewer premarital sexual partners (Kinsey et al., 1953; Hunt, 1974). Women's sexual difficulties, therefore, may reflect these limitations in early sexual experience, rather than indicate an inherent "frigidity," sexual repression, or biological lack of sex drive. In short, many women have not taken the opportunity to learn *how* to be sexual.

In contrast, most adolescent boys (who are given far more cultural permission, if not encouragement) practice adult masculine sexual behavior (i.e., genital sex) through masturbation and actual or fantasized intercourse. With such experience they become familiar with, and facile at, producing the *genital* sensory patterns of arousal that facilitate their orgasms. In addition, they may eroticize a wide array of stimuli through fantasy and, with the pleasurable experience of orgasm, are likely to develop a positive sexual self-image and pro-sexual attitudes (Gagnon & Simon, 1973). Adolescent girls, on the other hand, practice only the outward *appearance* of sexuality; that is, girls learn a *social* repertoire (e.g., flirting behavior) to enhance their sexual appeal but fail to learn (if they are "good" girls) genital sexual expression.

Deficits in such genital practice delays sexual learning. Research and clinical reports show that, with practice, women can and do learn to experience orgasms (Kaplan, 1974; Masters & Johnson, 1970). Kinsey et al. (1953) found that women who had engaged in premarital intercourse were more likely to report orgasm during the early years of marriage than women without such early sexual experience. The more inexperienced women, however, became more orgasmic as they became more familiar with sexual activity. In fact, orgasmic regularity increased with the duration of marriage, presumably a result of increased practice and experience.

Deficits in masturbation are particularly critical in understanding female sexual dysfunction. Results of the Hite survey (1976) indicated that women who had never masturbated were five times more likely to report primary orgasmic dysfunction than women who had masturbated. Masturbation, then, would seem to be the easiest way for women to experience orgasm, probably because there is more direct and intense clitoral stimulation than during intercourse. Through masturbation, a woman learns to identify her clitoris as a source of sexual arousal and pleasure; learns to experiment with and control patterns of genital stimulation (e.g., pressure, pace, and location) that produce heightened arousal and orgasm; and, finally, learns to focus on her own pleasure without inhibiting distractions from a partner.

Practice in genital sexual activity also is critical in learning to recognize and label accurately the signs of sexual arousal. Since the early indications of female sexual arousal are neither visually obvious (in contrast to a male's erection) nor easily detected (Heiman, 1977), a woman with little sexual practice and experience may fail to identify low levels of arousal and mistakenly conclude she is not "turned on" (Rook & Hammen, 1977). Moreover, since the early cues of female arousal are nonspecific and similar in nature to the physiological arousal experienced during nonerotic emotional reactions (Masters & Johnson, 1966), a woman with little experience may mislable her arousal as nonsexual. It is not unusual, for example, for sexually naive women to label low levels of arousal as fear, guilt, or a "ticklish" sensation, rather than as erotic feelings. The importance of learning accurate perception and labeling of arousal is underscored by recent findings that women who report high orgasmic consistency are significantly more aware of the physiological changes of sexual arousal than women reporting low orgasmic consistency (Hoon & Hoon, 1978).

Despite the fact that inadequate learning experiences are frequently at the root of a variety of female sexual difficulties, many women do not label such problems as skill deficits, but rather blame themselves or their partners. Thus, the *cognitive* consequences of such experiential deficiencies (self-blame, guilt, anger, resentment, distrust) may contribute further to dysfunction by inhibiting arousal or prompting premature termination of genital stimulation.

Sexual Naiveté.   In order to conform to the culture's image of a woman as "pure, innocent, and nonsexual," many women have learned to maintain a sexual naiveté that includes learning not to ask questions, not to be too curious or knowledgeable about sex, and not to talk about their sexual thoughts, desires, or experiences, even among female peers. Furthermore, a girl is assured that she need not learn about sex, since her husband will be able to teach, guide, and instruct her in everything she will ever need to know (Leiblum, 1980).

Whereas a man may be an "expert" in showing a woman what she can do to enhance *his* sexual pleasure, he cannot know automatically what will be pleasing to his partner, especially since female sexual responsiveness is quite variable. A woman who expects her male partner to be omnisciently knowledgeable about sex—and to be expert in his understanding of when and where she must be stimulated during each sexual encounter—is likely to be disappointed. Not only is it unlikely that she will receive adequate physical stimulation for arousal and orgasm, but she also may inhibit her own arousal by resenting her partner for not "knowing" how to arouse her. Women with arousal or orgasmic problems who seek sex therapy are often surprised that their partners are not able to "read their minds." Such women learn that it is their responsibility, in part, to communicate specific sexual needs to their partners.

Female sexual naiveté also may contribute to sexual problems in more subtle ways. Men who accept the cultural stereotype of sexual expert may blame themselves for their partner's lack of sexual response. Such self-blame and the pressure on him to be responsible for both his own and his partner's sexual satisfaction may lead to anxiety, which frequently is associated with male sexual dysfunction (Zilbergeld, 1978). Erectile problems from such anxiety (especially when intercourse is the only acceptable mode of sexual behavior) are, in fact, important antecedents to female sexual dissatisfaction and dysfunction.

Women Are Passive; Men Are Aggressive

Women in this culture traditionally have been stereotyped as weak, passive, and dependent, in contrast to men, who are described as strong, aggressive, and independent. Men, by their very "nature," are presumed to be active initiators, authoritative leaders, and individuals who take control of and master their environment. Women, on the other hand, are presumed to react passively to situations and submissively (and even willingly) defer to authority. Men assert and request; women accommodate and comply.

Passivity and submission have been traditional feminine roles in the romantic sexual script. Most modern women have grown up viewing a score of beautiful and feminine movie stars submit obediently (after an initial "struggle" to prove her purity) to the overpowering advances of her hero. The more explicit bedroom scenes of films today foster the belief that only one preliminary embrace or kiss and remarkably brief intercourse are sufficient for passionate arousal and orgasm for *both* partners. Thus a woman learns the myth (from the male-dominated media) that passive submission to "true love" automatically will assure her own sexual satisfaction.

While enactment of the traditional feminine role during sex may be highly erotic for *some* women, passive sexual behavior, for most women, more likely masks their sexual ignorance and a variety of fears about being sexually assertive. Until quite recently, passivity in women reflected the historic reality of women's dependence on men's economic security. Many women, therefore, learned to adopt passive behavioral styles in order to minimize the risk of losing the love, approval, and support of men. Especially during sex, women have been afraid to assert themselves for fear of challenging men in a sphere considered so vitally central to masculine identity and pride (Dinnerstein, 1976; Fisher, 1973; Friday, 1977; Gross, 1978).

Since sexual assertion for many women has been associated with guilt, shame, and especially fear of male anger and rejection, it is not surprising that many women have *preferred* a passive role during sex. However, while such passivity may have been adaptive in the past, when the implicit goal of nonprocreative sex was solely *male* pleasure, current adherence to these traditional passive stereotypes may interfere with a woman's ability to obtain her *own* pleasure.

According to the traditional sexual script, the male is supposed to play the active or aggressive role, "orchestrating" the entire sexual encounter. He is the one who is required to initiate, who determines which sexual activities the couple will (or will not) try, and the one who decides the position, duration, frequency, and sequencing of sexual behaviors. With such little control over the sexual script, it is unlikely that a woman's needs will be satisfied properly. Despite the fact that most women rarely receive adequate clitoral stimulation (useful for arousal and orgasm) through intercourse alone, many women are reluctant to request nonpenile forms of stimulation. Since intercourse is generally the most acceptable (and preferable) form of sexual behavior for heterosexual men, even women who are capable of orgasm when they are alone (i.e., through masturbation) may be afraid to challenge a man's preference for "no-hands" intercourse.

Similarly, many women are afraid to ask for oral stimulation, frequently the easiest means (other than masturbation) by which women reach orgasm. Fearful of their partner's disgust or resentment, women do not request what will please them most. Even when a woman has a partner who enjoys or is willing to provide oral stimulation, she may terminate the activity before reaching maximal arousal because she fears he is getting tired or she is afraid of appearing selfish by focusing entirely on her own pleasure.

In addition, women may passively accept male orgasm as the signal to terminate sexual activity. Not only are they reluctant to disturb their partners, who are "spent," they also are fearful of embarrassing the male who has ejaculated prematurely. Early ejaculation, in fact, has been shown to be a major cause of female anorgasmia (Masters & Johnson, 1970), perhaps because women are unwilling to request nonpenile forms of stimulation once the male has climaxed.

Another passive behavior style women frequently adopt during sex is the dependence on the male's timing and pace of sexual activities. A woman, for example, may allow the male to determine the duration of "foreplay" and the start of intercourse. If the male prefers only brief foreplay (a term that obviously implies that intercourse is the preferred or main activity), a woman may be deprived of affectional and sexual behavior she finds enjoyable and arousing. Moreover, she may not have sufficient time to become lubricated, making penetration and the act of intercourse painful or uncomfortable. Finally, she may not have sufficient time to reach a level of arousal that would enhance her detection of and pleasure in vaginal stimulation.

In view of the evidence that relatively long periods of foreplay (15 to 20 minutes or longer) are more likely to produce consistent female orgasms than limited foreplay (1 to 10 minutes) (Gebhard, 1978), a woman's passive acceptance of the male's preference for brief foreplay may interfere not only with a woman's pleasure but also with her orgasmic consistency.

Similarly, a woman may accept passively the male's pace and duration of intercourse despite her own needs and preferences. In light of cross-cultural evidence indicating that women need longer intercourse to reach orgasm than men (Gebhard, 1971), dependence on the male's lead may preclude a woman's own sexual pleasure and response. Although a woman may feel that sex is over before it has begun, she may be extremely reluctant to ask her partner to "last longer." Cross-cultural research, however, indicates that men in other societies intentionally learn to prolong intercourse, in order to insure or increase the likelihood of female orgasm. Thus the "slam-bang" pace does not appear to be a biological requirement (Gebhard, 1971).

Since the cultural stereotype reinforces female passivity, especially during sex, many women learn passive fantasies as well. Sexual fantasies that portray women in passive roles (even to the extreme of violence, domination, and rape) actually may fulfill the stereotyped expectation of femininity. Such cognitive rehearsal of passivity, however, may make it far more difficult for a woman to take an active role in sex.

A major consequence of female passivity and the acceptance of the male's lead in sex is that the sexual behaviors in which the couple engage are likely to be nonarousing for the woman. Because such activity is motivated by and timed to *his* arousal, a woman may find that sex is rarely associated with her own erotic pleasure. Repeated association of sexual activity with low (or nonexistent) levels of arousal may limit a woman's sexual pleasure and contribute to problems in sexual functioning (Rook & Hammen, 1977). Further, a woman who repeatedly engages in unsatisfactory sexual activity may begin to doubt her own sexual capabilities, question and perhaps resent her partner's level of sexual expertise, and finally conclude that she "just doesn't like sex."

Women who take an active role in sex are far more likely to experience sexual pleasure than those who remain passive (Levine & Levine, 1975). Such women are more likely to communicate their sexual needs and desires and are less likely to engage in nonarousing and nonenjoyable activities. For example, in a study of female college students, orgasmic women were found to be significantly more active during sex and far less likely to accept male demands passively, as compared to nonorgasmic women (Shope, 1975). Similarly, results of a *Redbook Magazine* survey (Levine & Levine, 1975), which studied the attitudes of over 100,000 women, indicated that those women who rated sex as "very good" were far more likely to play an active rather than passive sexual role.

Whether a woman is active or passive during sex is not the result of inherent personality traits or characteristics but rather the result of complex learning. Despite independent and assertive behavior in nonsexual spheres, heterosexual encounters frequently elicit passive behaviors from most women. Such overlearned female sexual passivity is markedly illustrated in a recent study of the sexual behavior of ambisexual men and women (Masters & Johnson, 1979). When ambisexual women (women who showed equal preference for, and responsiveness to, male and female sexual partners) engaged in sex with a female partner, they were far more active and expressive than during sex with male partners. With female partners, ambisexual women evidenced more initiation, more comfort in giving and receiving pleasure, and more variation in the pace of genital stimulation and reflected, in general, far greater equality (turn taking and sharing) than when engaged in sex with male partners. In heterosexual encounters, ambisexual women let the men initiate and passively allowed them to decide the pace, position, and sequencing of sexual activities. In a similar fashion, ambisexual men showed more equal and flexible sexual behaviors when engaged in sexual activity with male partners and took on a more dominant role when engaged in sexual activity with female partners.

In sum, it appears that sexual encounters between women and men are highly scripted in ways that encourage each sex to conform to stereotyped notions of appropriate sex-role behavior. Unfortunately, these roles often impede the sexual expression of women.

Women Are Emotional and "Romantic"; Men Are Instrumental and Rational

According to the traditional sex-role stereotype, females are emotional. They are thought to be especially gifted in expressing and understanding feelings and are most interested in the emotional aspects of relationships. Men, on the other hand, are instrumental. They are expected to be skilled in achieving and accomplishing important goals and to require rationality, logic, and emotional control for such performance. In short, women "feel"; men "do."

Women's expectations for sex clearly reflect an emotional orientation to relationships. In the absence of explicit sexual learning and in the presence of the culture's prohibition against female sexual expression, women learn to view sex as an expression of emotional commitment and romantic love (Offit, 1977). While males learn a more explicit and genital orientation to sex through actual or vicarious experience, it is likely that "good girls" have only vague notions about what actually happens during sex and probably never learn to incorporate images of genital sex in their fantasies of sexual self-image (Gagnon & Simon, 1973).

Instead, images of "romantic love" (e.g., falling madly in love with Mr. Right; being "swept off her feet" in a romantic courtship of wine, roses, and declarations of love) play an integral part in traditional females' expectations for sexual encounters and in fact may provide the strongest cues for sexual arousal (Offit, 1977). It is not surprising that adolescent girls reported arousal to romantic rather than erotic words and descriptions (Gagnon & Simon, 1973), or that some women report that the romantic and affectional aspects of sex are sufficient for them to report satisfaction with their sexual lives (Hite, 1976; Levine & Levine, 1975).

The importance of love and romance for women's sexual responsiveness cannot be overestimated, in view of the fact that love and emotional commitment within marriage are seen by most women as the *only* appropriate context or justification for sex. Moreover, since most women assume that men generally do not require such emotional commitment for sex, and since many women are afraid of the stereotypic "love 'em and leave 'em" male attitude toward relationships, women often need to feel the trust of a secure and loving relationship before they are able to relax and feel aroused during sex (Fisher, 1973). Even married women may need to hear the reassuring words of love before they are able to "let go." Thus, the traditional female script of candlelight dinners and romantic expressions of love as a prelude to genital sex not only may serve to provide learned cues for arousal but also may help reduce a woman's anxiety about engaging in sex.

A romantic script, while valued and perhaps even necessary for a woman's arousal, may be incompatible with the expectations and preferences of her partner. According to the stereotype, men value action rather than the romance of intimate conversations, words of endearment, and the like. It is the sexual activity *itself* that not only provides the physical pleasures of sex but also reinforces a man's sense of masculinity. Since a man often believes that female submission is a woman's ultimate sign of acceptance, approval, and love, it is the actual conquest (i.e., intercourse) rather than the chase (i.e., seduction) that plays the crucial emotional role in many men's sexual scenarios. Eager to prove his desirability and ignorant of the role romantic expressions of love may play in female arousal, a male may initiate intercourse with only brief, if any, romantic prologue.

Moreover, the expressions of tender, caring, and loving feelings may play only a small role in a traditional male's sexual repertoire because they are incompatible with the stereotyped masculine ideal (Gross, 1978; Lazarus, 1978; LoPiccolo & Heiman, 1977). Sexual activity may be, in fact, a substitute for intimacy or emotional expression for many men (Zilbergeld, 1978).

While love and romance probably enhance the meaning and pleasure of sex for most women, extreme dependence on a romantic script most likely will interfere with a woman's sexual functioning. Expectations for romantic love are likely to be unrealistic and thus remain unfulfilled. Note, for example, the connotations of "romance": mystery, illusion, and perfection (Merriam-Webster, 1976). While dating and courtship may have reinforced a woman's romantic notions of love, the inevitable reality of daily marital life is unlikely to be ideal, providing far fewer romantic cues for arousal than expected or required (Offit, 1977). Since most men do not require "romantic stimuli" for their own arousal and performance and are readily able to perform in relatively "neutral" situations, a woman who continues to depend on romance for her arousal may be unresponsive, disinterested, or annoyed ("How *could* he be interested in sex at a time like this?") when her partner initiates.

Finally, acceptance of the stereotypic romantic belief that love ensures naturally perfect sex makes the development of sexual dysfunction far more likely. Such myths deny the essential role that communication, learning, and active responsibility play in mutually pleasurable and satisfying sexual functioning.

**Women Are Beautiful;
Men Are Successful**

Probably one of the most prominent characteristics of ideal femininity is physical beauty. Since a girl is taught that her physical beauty, above all other qualities, determines her appeal to men, a girl typically learns to attach enormous value to her physical appearance. In order to improve her desirability and enhance her opportunities for marriage, a young woman is encouraged to keep a trim figure, wear the most fashionable clothing (makeup, hairdo), and buy any and all commercial beauty products to help her "make the most of what she's got."

Since it is impossible for the average woman to live up to the idealized standards of beauty portrayed by the media, most women learn to be quite dissatisfied with their bodies. A woman is likely to feel, for example, that she is not thin enough, that her breasts are the wrong size (too big, too small, not firm enough), or that her frame is not delicate or petite.

A woman who believes that she must embody the culture's stereotyped feminine ideals of beauty in order to be sexually attractive to her partner most likely will be inhibited during sex. Rather than concentrate on physical sensations of arousal, a woman may worry about her physical appearance. She may even try to assume positions that she thinks will be more flattering (e.g., lying on her back so that her stomach will appear flatter), rather than try positions that are more likely to facilitate her arousal (e.g., female-superior position during intercourse) (Leiblum, 1980). Such self-conscious monitoring may contribute to the "spectatoring" of the sexual encounter, a primary factor in the inhibition of female arousal and orgasm (Masters & Johnson, 1970).

Besides physical characteristics, cultural stereotypes of femininity dictate the standards for the way a woman moves. Restricted rather than exaggerated movements are considered more "ladylike," and a feminine woman is expected to be graceful, poised, and relatively passive at all times (Eakins & Eakins, 1978). A woman who is overly concerned with being beautiful in both sexual and nonsexual spheres, therefore, may be far more likely to inhibit spontaneous movement, fearing that such behavior will seem too active or that she will be labeled a "jock" or an "Amazon." Such restrictions may limit severely the physical freedom necessary for a woman's arousal or expression of erotic excitement. Physical inhibition, in fact, is often so extreme that sex therapists frequently must prescribe role-playing exercises in which women exaggerate what they imagine an orgasm is like (Lobitz & LoPiccolo, 1972). In this way, a woman may learn to overcome her fear that sweating, thrashing, and "moans of erotic pleasure" will detract from her femininity.

The cultural equation of sexual attractiveness with physical beauty may be particularly detrimental to a woman's sexual self-image when the criteria for such beauty are defined so narrowly. With a social premium placed on youth and slenderness, women who are overweight, pregnant, or over 30 (the majority of American women) may be especially self-conscious about their bodies and concerned about their sexual attractiveness to their partners, particularly if those men have accepted the same cultural stereotypes of feminine beauty. Such concerns, in fact, often lead to the reduced sexual activity found in many postmenopausal women. Not only have they bought into the myth that sex ends after 50, but they find it hard to believe that their no-longer-youthful bodies still can elicit or experience sensual arousal. Mature women often are far more rejecting of their bodies than their partners, and their lack of self-acceptance can subdue the sexual interest of actual and potential lovers (Bachmann & Leiblum, 1981).

The emphasis on physical or surface qualities may be especially destructive to the woman who, for example, has had a mastectomy or is physically deformed or disabled. Ironically, even a physically beautiful woman may be vulnerable to the detrimental effects of the cultural standards of beauty, since she may be far less confident that a man actually loves her as a whole person. Such women frequently are far more concerned about the inevitable fading of their beauty as they grow older.

While a woman often is described by (and valued for) her physical characteristics, a man usually is judged by his achievements. According to traditional notions, a man's sense of masculinity is based in large part on the successful attainment of tangible goals. In sex, a man is concerned, as he is at work, with goals, performance, and products. Rather than an enjoyable process of mutual sensory pleasure, sex has become for many men another "proving ground" of masculinity, with an objective measure of success: orgasm (Gross, 1978; Zilbergeld, 1978). Such goal orientation toward sex has interfered with the sexual pleasure of many women, who often complain, for example, that men seem preoccupied with "producing" orgasms (both his and hers) rather than sharing emotional and physical intimacy. Sex, then, becomes rushed and impersonal and even the experience of orgasm often is described as emotionally disappointing.

Since women who adopt traditional stereotypes may feel obligated to reassure their partners and protect their masculinity, they also may accept goal orientation toward sex. They, like their male partners, may be preoccupied with "achieving" orgasm.

While lovemaking certainly may be a pleasurable experience, the *demand* for orgasm has interfered with many women's ability to enjoy sex at all. For many, in fact, sex has become a chore or a frustrating experience of failure. Ironically, the harder a woman tries to reach orgasm, the less likely she is to relax and feel aroused. Resultant maladaptive cognitions ("I *must* have an orgasm; what's wrong with me/him?; maybe *this* time . . .") and "spectatoring" are more likely to inhibit arousal and orgasm than to achieve the desired results. Continued experiences of such failure may maintain and exacerbate, in a cyclical fashion, a woman's sexual difficulties. For example, she may begin to dislike sex, resent her partner's initiations, and develop ways to avoid sexual contact. Such avoidance not only becomes a critical source of conflict for many couples but also prevents important corrective learning (Kaplan, 1974).

For some women, "failure" may not even be an option. Since their own orgasm seems necessary to reinforce a man's sexual self-esteem, many women have chosen to *appear* aroused and to fake orgasm. One survey, in fact, reported as many as two-thirds of the women feigned orgasm (Tavris, 1973). These findings are supported by the *Hite Report* (Hite, 1976), which showed that more than 34 percent of women respondents faked their sexual responses. Unfortunately, pretending to be sexually aroused (or satisfied) not only ensures sexual disappointment but also provides inaccurate feedback (and reinforcement) to one's partner, impeding facilitative and corrective communication.

In sum, stereotyped demands for feminine beauty and masculine success may inhibit rather than enhance a couple's sexual satisfaction. It is the expression of genuine feelings rather than a quest for superficial characteristics or "quantitative" outcomes that ultimately will contribute to sexual pleasure and responsiveness.

SUMMARY AND CONCLUSION

It seems evident that a variety of traditional sex-role stereotypes have influenced female sexuality and contributed to sexual problems in women. Enactment of the asexual, passive, romantic, and "beautiful" stereotypes (and a variety of other "feminine" attributes) may be directly responsible for problems of desire, arousal, and orgasm. Recent changes, however, in cultural attitudes toward sexuality may have significant impact on women's (and men's) sexual behavior.

The last generation has witnessed a "sexual revolution," especially in the media. It seems clear that women have been given far greater permission (if not the demand) to be sexual. Popular books, magazines, television programs, and films have made it increasingly possible for women to become more knowledgeable about sex. Evidence exists that girls are learning to masturbate earlier and more frequently than a generation ago and are accepting a more genital orientation toward sex (Hunt, 1974). As they begin to have more positive experiences, it is likely that many of the learning deficits and the negative influence of the traditional sex-role stereotypes will be diminished. Even many liberal clergy have recognized that sexual compatibility and satisfaction are important, if not critical, components of happy marriages and increasingly have given greater "permission" for a variety of sexual behaviors.

As some of the sexual stereotypes change and women learn to be more assertive, instrumental, and responsible for their own lives, sexual satisfaction likely will improve. Moreover, as women learn to take greater responsibility for their own sexual needs and satisfaction (and thereby relieve some of the pressure for men to be successful and orchestrate every sexual encounter), sexual pleasure for both women and men may be enhanced.

The impact of traditional sex roles on sexual functioning cannot be overestimated, even by sex therapists. Professionals need to become more aware of the influence of feminine and masculine stereotypes on sexual dysfunction so that they can understand more fully their client's sexual difficulties and can develop more effective treatment strategies. While a variety of therapeutic techniques exist for the amelioration of sexual problems, therapists must not lose sight of the real goal of sexual behavior — which is mutual pleasure rather than the achievement of any particular result. Thus, it may be necessary to redefine what we mean by "dysfunction," adopting instead concepts of distress and dissatisfaction (rather than anorgasmia or erection failure). In this way, orgasm for both men and women may be offered as an *option* rather than a necessary goal to achieve. Further, sex therapists must be extremely sensitive to the inevitable stress that accompany any change in sexuality. Sexual roles undoubtedly will shift as sexual behavior changes, and therapists need to be acutely aware of the side effects of sex therapy and become competent to handle a wide variety of relationship difficulties, as well as problems of sex dysfunction (Leiblum & Pervin, 1980).

Despite recent challenges to sex-role stereotypes, it is evident that cultural mores change slowly. The need, therefore, for increased and widespread sex education and prevention of sexual difficulties is obvious. Not only must schools and the mass media continue to educate children and adolescents in the "facts of life" (anatomy, physiology, and even technique), but (perhaps more importantly) they also must start to reflect changes in the attitudes, demands, and expectations of more functional and appropriate "masculine" and "feminine" behavior in this society. In addition, it seems necessary that the emphasis of the media on female youth and beauty must be replaced with a more realistic portrayal of women.

As we have indicated, sex-role expectations of passivity and asexuality have significant influence on female sexuality. In order to insure positive changes, it seems essential that women's fear of the negative consequences of sexual behavior be diminished. Through more enlightened media presentations, for example, women may learn that the result of sexual behavior need not be social stigma or desertion. More importantly, they must be assured of control over pregnancy, through access to contraception and abortion. Finally, in order for women to become assertive, independent, and free of the fear of male disapproval, they must be able to have control over the economic conditions and realities that make independent and assertive behavior possible.

In summary, it seems clear that a number of female sexual difficulties may have at their root a variety of cultural sex-role stereotypes dictating "appropriate" masculine and feminine behavior. It is strongly felt that, through modification of such role expectations, the lives of both women and men will become more positive, satisfactory, and happy. We are not naive, however, in assuming that such radical change in the very nature of the social and economic network of this society will occur quickly or without struggle. We do feel, nevertheless, that such change — ultimately beneficial to all — is realizable. There seems, then, to be room for cautious optimism.

REFERENCES

American Psychiatric Association. *Diagnostic and statistical manual of mental disorders*, 3rd ed. Washington, D.C.: APA, 1980.

Bachmann, G., & Leiblum, S. Sexual expression in menopausal women. *Medical Aspects of Human Sexuality*, 1981, *15* (10), 96B–96H.

Barbach, L. G. Group treatment of anorgasmic women. In S. Leiblum, & L. Pervin, *Principles and practice of sex therapy*. New York: Guilford Press, 1980.

Bell, A. P., & Weinberg, M. S. *Homosexualities: A study of diversity among men and women*. New York: Simon & Schuster, 1978.

Bem, S. L. The measurement of psychological androgyny. *Journal of Consulting and Clinical Psychology*, 1974, *42* (2), 155–162.

Dinnerstein, D. *The mermaid & the minotaur: Sexual arrangements and human malaise*. New York: Harper & Row, 1976.

Eakins, B. W., & Eakins, R. G. *Sex differences in human communication*. Boston: Houghton Mifflin, 1978.

Fisher, S. *The female orgasm*. New York: Basic Books, 1973.

Ford, C. S., & Beach, F. A. *Patterns of sexual behavior*. New York: Ace Books, 1951.

Frank, E., Anderson, C., & Rubinstein, D. Frequency of sexual dysfunction in "normal" couples. *New England Journal of Medicine*, 1978, *299*, 111–115.

Friday, N. *My mother/myself: The daughter's search for identity.* New York: Dell, 1977.

Frieze, I. H. Sexual roles of women. In I. H. Frieze, J. E. Parson, P. B. Johnson, D. N. Ruble, & G. L. Zellman (Eds.), *Women and sex roles: A social psychological perspective.* New York: W. W. Norton, 1978.

Gagnon, J. *Human sexualities.* Glenview, Ill.: Scott, Foresman, 1977.

Gagnon, J., & Simon, W. *Sexual conduct: The social sources of sexuality.* Chicago: Aldine, 1973.

Gebhard, P. H. Human sexual behavior: A summary statement. In D. S. Marshall & R. Suggs (Eds.), *Human sexual behavior.* Englewood Cliffs, N.J.: Prentice-Hall, 1971.

Gebhard, P. H. Factors in marital orgasm. In J. LoPiccolo & L. LoPiccolo (Eds.), *Handbook of sex therapy.* New York: Plenum Press, 1978.

Gross, A. E. The male role and heterosexual behavior. *Journal of Social Issues,* 1978, *34* (1), 87–107.

Heiman, J. R. A psychophysiological exploration of sexual arousal patterns in females and males. *Psychophysiology,* 1977, *14,* 266–274.

Hite, S. *The Hite report: A nationwide study of female sexuality.* New York: Dell, 1976.

Hoon, E. F. & Hoon, P. W. Styles of sexual expression in women: Clinical implications of multivariate analyses. *Archives of Sexual Behavior,* 1978, *7* (2), 105–116.

Hunt, M. *Sexual behavior in the 1970's.* Chicago: Playboy Press, 1974.

Kaplan, H. *The new sex therapy.* New York: Brunner/Mazel, 1974.

Kaplan, H. *Disorders of sexual desire.* New York: Brunner/Mazel, 1979.

Kinsey, A., Pomeroy, W. B., Martin, C. E., & Gebhard, P. H. *Sexual behavior in the human female.* Philadelphia: W. B. Saunders, 1953.

Lazarus, A. Overcoming sexual inadequacy. In J. LoPiccolo & L. LoPiccolo (Eds.), *Handbook of sex therapy.* New York: Plenum Press, 1978.

Leiblum, S. Sexual problems of women: Treatment perspectives. BMA audio cassette. New York: Guilford Publications, 1980.

Leiblum, S. R., & Pervin, L. A. *Principles and practice of sex therapy.* New York: Guilford Press, 1980.

Levine, R. J., & Levine, A. Sexual pleasure: The surprising preferences of 100,000 women. *Redbook Magazine,* 1975, *145* (5), 51–58.

Lobitz, W. C., & LoPiccolo, J. New methods in the behavioral treatment of sexual dysfunction. *Journal of Behavior Therapy and Experimental Psychiatry,* 1972, *3,* 265–271.

LoPiccolo, J., & Heiman, J. Cultural values and the therapeutic definition of sexual function and dysfunction. *Journal of Social Issues,* 1977, *33* (2), 166–183.

Masters, W. H., & Johnson, V. E. *Human Sexual Response*. Boston: Little, Brown, 1966.

Masters, W. H., & Johnson, V. E. *Human sexual inadequacy*. Boston: Little, Brown, 1970.

Masters, W. H., & Johnson, V. E. *Homosexualities in perspective*. Boston: Little, Brown, 1979.

Merriam-Webster. *Webster's New Collegiate Dictionary*. Springfield, Mass.: G. & C. Merriam Company, 1967.

Mischel, W. A social-learning view of sex differences in behavior. In E. E. Maccoby (Ed.), *The development of sex differences*. Stanford, Calif.: Stanford University Press, 1966.

Offit, A. K. *The sexual self*. Philadelphia/New York: Lippincott, 1977.

Rook, K. S., & Hammen, C. L. A cognitive perspective on the experience of sexual arousal. *Journal of Social Issues*, 1977, 33 (2), 7–27.

Shope, D. F. *Interpersonal sexuality*. Philadelphia: W. B. Saunders, 1975.

Tavris, C. Woman and man. In C. Tavris (Ed.), *The female experience*, Del Mar, Calif.: CRM Publishing, 1973.

Zilbergeld, B. *Male sexuality: A guide to sexual fulfillment*. New York: Bantam Books, 1978.

■ three
SPECIAL
PROBLEMS
OF LIVING

■ 8
Women's Assertion and the Feminine Sex-Role Stereotype

CHARLENE L. MUEHLENHARD

Assertion training — especially assertion training for women — has become increasingly popular during the past decade. This is evidenced by a proliferation of assertion-training groups for women and a growing number of self-help books and magazine articles encouraging women to be more assertive (e.g., Baer, 1976). Assertion training for women also has become a concern in the professional literature (e.g., Brockway, 1976; Jakubowski-Spector, 1973).

One possible reason for this emphasis on assertion training for women is that women are less assertive than men. To evaluate this hypothesis, Hollandsworth & Wall (1977) reviewed 108 articles dealing with assertion and found 14 comparisons of women and men, all using self-report measures that sampled a wide range of situations involving assertion. In all 14 cases, male subjects reported being more assertive than female subjects; 4 of these differences were significant.

If women are indeed less assertive than men, this could have important ramifications. A woman who cannot act assertively — who cannot refuse an unreasonable request or ask for what she wants — has little control over her life. Empirically, a significant negative relationship has been found between daily levels of depression and rates of assertive behavior; cross-lagged correlations showed that rates of assertive behavior predicted subsequent depression, but not vice versa (Sanchez & Lewinsohn, 1980). A significant positive relationship has been found between assertion and sexual satisfcation, although the direction of causality has not been established (Whitley & Poulsen, 1975). Assertion training has been useful in treating a variety of disorders, including obsessive–compulsive disorders (Walton & Mather, 1963), sexual deviation (Edwards, 1972; Stevenson & Wolpe, 1960), heterosexual anxiety (Burgess, 1969), aggressive and explosive behaviors (Foy, Eisler, & Pinkston, 1975), juvenile delinquency (Sarasan & Ganzer, 1973), and skills deficits of psychiatric inpatients (Goldsmith & McFall, 1975). These studies suggest that assertion is important and that women's unassertiveness is a potentially significant problem worthy of further investigation.

The first step in examining this issue is to clarify what is meant by "assertion." A perusal of the literature reveals a number of different definitions. This paper begins by discussing these definitions, with no intention to promote any one in particular but rather to identify different uses of the term and clarify subsequent discussion.

The popularity of assertion training for women and the finding that men consistently reported being more assertive than women lead us to ask why this might be occurring. One approach to investigating this question — and the second step in the present paper — is to examine the relationship between the feminine sex-role stereotype and women's problems with assertion. On the basis of this stereotype, what aspects of assertion would we expect to be problematic for women?

The third step is a review of the relevant literature. Is there evidence to support the predictions based on the sex-role stereotype? Are there data on the consequences of behaving assertively?

Finally, the implications of these findings for women of the 1980s are discussed.

DEFINITIONS OF ASSERTION

Assertion has been defined in different ways. In order to discuss meaningfully issues related to assertion, the use of the term must be specified clearly.

Definitions Focusing on Content versus Consequences

Definitions of assertion vary as to whether they specify the content or the consequences of the behavior. Some definitions focus exclusively on content. For example, Wolpe (1969) stated, "The word assertive is applied to the outward expression of practically all feelings other than anxiety" (p. 61). Lazarus (1973) suggested that assertive behavior can be divided into four content areas: (1) the ability to say no; (2) the ability to ask for favors and make requests; (3) the ability to express positive and negative feelings; and (4) the ability to initiate, continue, and terminate conversations. Using such definitions, determining what behaviors are assertive involves simply identifying the content of the behavior.

Other definitions specify nothing about the content of the behaviors; they focus entirely on the consequences. For example, Heimberg, Montgomery, Madsen, and Heimberg (1977) suggested that assertive behavior be conceptualized as effective social problem solving. Using this definition, any behavior would be considered assertive as long as it was socially effective, even if it did not involve the expression of feelings.

Still other definitions of assertion specify both the content and the consequences of the behavior. McDonald (1978) defined it as "the open expression of preferences (by words or actions) in a manner causing others to take them into account" (p. 890). Rich and Schroeder (1976) also combined content and consequences when they stated, "Assertive behavior is the skill to seek, maintain, or enhance reinforcement in an interpersonal situation through an expression of feelings or wants when such expression risks loss of reinforcement or even punishment" (p. 1082). Based on these definitions, for a behavior to be assertive, it not only must be an expression of feelings but it also must be effective.

Content Areas of Assertion

Negative Assertion. Among definitions of assertion that emphasize content, there is disagreement as to what content areas should be included. Most definitions of assertion include expressing negative feelings and standing up for one's rights. This also has been called "hostile assertion" (Wolpe, 1969) or "negative assertion" (Bellack, Hersen, & Turner, 1978). Examples include expressing dissatisfaction, refusing unreasonable requests, and requesting change in someone's behavior.

Positive Assertion. There is a disagreement, however, as to whether the expression of positive feelings — sometimes referred to as "commendatory assertion" (Wolpe, 1969) or "positive assertion" (Bellack et al., 1978) — should be included as assertive behavior. Many researchers have included the expression of positive feelings, such as friendly, affectionate feelings (Wolpe, 1969); warm, complimentary feelings (Kelly, Frederiksen, Fitts, & Phillips, 1978); and praise, appreciation, liking, empathy, and self-disclosure (Warren & Gilner, 1978). Others have chosen not to consider the expression of positive feelings to be assertive. Jakubowski-Spector (1973), for example, argues that including the ability to give and take affection "would stretch the term beyond its lexical boundaries. Assertion would become so broad that it would become a relatively meaningless concept" (p. 76).

Social Initiation. Still other researchers have chosen to include a range of behaviors even broader than the expression of positive and negative feelings. These behaviors generally involve initiating social contacts and could be labeled "social initiation." They include behaviors such as initiating conversations or asking for dates. (Gambrill & Richey, 1975; Kirschner, 1976; Lazarus, 1973; Rathus, 1973).

THE FEMININE SEX-ROLE STEREOTYPE AND ASSERTION

These definitions of assertion can provide structure for our investigation of the relationship between the feminine sex-role stereotype and assertion. The present section discusses how assertive a stereotypic woman would be in the content areas of negative assertion, positive assertion, and social initiation. The consequences of these behaviors will be discussed in a subsequent section.

An empirically derived feminine stereotype was obtained from Broverman, Broverman, Clarkson, Rosenkrantz, and Vogel (1970). They presented 38 bipolar items characterizing female and male stereotypes. Groups of female and male college students previously had judged, with 75 percent or greater agreement, which poles of these items characterized women and which characterized men (Rosenkrantz, Vogel, Bee, Broverman, & Broverman, 1968). The feminine pole of these items can be regarded as the feminine stereotype.

Items related to assertion are presented in Table 8-1. The feminine-stereotype characteristics relevant to negative assertion suggest that a stereotypic woman would not be very negatively assertive. A woman who is influenced very easily and very submissive probably would be unlikely to refuse unreasonable requests. A woman who is very sneaky (as opposed to being direct, the masculine pole) is unlikely to request a change in someone's behavior. Instead, she is likely to try to get her way by more subtle and devious means. A woman who is very tactful (as opposed to being blunt) and very aware of the feelings of others is unlikely to state her opinions or express dissatisfaction.

Would a woman who is not at all aggressive or very uncomfortable about being aggressive be negatively assertive? This depends on how *aggressive* is defined. Currently, in the psychological literature, a distinction is made between being assertive and aggressive (e.g., Hollandsworth, 1977; MacDonald, 1978); thus, a woman who is not at all aggressive could still be quite assertive. In popular usage, however, assertion and aggression often are used interchangeably. In *The American Heritage Dictionary of the English Language*, for example, one definition of

TABLE 8-1. Feminine-stereotype characteristics relevant to assertion

Relevant to negative assertion:
  Very easily influenced
  Very submissive
  Very sneaky
  Very tactful
  Very aware of the feelings of others
  Not at all aggressive
  Very uncomfortable about being aggressive
  Does not hide emotions at all
Relevant to positive assertion:
  Easily expresses tender feelings
  Very emotional
  Does not hide emotions at all
  Very aware of the feelings of others
Relevant to social initiation:
  Very passive
  Not at all self-confident
  Almost never acts as a leader
  Very dependent

aggressive is "assertive; bold; enterprising" (Morris, 1975, pp. 24–25). When aggressive is defined in this way, a woman who is not at all aggressive and is uncomfortable about being aggressive is not likely to engage in negative assertion.

The only feminine-stereotype characteristic that might be conducive to being negatively assertive is not hiding emotions at all. A woman who felt and expressed anger or dissatisfaction would be regarded as negatively assertive.

Positive assertion seems to be entirely consistent with the feminine stereotype (see Table 8–1). A woman who easily expresses tender feelings, who is every emotional and does not hide her emotions at all, and who is very aware of the feelings of others is likely to express warm, positive emotions.

Social initiation, on the other hand, is inconsistent with the feminine stereotype (see Table 8–1). Stereotype items relevant to social initiation include being very passive, being not at all self-confident, almost never acting as a leader, and being very dependent. A stereotypic woman would tend not to engage in social initiation; instead, she would wait passively for someone else to initiate.

REVIEW OF THE RESEARCH PERTAINING TO EFFECTS OF WOMEN'S ASSERTION

Negative Assertion

Do women have more problems than men do with negative assertion, as the feminine stereotype suggests? Several studies have shown this to be the case. Hollandsworth and Wall (1977) had 702 subjects, aged 17 to 60, fill out the Adult Self-Expression Scale (Gay, Hollandsworth, & Galassi, 1975). They found that men reported being more assertive than women in several areas of negative assertion: refusing a boss's unreasonable request, asking a boss for favors, expressing anger or annoyance to the boss, standing up to a boss for their legitimate rights, stating opinions to a boss, asking a friend to pay a $5 loan, and stating their opinions in a discussion or debate. Women reported being more negatively assertive than men on only one item: expressing anger to their parents.

Although men report being more negatively assertive than women, these self-reports may be influenced by social desirability. Kiecolt and McGrath (1979) found that high social-desirability scorers, when compared with low scorers, described themselves in a self-report measure as being more assertive and less anxious, but responded less assertively on a behavioral role-play measure. It could be that it is more socially desirable for men than women to report behaving assertively; thus, it is important to determine whether other kinds of data also support the prediction that men are more negatively assertive than women.

Studies of women's and men's linguistic styles suggest that the way women speak is not conducive to being negatively assertive (Frieze & Ramsey, 1976; Haas, 1979; Parlee, 1979). Women's language is more tentative than men's; for example, the pitch of women's voices tends to rise at the end of sentences, causing their declarative sentences to sound like questions and women are more likely than men to end their sentences with tag questions, such as "don't you think?" Women tend to use modifiers such of "sort of" and "I guess" to qualify their statements. Furthermore, women are more likely than men to use excessively polite speech.

This linguistic style communicates hesitancy, insecurity, and shyness (Frieze & Ramsey, 1976). It is used by persons lacking power. For example, clients talking with police personnel tended to use "women's language" more than the police, regardless of the gender of the persons involved (Parlee, 1979). Parlee also reported that persons who use "women's language" are less likely to be believed by a jury. It is likely that women, by using such language, are not taken seriously and are ineffective in situations requiring negative assertion.

Making requests, another area of negative assertion, seems to be a problem for women. There is evidence that women make fewer requests than men. For example, Haas (1979) reported a naturalistic study of a married couple showing that the husband made far more requests than the wife. When women and men do make requests, their styles often differ: Women tend to make requests, whereas men tend to make commands (Haas, 1979).

In the business world, supervisors reported that businesswomen are less negatively assertive than is desirable. Leonard (1978) examined questionnaires filled out by 254 Fortune 500 firm executives who supervised businesswomen. She identified three major training needs, that is, skills at which the women's actual performance was well below what the supervisors desired. These three areas were delegating workloads, speaking up in meetings, and working under pressure. The first two involve negative assertion. Leonard also identified ten minor training needs. These fell in the general areas of making requests of others, persuading and motivating others, getting the floor during meetings, acting independently, and dealing with criticism. These also involve negative assertion.

Behavioral assessment also has shown that negative assertion is influenced by sex, or at least by sex role. Bem and her colleagues compared the behavior of masculine, feminine, and androgynous subjects. In one study, Bem (1975b) looked at the willingness of subjects to state their opinions, even when those opinions did not conform with others' opinions. She had subjects rate the humor of cartoons after hearing the bogus ratings of confederates. Bem found that feminine subjects conformed significantly more often than masculine or androgynous subjects. In another study (Bem, 1975a), subjects were telephoned with an unreasonable request. Of the feminine women, 67 percent said it was difficult to refuse, compared with 28 percent of the masculine men and androgynous women and men.

Thus, evidence based on self-reports, reports of others, and behavioral assessments supports the prediction that women — especially feminine women — have more trouble with negative assertion than do men.

Positive Assertion

The feminine stereotype suggests that women are better than men at positive assertion. Research has supported this prediction. On the Adult Self-Expression Scale, women reported being more assertive than men in complimenting and praising others and in expressing love, affection, and approval to their spouses or friends (Hollandsworth & Wall, 1977). There were no items on which men reported being more positively assertive than women.

Women are more positively assertive than men in their use of language. Haas (1979) reported that women are often more polite, supportive, and expressive when they talk. They are more likely to use emotional language, such as "lovely," "delightful," or "nice." This use of language is consistent with expressing warm feelings and compliments.

Haas (1979) reported that women tend to laugh more than men in mixed-sex dyads. Humor may be related to power: Senior staff members made more jokes than junior staff members; men made more jokes than women; and women laughed more (Haas, 1979). Laughing at another person's jokes could be construed as a way of being warm and complimentary, that is, as a form of positive assertion.

Women show more affection nonverbally than do men. For example, women tend to engage in more eye contact for longer periods of time and to smile more than men (Frieze & Ramsey, 1976).

The relationship between positive assertion and femininity also has been demonstrated using behavioral assessment (Bem, 1975a). Masculine, feminine, and androgynous subjects listened to a confederate's personal problems. Dependent variables included the subjects' reactions (such as nodding or making sympathetic comments) and their self-reported concerns. Results showed masculine men to be least responsive and feminine women to be most responsive — even more responsive than androgynous women.

Once again, a prediction based on the feminine sex-role stereotype has been supported: Women do seem to be more positively assertive than men.

Social Initiation

The feminine stereotype suggests that women have more trouble with social initiation than men do. This prediction is supported by research. Hollandsworth and Wall (1977) found that, among their subjects who responded to the Adult Self-Expression Scale, men reported being more assertive than women in initiating conversations with a person of the other sex at a party. This showed the largest sex difference of any item. A consistent result also has been found using a behavioral measure (Lipton & Nelson, 1980). When subjects engaged in conversations with other-sex confederates, women were better at the passive than the active initiation role; that is, they were better at responding to the male confederate's attempts to initiate a conversation than they were at actively initiating a conversation.

Dating initiation is another area of social initiation in which women have more difficulty than men. A survey of college students revealed that women had significantly more trouble than men making contact with prospective dates (Klaus, Hersen, & Bellack, 1977). Gambrill & Richey (1975) found that women reported being less likely than men to request a date with someone, but more likely than men to turn down requests for dates and to resist sexual overtures. These results suggest that men are taking the active initiation role, while women are waiting passively to be asked and then deciding whether to accept or reject the man's offer.

Thus, research shows that women have more trouble than men initiating conversations and dates with the other sex. The prediction about women's social initiation, based on the feminine stereotype, is supported, at least with respect to the other sex.

In conclusion, women seem to be less assertive than men in the areas of negative assertion and social initiation and more assertive than men in the area of positive assertion. Whether men are generally more assertive than women depends on how heavily these different areas are weighted.

DATA ON THE CONSEQUENCES
OF BEHAVING ASSERTIVELY

Should women be encouraged to behave more assertively in the areas in which they are now less assertive than men? Should they be encouraged to refuse unreasonable requests, state their opinions, express their anger, and stand up for their rights? Should they be encouraged to initiate social interactions with the other sex? These are controversial questions. The answers depend, in part, on women's values. There are, however, some interesting data on the consequences of these behaviors that may help women make these decisions.

Women and Negative Assertion

Being able to be negatively assertive can be a useful skill. Being able to refuse unreasonable requests can enable a person to avoid doing things she or he does not want to do. Being able to make requests can enable a person to get what she or he wants. There is evidence, however, that persons who use negative assertion are perceived as being effective but not very pleasant. For example, Woolfolk and Dever (1979) had subjects read vignettes of situations calling for assertion, such as a nonsmoker bothered by cigar smoke in a no-smoking area, or an unwelcome visit from an aunt. The offended person in these vignettes responded either nonassertively, assertively, or aggressively. Subjects rated assertion as being more appropriate and efficacious than either nonassertion or aggression. When compared with nonassertion, however, assertion was seen as being less polite, less kind, more hostile, and less satisfying to the recipient. Subjects responded similarly to female and male models.

In another study, subjects interacted with a female confederate who behaved either nonassertively, assertively, or aggressively in role-play situations involving refusals and requests for behavior change (Hull & Schroeder, 1979). Subjects' ratings indicated that nonassertion would not allow the confederate to achieve her immediate goals, but they generally responded positively to it. Subjects indicated that both aggression and assertion would allow her to achieve her goals. They evaluated aggression negatively. They had mixed reactions to assertion. The assertive person was rated as being nonrevengeful and friendly but also as being dominant, unsympathetic, and aggressive. On many ratings, subjects responded similarly to assertion and aggression. Hull and Schroeder concluded that assertion training needs to be concerned with more than just the effectiveness of the response; if an assertive person is perceived as being dominant, unsympathetic, and aggressive, her or his interpersonal relationships might be damaged.

Some persons believe that assertive women are perceived more negatively than assertive men. For example, I once saw this sign taped to a delicatessen cash register:

How to Tell a Businessman from a Businesswoman

He's aggressive; she's pushy.
He's firm; she's stubborn.
He loses his temper because he's involved with his job; she's bitchy.
He exercises his authority; she's tyrannical.
He follows through; she doesn't know when to quit.
He's careful about details; she's obsessive.
He's a man of the world; she slept her way to the top.

There is some empirical evidence to support the notion that assertive women are regarded especially negatively. In one study, subjects viewed videotapes of assertive and nonassertive female and male models (Kelly, Kern, Kirkley, Patterson, & Keane, 1980). Assertive models were rated as being more skilled and able than nonassertive models, but also as being less likable than nonassertive models. Assertive women were evaluated even more negatively than men engaging in identical behavior. Assertive women, when compared with assertive men or nonassertive women or men, were rated as being less friendly, less pleasant, less considerate, less open-minded, less good-natured, less kind, less likable, less thoughtful, and less warm.

Lao, Upchurch, Corwin and Grossnickle (1975) also found a significant interaction between sex of model and level of assertion, in which highly assertive women were perceived negatively. They showed subjects videotapes of high-, medium-, and low-assertive males and females. Subjects rated these models on intelligence and likability. In every condition, males were perceived as being more intelligent and likable than females. For both sexes, medium-assertive models were rated as being more intelligent and likable than high- or low-assertive models. Being highly assertive had a much more negative effect for female models than for male models in ratings of both intelligence and likability. This phenomenon puts women in the double bind of having to choose between being effective and being liked. Lao et al. (1975) pointed out that this may exclude women from occupations that demand high assertion, intelligence, and likability.

Reactions to assertive women in business situations were studied by Solomon, Brehony, Rothblum, and Kelly (in press). Executives of a large corporation rated audiotapes of assertive and unassertive women and men. No significant differences were found with respect to the sex of the model. One explanation for this finding might be that businesspersons have different expectations of women and men than do the college students who often are used as subjects. An alternative explanation might be that gender is less salient in studies using audiotapes or written vignettes than in studies using videotapes.

One possible solution to the problem of negative perceptions of assertion might be what Woolfolk and Dever (1979) called "assertion plus extra consideration" or "assertion plus empathy." This involves making a special effort to acknowledge the needs of others and to be friendly and polite while at the same time standing up for one's rights. Subjects listened to audiotapes of models who responded either nonassertively, aggressively, assertively, or assertively with empathy. They found that assertion plus an empathy statement was rated as being just as effective and appropriate as assertion but was rated as being kinder, less hostile, and more satisfying to the recipient than assertion without an empathy statement. Thus, this style of responding might be a way for people — especially for women — to be effective while being perceived as likable.

Women and Social Initiation

Conversations. Women have more difficulty than men initiating conversations with the other sex, based on their self-reports and role-play tests. Does this imply that women should work harder at initiating conversations?

Parlee (1979) cites evidence that women already work harder at initiating conversations than do men. A naturalistic study was conducted with three couples who considered themselves liberated from traditional stereotypes. Topics introduced by the men succeeded — that is, led to a conversation — 96 percent of the time, whereas topics introduced by women succeeded only 36 percent of the time. Men often let the women's topics drop after giving only a minimal response, such as "uhmm," whereas women pursued the conversational topics introduced by the men. Thus, the men were able to control the conversation more easily than the women. This conversation style could be one reason why women have trouble initiating conversations with men.

Once a conversation does get started, men interrupt women more often than they interrupt other men, and more often than women interrupt men or other women (Parlee, 1979). Furthermore, women who have been interrupted are unlikely to protest (Haas, 1979).

Dating Initiation.   As we have seen, women have more trouble than men initiating dates (Klaus et al., 1977). If a woman wants to initiate a date with a man, what is the best action for her to take? If she asks him out, will she increase her chances of getting a date with him, or will she be regarded as too aggressive and decrease her chances of getting a date with him?

A study was conducted in which men were asked how they would respond to women who asked, hinted, or waited for a date (Muehlenhard & McFall, in press). Men reported that if a woman asked them for a date, they would gladly accept the date if they liked her. If, on the other hand, they did not like her, they reported that they would either refuse the invitation or make an excuse and would wish she had not asked. If the woman hinted about a date, men reported that they would ask her out only if they liked her. If a woman they wanted to date merely waited, neither asking nor hinting, 66 percent of the men said they would try to talk to her more often; 30 percent said they would not ask her out because they thought she was not interested in them. Even if they liked her and wanted to date her, only 4 percent said they would ask her out if she gave no indication that she wanted to date them.

Generally, then, men reported that if a woman takes the initiative, they would accept if they liked her and would not accept if they did not like her. Even men who said they generally preferred women to hint rather than to ask reported that they would be pleased and accept the invitation of a woman whom they liked and wanted to date. These results suggest that if a woman wants to date a man and is willing to face rejection, she has virtually nothing to lose by taking the initiative. The authors cautioned, however, that this study was done on a liberal university campus and that men in other populations might respond differently.

Recent evidence suggests that even though taking the initiative might not be risky in terms of decreasing the probability of getting a date, it might be risky in other ways. Johnson and her colleagues at UCLA (Fingler, 1981; Johnson, 1981) studied the perceptions and attitudes of high-school students. They found that any initiative taken by a girl—even a casual phone call—was viewed by boys as a sign that she wanted to have sex. This is especially disturbing in light of another of their findings: Many of the students thought it was acceptable for a boy to force sex if the girl had led him on. These two findings suggest that taking the initiative might increase the possibility of rape—or at least make rape more acceptable. Clearly, more research is needed in this area.

Conclusion

Women do appear to be less assertive than men in the areas of negative assertion and social initiation. If we teach women to be more assertive, however, we cannot assume that the consequences will always be positive. In some cases, an assertive woman might face negative reactions from others. Many women, however, would be willing to face this possibility in exchange for increased control over their lives. It is important that women have a repertoire of ways to handle problem situations and that they know the consequences of these alternatives. Important consequences include not only whether the woman is effective in reaching her goal but also how people feel about her and how she feels about herself. As women increase their behavioral repertoires and knowledge of likely consequences, they will have more options for effectively reaching their goals and will be better able to make informed decisions about how they want to behave.

IMPLICATIONS FOR THE 1980s

Women's Assertion and the
Feminine Sex-Role Stereotype

Women's assertion and the feminine sex-role stereotype are related in at least two ways: (1) women tend to show deficits in negative assertion and social initiation, consistent with the stereotype, and (2) some people re-act negatively to women whose behavior does not fit the stereotype. Be-cause both these have negative implications, changes in the stereotype probably would benefit women.

Although more research is needed on the direction of causality be-tween women's unassertive behavior and the feminine stereotype, it is likely that they perpetuate each other, thus maintaining the status quo. This cycle could be broken by intervening at two levels: changing the stereotype and changing women's behavior.

Changing the Stereotype. To the extent that the feminine stereotype is perpetuated by women's behavior, women could change the stereotype by changing their behavior. There are other influences on the stereotype over which women have less control, however, such as the portrayal of women in the mass media.

In an excellent review of women and the media, Butler and Paisley (1980) presented study after study finding that the media either neglect women or portray them stereotypically. Women are found less often than men in movies, newspapers, and television programs aimed at adults and in commercials, Saturday morning cartoons, and other tele-vision programs aimed at children. Women who do appear tend to con-form to the sex-role stereotype, which includes being unassertive. For example, in prime-time dramas, males gave 70 percent of the directives. In television commercials, about 90 percent of the voice-overs — the authoritative voices telling us what to buy — are spoken by men. Twenty-four percent of the ads portrayed women as submissive. In *New Yorker* cartoons and the Sunday comics, women used weaker, more restricted language and fewer exclamations and curse words than men. Female characters in Saturday morning cartoons were passive: 12 percent of the girls and women initiated action, compared with 57 percent of the boys and men; 50 percent of the girls and women were acted on, compared with 14 percent of the boys and men. "Male [cartoon] characters were shown as adventuresome, knowledgeable, independent, aggressive, sturdy, and bold; female characters were shown as romantic, submissive, emotional, fragile, timid, and patient" (Butler & Paisley, 1980, p. 90). Similarly, in children's literature, "[t]he themes of achievement, aggression, activity, independence, ingenuity, industry, strength, creative helpfulness, acquisition, and adventure are primarily associated with boys/men. The themes of harm avoidance, rejection avoidance, nurturance, passivity, dependence, goal constriction, and humiliation are primarily associated in stories with girls/women" (Butler & Paisley, 1980, p. 128).

Perhaps most disturbing is that this situation does not seem to be improving very much. Butler and Paisley (1980) reported that the number and significance of movie roles for women have decreased over the years. The percentage of women in commercials who engaged in sex-typed tasks (cooking, cleaning, etc.) rose from 66 percent in 1972 to 82 percent in 1974, and male voice-overs continued to be the voices of authority. In California there is a code prohibiting sexist portrayals of women in material purchased with state funds; however, a study of first-, second-, and third-grade readers adopted there in 1977 revealed that males were twice as likely as females to be portrayed in business settings; females were almost four times as likely as males to be portrayed in school settings. Between 1972 and 1977, stereotypes had become somewhat less rigid, but they had not disappeared (Butler & Paisley, 1980).

Changing Women's Behavior.   Much of the assertion literature has focused on how to teach persons to be assertive. An equally important issue — one that needs further study — is identifying the consequences of assertion. Certainly there are positive consequences: Assertion is a way for women to take control of their lives. Subjects consistently rated assertion as an effective way to achieve goals. They also rated assertive individuals as being more intelligent and competent than nonassertive individuals. On the other hand, assertion can have negative consequences: An assertive woman is likely to be regarded as less likable than an unassertive woman. A woman attempting to initiate conversations with men might be frustrated by their unresponsiveness. Attempts to initiate dates might be perceived by males as attempts to initiate sex, and leading a male on could be regarded as an excuse for rape.

Given such potential positive and negative consequences, a woman's values become important in her decision to act assertively. Perhaps psychologists can serve women best by helping them see what their options are, teaching them to make assertive responses comfortably, and making them aware of the likely consequences and the important situational factors affecting these consequences. With this information, women will be prepared to make their own choices about how to act.

REFERENCES

Baer, J. *How to be an assertive (not aggressive) woman in life, in love, and on the job: A total guide to self-assertiveness.* New York: Signet, 1976.

Bellack, A. S., Hersen, M., & Turner, S. M. Role-play tests for assessing social skills: Are they valid? *Behavior Therapy,* 1978, *9,* 448–461.

Bem, S. L. Androgyny vs. the tight little lives of fluffy women and chesty men. *Psychology Today,* 1975, *9,* 58–59, 61–62. (a)

Bem, S. L. Sex role adaptability: One consequence of psychological androgyny. *Journal of Personality and Social Psychology,* 1975, *31,* 634–643. (b)

Brockway, B. S. Assertive training for professional women. *Social Work,* 1976, *21,* 498–505.

Broverman, I. K., Broverman, D. M., Clarkson, F. E., Rosenkrantz, P. S., & Vogel, S. R. Sex-role stereotypes and clinical judgments of mental health. *Journal of Consulting and Clinical Psychology,* 1970, *34,* 1–7.

Burgess, E. P. Elimination of vomiting behavior. *Behaviour Research and Therapy,* 1969, *7,* 173–176.

Butler, M., & Paisley, W. *Women and the mass media: Sourcebook for research and action.* New York: Human Sciences Press, 1980.

Edwards, N. Case conference: Assertive training in a case of homosexual pedophilia. *Journal of Behavior Therapy and Experimental Psychiatry,* 1972, *3,* 55–63.

Fingler, L. Teenagers in survey condone forced sex. *Ms. Magazine,* 1981, *9,* 23.

Foy, D. W., Eisler, R. M., & Pinkston, S. Modeled assertion in a case of explosive rages. *Journal of Behavior Therapy and Experimental Psychiatry,* 1975, *6,* 135–138.

Frieze, I. H., & Ramsey, S. J. Nonverbal maintenance of traditional sex roles. *Journal of Social Issues,* 1976, *32,* 133–141.

Gambrill, E. D., & Richey, C. A. An assertion inventory for use in assessment and research. *Behavior Therapy,* 1975, *6,* 550–561.

Gay, M. L., Hollandsworth, J. G., & Galassi, J. P. An assertiveness inventory for adults. *Journal of Counseling Psychology,* 1975, *22,* 340–344.

Goldsmith, J. B., & McFall, R. M. Development and evaluation of an interpersonal-skill training program for psychiatric inpatients. *Journal of Abnormal Psychology*, 1975, *84*, 51–58.

Haas, A. Male and female spoken language differences: Stereotypes and evidence. *Psychological Bulletin*, 1979, *86*, 616–626.

Heimberg, R. G., Montgomery, D., Madsen, C. H., & Heimberg, J. S. Assertion training: A review of the literature. *Behavior Therapy*, 1977, *8*, 353–371.

Hollandsworth, J. G. Differentiating assertion and aggression: Some behavioral guidelines. *Behavior Therapy*, 1977, *8*, 347–352.

Hollandsworth, J. G., & Wall, K. E. Sex differences in assertive behavior: An empirical investigation. *Journal of Counseling Psychology*, 1977, *24*, 217–222.

Hull, D. B., & Schroeder, H. E. Some interpersonal effects of assertion, nonassertion, and aggression. *Behavior Therapy*, 1979, *10*, 20–28.

Jakubowski-Spector, P. Facilitating the growth of women through assertive training. *The Counseling Psychologist*, 1973, *4*, 75–86.

Johnson, P. Personal communication, June 3, 1981.

Kelly, J. A., Frederiksen, L. W., Fitts, H., & Phillips, J. Training and generalization of commendatory assertiveness: A controlled single subject experiment. *Journal of Behavior Therapy and Experimental Psychiatry*, 1978, *9*, 17–21.

Kelly, J. A., Kern, J. M., Kirkley, B. G., Patterson, J. N., & Keane, T. M. Reactions to assertive versus nonassertive behavior: Differential effects for males and females and implications for assertiveness training. *Behavior Therapy*, 1980, *11*, 670–682.

Kiecolt, J., & McGrath, E. Social desirability responding in the measurement of assertive behavior. *Journal of Consulting and Clinical Psychology*, 1979, *47*, 640–642.

Kirschner, N. M. Generalization of behaviorally oriented assertive training. *The Psychological Record*, 1976, *26*, 117–125.

Klaus, D., Hersen, M., & Bellack, A. S. Survey of dating habits of male and female college students: A necessary precursor to measurement and modification. *Journal of Clinical Psychology*, 1977, *33*, 369–375.

Lao, R. C., Upchurch, W. H., Corwin, B. J., & Groosnickle, W. F. Biased attitudes toward females as indicated by ratings of intelligence and likeability. *Psychological Reports*, 1975, *37*, 1315–1320.

Lazarus, A. A. On assertive behavior: A brief note. *Behavior Therapy*, 1973, *4*, 697–699.

Leonard, M. R. Assertiveness training needs of professional businesswomen. Unpublished paper, 1978.

Lipton, D. N., & Nelson, R. O. The contribution of initiation behaviors to dating frequency. *Behavior Therapy*, 1980, *11*, 59–67.

McDonald, M. L. Measuring assertion: A model and a method. *Behavior Therapy*, 1978, *9*, 889–899.

Morris, W. (Ed.). *The American Heritage Dictionary of the English Language.* Boston: Houghton-Mifflin, 1975.

Muehlenhard, C. L., & McFall, R. M. Dating initiation from a woman's perspective. *Behavior Therapy,* in press.

Parlee, M. B. Conversational politics. *Psychology Today,* 1979, *12,* 48–56.

Rathus, S. A. A 30-item schedule for assessing assertive behavior. *Behavior Therapy,* 1973, *4,* 398–406.

Rich, A. R., & Schroeder, H. E. Research issues in assertiveness training. *Psychological Bulletin,* 1976, *83,* 1081–1096.

Rosenkrantz, P., Vogel, S., Bee, H., Broverman, I., & Broverman, D. M. Sex-role stereotypes and self-concepts in college students. *Journal of Consulting and Clinical Psychology,* 1968, *32,* 287–295.

Sanchez, V., & Lewinsohn, P. M. Assertive behavior and depression. *Journal of Consulting and Clinical Psychology,* 1980, *48,* 119–120.

Sarasan, I. G., & Ganzer, V. J. Modeling and group discussion in the rehabilitation of juvenile delinquents. *Journal of Counseling Psychology,* 1973, *20,* 442–449.

Solomon, L. J., Brehony, K., Rothblum, E. D., & Kelly, J. A. The relationship of verbal content in assertive responses to perceptions of the businessperson. *Journal of Organizational Behavior Management,* in press.

Stevenson, I., & Wolpe, J. Recovery from sexual deviations through overcoming nonsexual neurotic responses. *American Journal of Psychiatry,* 1960, *116,* 737–742.

Walton, D., & Mather, M. D. The application of learning principles to the treatment of obsessive–compulsive states in the acute and chronic phases of illness. *Behaviour Research and Therapy,* 1963, *1,* 163–174.

Warren, N. J., & Gilner, F. H. Measurement of positive assertive behaviors: The behavioral test of tenderness expression. *Behavior Therapy,* 1978, *9,* 178–184.

Whitley, M. P., & Poulsen, S. B. Assertiveness and sexual satisfaction in employed professional women. *Journal of Marriage and the Family,* 1975, *37,* 573–581.

Wolpe, J. *The practice of behavior therapy.* New York: Pergamon, 1969.

Woolfolk, R. L., & Dever, S. Perceptions of assertion: An empirical analysis. *Behavior Therapy,* 1979, *10,* 404–411.

■ 9
Women, Weight, and Health

MARILYN A. ZEGMAN

Obesity is one of the nations' major health problems. The prevalence of obesity has reached epidemic proportions in the United States. Moreover, it is widely acknowledged that obesity is associated with increased morbidity and mortality. Obesity constitutes one of the most critical medical and public health problems in terms of increased illness, shorter life expectancy, and emotional and monetary costs to society (U.S. Department of Health, Education, and Welfare, 1979).

Although obesity long has been recognized as an important health problem, the causes of this complex disorder remain poorly understood (Salans, 1979). It is recognized, however, that social and cultural factors play an important etiological role (Stunkard, 1979). The purpose of this chapter is to explore the contribution of sex roles and sex-role stereotypes to the development of obesity. As an introduction, problems in defining and measuring obesity will be discussed, followed by statistics on the prevalence of obesity and its medical complications. Sex differences in prevalence rates will be highlighted in these sections because they provide clues to the etiological importance of sex-role expectations in obesity and its attendant problems. Established theories on the causes of obesity will be reviewed, with particular emphasis given to patterns of eating and physical activity. Conservative and radical approaches to the treatment will be discussed also. Finally, the implications for the next decade will be discussed.

172

The thesis being advanced is that sex-role expectations of lifestyle patterns of behavior contribute to the development of obesity and related health risks. Sex-role expectations also influence decisions regarding treatment; indeed, recent data suggest that dieting, a treatment chosen most often by women, worsens rather than alleviates the problem of obesity (Wooley & Wooley, 1979; Wooley, Wooley, & Dryenforth, 1979a, 1979b).

PROBLEMS OF DEFINITION AND MEASUREMENT

Obesity has been defined as a condition involving an excessive accumulation of fat or adipose tissue in the body. The diagnosis of obesity thus depends on the demonstration of increased body fat. There are two problems in making this diagnosis: how to measure body fat and how to determine what is excessive adiposity (Salans, 1979). The most frequently used measure of obesity is degree overweight, assessed by comparisons of actual weight to norms provided by height and weight tables. This method implies that overweight is synonymous with obesity. Evidence suggests, however, that body weight is a poor predictor of body fat (Mayer, 1968; Rogers, Mahoney, Mahoney, Straw, & Kenigsberg, 1980; Zegman, Wilson, Dubbert, & Lamon, 1979). There are several highly objective yet impractical procedures for measuring body fat directly. One practical method that can be applied on a wide-scale clinical basis is skin-fold assessment. Unfortunately, skin-fold assessments often suffer from problems of reliability (Franzini & Grimes, 1976; Johnson & Stalonas, 1977).

Obesity has statistical, operational, and social meanings (Sims, 1979). The statistical definition refers to the amount of body fat or body weight regarded as excessive. The optimal percentage of body fat generally is considered to be 15 percent to 20 percent in males and 20 percent to 25 percent in females (Montoye, 1978). Weight deviations of 10 percent to 20 percent overweight generally are considered indicative of obesity. These criteria are somewhat arbitrary, and they obscure the importance of making a diagnosis in the context of an individual's health and social status.

The operational definition of obesity refers to the influence of obesity on illness and death, that is the level of overweight and/or adiposity below which there is no discernable improvement in morbidity or mortality (Sums, 1979).

Obesity defined socially alludes to societal attitudes toward the appearance of overweight. In former European cultures, obesity was considered a social asset (Dwyer, Feldman, & Mayer, 1970). Renaissance painters and sculptors favored endomorphic women as subjects. Obesity is also considered desirable in several present-day, non-Western cultures; however, an obese appearance in present-day Western cultures is considered a social liability, especially for females (Dwyer et al., 1970; Wooley & Wooley, 1979; Wooley et al., 1979a).

Several researchers have argued that obesity be considered a heterogeneous group of disorders rather than a unitary problem (US DHEW, 1979). To aid in greater understanding of the disorder, obesity has been classified by age of onset (juvenile or adult), adipose cell number and size (hypertrophic or hyperplastic), and patterning of fat in the body (general or central).

PREVALENCE OF OBESITY

Figures on the prevalence of obesity vary with the criteria used. All indicators suggest that an epidemic continues in this nation. The U.S. Department of Health, Education, and Welfare (1967) estimated that as many as 50 million Americans are significantly overweight. According to the Seven Country Study (USDHEW, 1979), Americans have the greatest prevalence of obesity when measured by both weight and skin folds.

Generally, the prevalence of obesity is greater in women than in men. Among individuals 20 to 74 years of age, 14 percent of the men and 24 percent of the women are at least 20 percent overweight (US DHEW, 1979). These figures are modified when race and social class are considered and narrower age ranges are examined:

1. *Race.* The prevalence of obesity among black women is significantly higher than that of white women, regardless of age or income level (USDHEW, 1979). These racial discrepancies are not as great for males.
2. *Social class.* The Midtown Manhattan study, a survey of the epidemiology of mental illness involving 110,000 adults ages 20

to 59, revealed that 37 percent of women of low socioeconomic status where obese, compared to 2 percent in the high social class. The results for males were similar but not as striking: 32 percent of the males of low socioeconomic status were obese, compared to 16 percent in the high social class (Srole, Langner, Michael, Kirkpatrick, Opler, & Rennie 1962).

3. *Age.* Among white, nonpoverty-level populations, obese men outnumber obese women during the early stages of adulthood, but this trend is reversed during middle age (Stuart & Davis, 1972.)

MEDICAL COMPLICATIONS OF OBESITY

We are unanimous in our belief that obesity is a hazard to health and a detriment to well being. [James, 1977, cited in USDHEW, 1979]

These sentiments of a British researcher expressed the feelings of the participants at the recent Conference on Obesity in America. It is well recognized that obesity is associated with morbidity and mortality. Obesity is related to the following conditions: hypertension, diabetes mellitus, gout, pulmonary and renal disorders, menstrual and ovarian abnormalities, endometrial carcinoma, complications during pregnancy, atherosclerosis, gall bladder disease, and surgical risk (Bray, 1976; Rimm & White, 1979).

The most common medical complication of obesity is coronary heart disease. Obesity affects cardiovascular condition through its influence on blood pressure, blood lipids, and carbohydrate methabolism (Gordon & Kannel, 1973). Moreover, weight reduction is associated with improvements in hypertension, hyperlipidemia, and carbohydrate tolerance (Brownell & Skunkard, 1980). Data selected from the Framingham study suggested that, in the United States, coronary heart disease would be reduced by 25 percent and congestive heart failure by 35 percent if Americans were of normal weight (Kannel & Gordon, 1979). Some researchers believe that obesity is not a coronary risk factor independent of its influence on blood pressure and serum lipids (Mann, 1974). Others claim that obesity influences cardiovascular condition directly (Kannel & Gordon, 1979). A strong correlation between obesity and cardiovascular disease is found even after correcting for other risk factors.

The relationship between obesity and ill health is complex and depends upon several factors, including the extent of excess weight, the person's age, the distribution of body fat, and the age at which obesity develops (USDHEW, 1979). This relationship also differs for men and women (Dublin & Marks, 1958; Stuart & Jacobson, 1979; USDHEW, 1965, 1979). From early adulthood onward, obese men face a greater health risk than do obese women. Results from the Build and Blood Pressure study (Society of Actuaries, 1959) revealed that the mortality rate of men who were 20 percent above average weight was approximately 25 percent greater than men of normal weight. Men 40 percent to 60 percent above average weight showed a 67 percent to 150 percent increase in mortality. The rise in mortality among obese women was substantially lower. Excessive weight does not appear to exert a strong influence on the mortality of women until their fifties (Johnson, 1977).

Mortality rates for coronary heart disease are twice as high for males than females in the United States. Waldron (1976) determined that the sex differential in the prevalence of coronary heart disease is responsible for 40 percent of the total sex difference in mortality. Although these figures do not pertain to obesity directly, they are important to consider in light of the documented relationship between obesity and coronary heart disease.

CAUSES OF OBESITY

The recent Task Force on the Pathogenesis of Obesity (USDHEW, 1979) concluded that "large and significant gaps remain in our understanding of why obesity develops" (p. 10). Obesity has been attributed historically to overeating. This assumption is inherent in the etymology of the term itself: *ob* meaning "over" and *edere* meaning "to eat." Only recently has evidence begun to accrue that challenges the notion that obesity is the result of overeating. The numerous explanations of obesity can be divided roughly into biological, psychosocial, and behavioral theories.

Biological Theories

Biological contributions to obesity include the role of genetics, metabolism, hormones, and the physiology of hunger, satiety, and adiposity. Only those theories relevant to sex differences will be reviewed here.

Understanding the energy-balance equation is essential to comprehending the influence of basal metabolism on body weight. Energy is consumed during food intake; energy also is expended during physical activity, food digestion, and basal metabolism for the sustenance of basic life functions. Basal metabolism accounts for the greatest percentage of total energy expenditure. Obesity develops when more energy is consumed than is needed to maintain body functions and to meet the energy requirements of daily activities (Garrow, 1974). Excess energy is stored as adipose tissue.

Studies with animals have shown that the gonadal hormones influence metabolism and basal metabolic rate (Hoyenga & Hoyenga, 1979). Androgens, the male sex hormones, facilitate the synthesis of proteins. Estrogens, the female hormones, increase the production of fatty tissue. Because protein synthesis requires more energy than fat production, basal metabolic rates are generally higher for males. Higher metabolic rates are associated with slimness because more calories are expended in the process of sustaining basic life functions.

Adipose tissue partially determines body weight and is the portion of body composition that is the target of weight reduction programs. Adipose tissue influences body weight through cellular multiplication and/or enlargement. The adipose cellularity theory (Hirsch & Knittle, 1970) was derived in an attempt to explain the marked resistance to weight loss in some obese individuals. According to the adipose cellularity theory, fat cells differentiate in childhood. Juvenile-onset obesity is characterized by an increased number of fat cells (hyperplasia), sometimes approaching five times the number of fat cells in children of normal weight. Past childhood, fat cells no longer are reproduced, nor can existing cells be eliminated. Adult-onset obesity results from an increase in the size of existing fat cells (hypertrophy). In hyperplastically obese individuals, weight loss is accomplished by a decrease in the size of adipose cells; the large number of adipocytes remains unchanged. The theory contends that a mechanism that initiates feeding behavior is triggered when fat cells become depleted during weight loss, in order to restore the cells with lipids. The theory predicts that juvenile-onset obesity is more resistant to weight loss than adult-onset obesity. Studies have not borne out this prediction, however: individuals with juvenile-onset obesity do not respond differently to treatment than adult-onset obese persons (Brownell & Venditti, in press). Nevertheless, recent findings suggest that cellularity does influence weight reduction. Björntörp and his colleagues (Björntörp, Carlgren, Isaksson, Krotkiewski, Larson, & Sjöström, 1975) found that fat cell size of hypertrophic and hyperplastic obese women decreased to normal size during treatment, but the number of adipocytes remained unchanged; thus, hypertrophic obese women had a normal amount of body fat following treatment while hyperplastic obese subjects remained obese. These findings suggest that weight loss in hyperplastic obese subjects may cease prior to obtaining ideal body weight. "Adipose cellularity may be a major determinant of obesity and an important predictor of success in weight reduction" (Brownell & Venditti, in press).

These findings on adipose cellularity are relevant to a discussion on sex differences in obesity because females are born with a greater amount of body fat than males and this difference persists throughout life (Keys, 1955; Moumtoye, Epstein, & Kjelsberg, (1965); Stuart & Davis, 1972; Stuart & Jacobson, 1979; U.S. Public Health Service, 1970). Extrapolating from the adipose cellularity theory, females are more likely to become obese because of their greater number of fat cells. Moreover, as discussed in the last section, estrogens facilitate the production of fatty tissue and females have slower basal metabolic rates. It appears then that females have a biological predisposition favoring obesity. Indeed, the increase in body fat that characterizes the onset of puberty in both sexes is more pronounced in females. Throughout adolescence the differences become more apparent as girls continue to put on fat while boys become thinner (Forbes, 1979).

Pregnancy and parturition are associated commonly with weight gain (Salans, 1979). The reasons for this are not well understood. The phenomenon may be endocrinogenic or it may result from psychosocial factors that will be discussed in later sections.

Psychosocial Factors

The association between obesity and emotional disturbance has been researched extensively. Much of the research is correlational in nature and therefore suffers from third-variable and directionality problems. Consequently, little actually is known about the etiological significance of psychological factors. Beliefs that obese persons are emotionally disturbed and overeat to decrease anxiety and depression are common. These notions are not supported by research (Rodin, 1977). Negative affective states might precipitate overeating and obesity in some persons but certainly not all of them.

The most disabling psychological characteristic of some obese persons, particularly those who have been obese since childhood, is body-image disturbance.

> Body image disturbance in the obese is characterized by a feeling that one's body is grotesque and detestable, and that others view it with contempt and hostility. . . . This disturbance can lead to intense self-consciousness and to feelings that others are uniformly negative in their view of overweight people. Consequently, obese persons with negative body images tend to be withdrawn, shy, and socially immature. These reactions are similar to those of persons suffering from deformities of the face, breasts and genitals. [Brownell & Venditti, in press]

There is considerable evidence that the emotional problems of obese individuals are the result, rather than the cause, of their obesity. Discrimination, stigmatization, and prejudice characterize societal attitudes toward obese persons. Obesity evokes negative stereotypes even among young children. Staffieri (1967) asked boys aged 6 to 10 to assign characteristics to silhouettes of thin fat, and muscular children. The muscular body received uniformly positive responses. In contrast, the fat silhouette received offensive labels such as lazy, ugly, stupid, sloppy, and the like. In two other studies, adults and children consistently rated line drawings of an obese child as less likable than drawings of handicapped children. These findings suggest that the psychological problems of obese persons may result from social stresses that interfere with normal socialization (Rimm & White, 1979). These problems become manifest in body-image disturbances, an obsession with body weight, antagonism toward more obese persons, and envy toward thin persons. This preoccupation with weight can affect intellectual and physical performance adversely (Brownell & Venditti, in press).

Dieting also is associated with untoward psychological reactions.

> The obese person is under unrelenting pressure from family, friends, acquaintances, and society in general to lose weight. The value of thinness is internalized at an early age and most of these persons embark on a career of repeated diets. . . . This desire to reduce is so powerful that ordinary rational people can be seduced into buying miracle devices, cremes, pills, and diets. [Brownell & Venditti, in press]

Stunkard and others have reported that a high percentage of dieting patients experience nervousness and depression (Silverstone & Lascelles, 1966; Stunkard, 1957, 1976; Stunkard & Rush, 1974).

The Behavioral Model

This model of obesity assumes that weight gain results from excessive eating because of faulty eating habits, such as consuming large quantities of food, eating rapidly and frequently, and taking large bites. These habits are viewed as operant behaviors that are under the control of environmental cues related to food and the pleasure associated with eating.

The behavioral model derives partially from the work of Schachter (1968), a social psychologist who focused on the external influences of eating. Schachter and his colleagues argued that, relative to normal-weight individuals, obese persons are highly responsive to such external cues as time and the sight, taste, and availability of food. Recently, this externality hypothesis has been challenged, as it has been shown that environmental cues related to food appear to influence the eating of non-obese individuals as much as they do obese persons (Wooley & Wooley, 1975).

Another aspect of the behavioral model that has been criticized for being accepted on nonempirical grounds is the assumption that obese persons overeat (Mahoney, 1975; Wooley, et al., 1979b). The literature suggests that obese persons eat amounts less than or equivalent to normal-weight individuals (Garrow, 1974).

REMEDIAL EFFORTS

Reduction of Caloric Intake

The vast majority of weight control methods are designed to reduce caloric intake. Conservative approaches to treatment have involved fasting, protein-sparing fasts, low-calorie diets, behavior therapy, and self-help groups that may use one or more of the preceding methods. More radical treatment approaches include anorectic medication, bypass surgery, acupuncture, and jaw wiring (USDHEW, 1979). These treatments vary in effectiveness and likelihood of serious side effects. All methods have been successful for some patients and unsuccessful for others. Moreover, 75 percent to 95 percent of the patients receiving dietary, behavioral, or pharmacological treatment eventually regain some or all of the weight they have lost (USDHEW, 1979).

The fact that an effective and long-lasting treatment for obesity does not exist yet has not been impressed adequately on the public. The search for slimness is especially prevalent among females. Concern with overweight is much more widespread among adolescent girls than boys. In one high school, 48 percent of the girls versus 28 percent of the boys interviewed believed they had a weight problem (Deischer & Mills, 1963). In a study of attitudes toward weight and physical characteristics among high-school students, Dwyer, Feldman, and Mayer (1967) found that, although 16 percent of the girls could be rated obese, 30 percent were on diets at the time of the study. Moreover, 60 percent had been on diets by the time they were seniors. In contrast, whereas 19 percent of the boys could be rated obese, only 6 percent currently were dieting and only 24 percent had ever dieted. In a poll involving adults, Dwyer and Mayer (1970) found that 45 percent of the women compared to 22 percent of the men wanted to lose weight; 14 percent of the women and only 7 percent of the men were on diets to do so. This sex differential in the prevalence of dieting is apparent in the greater numbers of women who join self-help programs such as Weight Watchers or Lean Line (Berman, 1975; Stuart & Jacobson, 1979).

Although females are generally more motivated to lose weight than are males, they rarely are provided with accurate information on obesity and dieting. Women's magazines continue to advertise untested and often bizarre methods that promise easy and rapid weight loss (Brownwell & Venditti, in press). Professionals contribute to the confusion surrounding the optimal methods of weight reduction. In England, Yudkin (1968) and Ashwell (1973) discovered that physicians prescribed anorectic medication more often for women than for men, although no drug has demonstrated long-term effectiveness. Craighead, Stunkard, and O'Brien (1978) found that treatment involving medication actually showed a higher rate of relapse than treatment without medication.

Women often attribute their inability to lose weight to a lack of willpower. Adolescent females who were overweight attributed their weight status to an inability to eat less and to the sins of gluttony and sloth (Bullen, Monello, Cohen, & Mayer, 1963). The depression, anxiety, and body-image disturbance that often accompany obesity and attempts to lose weight might reflect this self-deprecation. Women have not been informed properly of the large gaps that exist in our knowledge of treating obesity. The physical and psychological consequences for women that ensue from treatment failures render these methods iatrogenic.

Exercise

Examining the physiological and metabolic processes underlying weight change might provide clues to the failures of dieting to produce long-term weight losses. As discussed, the energy-balance equation describes the relationships between caloric intake, caloric output, and weight. It frequently is assumed that obesity is the result of overeating. The energy-balance equation implies, however, that weight gain results from overeating relative to the amounts of energy expended rather than from excessive eating per se. The total energy expenditure produced by the body consists of the energy needed for basal metabolism, food digestion, and physical activity. Researchers have not found consistent differences between the obese and nonobese in basal metabolic rates or in calories expended during food digestion (Straw, 1978). Physical activity therefore appears to be responsible for the energy imbalance leading to weight gain. Mayer (1968) has been outspoken in his belief that inactivity rather than overeating is the primary cause of obesity. He attributed the massive prevalence of overweight to the sedentary lifestyles of most Western societies. We live in a highly mechanized culture that has virtually eliminated the need for effortful activity for travel or to accomplish chores. Technology has provided us with entertaining yet sedentary pursuits to occupy our leisure hours. Generally, we are spectators rather than participants in sports events. "For many individuals, physical activity is depressed to such and extent that the sedentary state is reached and excessive calories accumulate as fat" (Mayer, 1968, p. 77).

Garrow (1974) and Brownell and Stunkard (1980) have reviewed the literature on obese/nonobese differences in activity levels among children and adults. Results are mixed. Several studies suggested that obese children and adolescents are much less active than their nonobese peers. Two of these studies used parents' self-reports of their children's activity (Johnson, Burke, & Mayer, 1956; Stefanik, Heald, & Mayer, 1959). One study used motion picture samples of adolescent girls engaged in sports at summer camp (Bullen, Reed, & Mayer, 1974), and one study used mechanical recordings of infants' activity (Rose & Mayer, 1968). In contrast, four studies that used either pedometer or heart-rate measures found no differences in activity level between obese and nonobese children (Bradfield, Paulos, & Grossman, 1971; Maxfield & Konishi, 1966; Stunkard & Pestka, 1962; Wilkenson, Parklin, & Pearloom, 1977). Using oxygen consumption as the measure of energy expenditure, Waxman and Stunkard (in press) found obese boys to expend more calories than nonobese boys.

The literature on obese/nonobese differences in energy expenditure among adults has been more consistent in demonstrating that obese adults are less active than normal-weight adults. This finding has emerged whether activity has been measured by self-report (Mayer, Roy, & Mitra, 1956; Rand & Stunkard, 1974), pedometer (Chirico & Stunkard, 1960), a device that discriminates standing from sitting (Bloom & Eidex, 1967), or behavioral observations of use of stairs instead of escalators (Brownell, Albaum, & Stunkard, 1978).

Research suggests that inactivity might play a greater role in the development of obesity in women than in men. Chirico and Stunkard (1960) compared obese and nonobese individuals in terms of miles walked per day as measured by a pedometer. The results for the women were striking. The obese women were far less active than their normal-weight control subjects. Although the nonobese men walked more miles than did the obese men, the discrepancy was not as great as it was for the women.

Setting forth the following arguments, others have challenged the hypothesis that inactivity is the primary cause of obesity. First, studies on differences in activity level between obese and nonobese persons have suffered from imprecision and obtrusiveness of measures of physical activity (Wooley et al., 1979b). Furthermore, there is evidence that subjects matched for age, weight, height, and sex may vary tremendously in total energy output and intake (Rose & Williams, 1961; Warwick, Toft, & Garrow, 1978). Finally, one could argue that inactivity is the effect rather than the cause of obesity (Brownell & Stunkard, 1980; Wooley et al., 1979b).

Although inactivity may not be the primary cause of obesity, it is acknowledged to perpetuate the disorder. There are physiological and metabolic reasons for considering exercise in combination with caloric restriction as a more effective weight-reduction strategy than dieting alone.

> While the mathematics of weight loss through caloric restriction may seem rather straightforward, uncomplicated, and encouraging, several basic assumptions could, if violated, reduce the effectiveness of weight loss through diet or even cause the energy balance equation to become unbalanced in the opposite direction. [Katch & McArdle, 1977, p. 197]

Metabolic research has demonstrated that changes take place during caloric restriction that affect the rate at which weight loss occurs. Decreases in basal metabolic rate of 15 percent to 30 percent have been found to accompany periods of caloric restriction (Bray, 1969; Garrow, 1974; Wooley, et al., 1979a, 1979b). This phenomenon is viewed as an adaptive energy-conserving response to periods of food deprivation. A decline in basal metabolic rate causes dieting to become less effective with extended periods of caloric restriction. Wooley and her colleagues have argued forcefully that the ineffectiveness of dieting is attributable to the lowered metabolic rates that diets produce; that is, dieting itself promotes weight gain (Wooley & Wooley, 1979; Wooley, et al., 1979a, 1979b). Exercise has been shown to increase basal metabolic rate (Allen & Quigley, 1977; Mayer, 1968). An increase in basal metabolism resulting from exercise might counteract the decrease in metabolic rate caused by caloric restriction (Brownell & Stunkard, 1980).

Several studies on small groups of women have suggested that exercise augments the short-term effectveness of dietary regimens (e.g., Dahlkoetter, Callahan, & Linton, 1979; Dudleston & Bennion, 1970; Gwinup, 1975; President's Council on Physical Fitness and Sports, 1975; Zegman, et al., 1979). Dahlkoetter and her colleagues (1979) compared three treatments for overweight women. One treatment group received instructions in behavioral methods to alter eating habits; one group received instructions to increase their exercise; the third group received instructions to modify both eating habits and exercise. After eight weeks, the group that had been instructed to alter both eating habits and exercise lost significantly more weight than the groups instructed in either component alone. A delayed treatment group received instructions to alter both sides of the energy balance equation and lost amounts comparable to the experimental group that focused on both eating and exercise. Zegman and her colleagues (1979) similarly found that a group given behavioral instructions to alter eating habits and exercise lost more weight after ten weeks of treatment than a group given instructions to alter eating habits alone.

Gwinup (1975) conducted a long-term weight-reduction program that involved exercise but not dietary restriction. Out of 34 patients, only 11 women in the study continued to exercise for a minimum of 30 minutes daily for at least a year. Average weight loss for these women in their first year of treatment was 22 pounds. Generally, the more these patients exercised, the more they lost. Skin-fold measurement on the upper arm suggested that loss of fat accounted for most if not all of the weight loss.

In addition to the physiological and metabolic benefits of including exercise in a weight-reduction program, there may be several psychological advantages. The discomforts associated with dieting could be minimized if caloric restriction is moderate and exercise is used to expand additional calories. Moreover, exercise is a behavioral alternative to inappropriate eating (Stuart & Davis, 1972). Finally, evidence suggests that exercise mitigates negative emotions such as anxiety (Bahrke & Morgan, 1978) and depression (Greist, Klein, Eischens, Faris, Gurman, & Morgan, 1978). As discussed, negative affective states are antecedents to inappropriate eating in some obese persons.

Exercise and Health

The relationships between obesity and health risks and obesity and inactivity have been discussed. Epidemiological research also suggests a link between inactivity and poor health. Results from the Framingham Study (Kannel & Sorlie, 1979) suggest that morbidity and mortality are inversely related to the level of physical activity in men. Although physical inactivity is not among the more critical risk factors, "at any level of risk factors, singly or in combination, those who are sedentary are at greater risk" (Kannel & Sorlie, 1979, p. 859). Because men have been subjects in virtually all epidemiological studies on physical activity, the relationship between inactivity and health risks among women is unknown (Thomas, 1979).

CONTRIBUTIONS OF SEX ROLES AND SEX-ROLE STEREOTYPES

It was learned in preceding sections that the prevalence of obesity is generally higher in females than males. At first glance, a biological explanation might account for the sex difference: females are born with a higher percentage of body fat, further increased in the presence of estrogen, and have slower basal metabolic rates. However, a biological theory is inadequate to account for the finding that the prevalence of obesity is not always greater in females. The Midtown Manhattan Study (Srole et al., 1962) showed a strong relationship between social class and the prevalence of obesity. Women in the lower social class showed twice the prevalence of obesity than women of higher socioeconomic status. Among men, the prevalence of obesity was only slightly greater in the lower than in the higher social classes (Stunkard, 1979). Taking sex and class variables into account, Dwyer and his collegues (1970) observed that "successful men are often overweight or obese; successful career women and the wives of famous men rarely are" (p. 279). Although researchers have progressed little in determining the causes of obesity, the demonstrated association between prevalence rates and social class imply that obesity is strongly influenced by social and cultural factors. Prevalence rates reveal that these social factors have a greater influence on women than men. Researchers recognize the importance of specifying the social factors that influence obesity (USDHEW, 1979).

Two intertwined social factors that have received scant attention in the obesity literature are sex roles and sex-role stereotypes. Sex roles are defined as behaviors considered appropriate for an individual on the basis of social definitions of his or her sex (Unger, 1979). A sex-role stereotype is defined as "an attitudinal or behavioral bias against individuals in identical situations engaging in identical behaviors because of their membership in some specific sexual group" (Unger, 1979, p. 27). Greater understanding of obesity and its medical psychological hazards might emerge from examining aspects of the traditionally defined man and woman and from exploring current sex-role stereotypes.

Eating Habits

Traditional sex-role expectations surrounding the realm of work have had profound effects on lifestyle patterns of behavior. Lifestyle habits most relevant to obesity include eating and exercise. Traditionally, the roles of mother and homemaker have been considered most salient for women and the role of wage earner most important for men. The traditional woman has had more exposure to food cues by virtue of spending more time at home and being relegated to the tasks of shopping for and preparing food. As discussed, food cues are antecedents to eating in obese as well as nonobese individuals. Behavioral conceptualizations of obesity consider poor management of these antecedents an important etiological factor. Lack of stimulus control is more likely with greater exposure to food.

Women at home watching television during the day also are barraged with commercials showing perfect wives and moms serving delectable food to their appreciating families. Advertisers knowingly include several sources of powerful behavioral control in these commercials: The appetizing appearance of food combined with the vicarious reinforcement for fulfilling the traditional female role help to insure that women will spend more time in the kitchen.

Physical Activity

In Jean Mayer's opinion (1968) the traditional woman is more physically active than the traditional male because "she does the housework, walks with the children, pushes little carts in supermarkets, [and] window-shops" (p. 79) while her husband goes to work each day to a sedentary office job. Nevertheless, Mayer believes that the woman herself is quite inactive because of all the push-button conveniences for the modern homemaker. Because we live in a highly technological society, the activities we engage in during leisure hours may be critical to our weight and health. Unfortunately, sex-role expectations of women also have provided major obstacles to their pursuing athletics (Leonard, 1980). Stereotypes of females as passive and noncompetitive are basically incompatible with athletic performance, which may require competitiveness and aggression — male stereotype characteristics (Broverman, Vogel, Broverman, Clarkson, & Rosenkrantz, 1972).

Throughout the ages, females have been considered inferior to males in athletics and have been excluded from competitive sports (Brodnar, 1980a, 1980b). Sex differences in athletic capability have been attributed historically to biological differences. Women have been considered weaker, their bones fragile, and their endurance minimal (Leonard, 1980; Rohrbaugh, 1979). Beliefs also have prevailed that physical activity will cause women to become muscular and that it is harmful to their reproductive functions (Klafs & Lyon, 1973). These contentions have now "thoroughly been exposed as myths" (Leonard, 1980, p. 193). Anatomically there are no differences between female athletes and nonathletes (Snyder & Kivlin, cited in Rohrbaugh, 1979). Female athletes do have a lower percentage of body fat than nonathletes, however (Krahenbuhl, Wells, Brown, & Ward, 1979). Exercise has been found to be beneficial, not harmful, to women's reproductive functions (Glover & Shepard, 1978; Klafs & Lyon, 1973). Finally, studies have demonstrated that when males and females are given similar opportunities in physical training they evince similar improvements in strength and endurance (Massicotte, Avon, & Corriveau, 1979; Wilmore, 1975).

A host of social barriers have prevented females from participating in athletics:

1. In early childhood, boys and girls are separated in sports, preventing children from learning that girls and boys can be equally proficient in athletics. Girls who show masculine interests in sports are called tomboys (Michener, 1976).

2. By puberty, girls are encouraged to relinquish their athletic interests. Neuman and his colleagues (Neuman, deNeuman, Valera, & Lindental, 1979) found that from puberty onward females were significantly more sedentary than males.

3. The mass media have contributed greatly to sex-role expectations where sports are concerned. In 1973 NBC televised 366 hours of live sports; one hour was devoted to women (Gilbert & Williamson, cited in Leonard, 1980). The Dallas Cowboy cheeleaders reflect prevailing views on women's role in athletics.

4. Unequal funds for coaching and equipment have been allotted to male and female professional and collegiate sports. Margaret Dunkle, author of *What Constitutes Equality for Women in Sports*, referred to one extreme case in which a large university spent more than $2.6 million for the men's intercollegiate athletic program and no money whatsoever for the women's program (cited in Michener, 1976).

5. Physicians are likely to advise overweight women to diet and prescribe medication to help them do so, while they are likely to advise overweight men to both diet and exercise. "These differentials . . . are more likely to be a reflection of the cultural bias of the physicians than of the idiographic needs of the patients" (Stuart & Jacobson, 1979, p. 251).

The influence of sex-role expectations on obesity perhaps is epitomized by the expectant mother. As discussed, pregnancy and childbirth often are associated with weight gain. Although biological explanations have been invoked, the weight gain could be attributed to a number of psychosocial factors: (1) the notion that she must "eat for two"; (2) restriction of the mother to the home in order to care for the child, thus decreasing her physical activity and increasing her exposure to food cues; and (3) eating to compensate for her limited personal activities (Salans, 1979).

Morbidity and Mortality

Apart from influencing eating habits and activity patterns, data suggest that sex-role expectations contribute to the medical complications of obesity. As discussed, men are more vulnerable to illness and death from obesity than are women. Obesity is a coronary risk factor. For over half a century men have had a higher prevalence of coronary heart disease and a shorter life expectancy than women (Johnson, 1977). Biological theories to explain this sex difference have emphasized the protective role of female hormones (Neuman et al., 1979) and a sex-linked difference in susceptibility to stress (Gadpaelle, 1972). The higher mortality rate among males is not universal, however. Higher mortality rates in women frequently are observed in developing countries (Waldron, 1976; Al-Issa, 1980).

The sex difference in the prevalence of coronary heart disease may be attributable to the effect of social factors and sex-role expectations in particular. Waldron (1976, 1978a) identified a sex difference in one set of behaviors she labeled collectively as the "coronary-prone behavior pattern." This pattern characterizes the traditional male occupational role — a rushed, hard-driving, aggressive, and competitive style of life. Because women traditionally have not worked outside of the home, the coronary-prone behavior pattern is discordant with traditional expectancies for women and with personality traits stereotypically ascribed to women; that is passivity, supportiveness, and dependency. The implication of this sociocultural hypothesis is that males have been socialized into patterns of behavior that predispose them to coronary heart disease (Johnson, 1977). For the traditional male, obesity, inactivity, and occupational stress represent a lethal combination of lifestyle habits.

Double Standard of Physical Attractiveness

As discussed, obesity is viewed with disdain in our culture. While obesity may be a greater medical problem for males, it appears to be a greater social hazard for females. Double standards of attractiveness for males and females exist in our culture. The billion-dollar beauty business, targeted mainly at women and involving cosmetics, clothes, plastic surgery, and breast augmentation, is an attempt to accentuate the physical differences between the sexes and reinforce the stereotype of the female as a sex object (Al-Issa, 1980).

There are many advantages conferred upon the attractive female. She is well liked and endowed with many socially desirable traits (Al-Issa, 1980). She also has economic advantages in that she is likely to marry into a higher social class than a less attractive woman.

Women know the importance of their physical appearance particularly in determining how the male half of the human race will regard them . . .

Men have always desired physical attractiveness in their mates and have valued it highly. [Dwyer, Feldman, & Mayer, 1970, p. 279]

Physical attractiveness is a better predictor of self-concept in females than in males (Al-Issa, 1980). Beautiful women tend to be happier, more satisfied with themselves, and more emotionally stable (Mathes & Kahn, 1975). Women hospitalized in psychiatric institutions have been rated less attractive than women living in the community. Those hospitalized longer tend to be rated even less attractive (Farina, Fischer, Sherman, Smith, Groh, & Mermin, 1977). Al-Issa (1980) put it aptly: "the beautiful female body [is the] key to mental health." Data on the relationship between physical attractiveness and mental health suggest that females who do not conform to the sex-role stereotype of physical beauty suffer debilitating effects from social and economic discrimination.

As applied to the body shape, there is evidence of a shared cultural norm for physical beauty epitomized by the slender, full-bosomed, Barbie doll. These ideals are pervasive within and perpetuated by the media. Children are exposed to these ideals early; by adolescence, females are more concerned with their physiques than are males. Because of the emphasis social messages place on attractiveness in women and because obesity is equated with ugliness in our culture, obesity is more of a social liability for females. Unattractive and obese females are unpopular, do not date, and face considerable job discrimination (Al-Issa, 1980). Obese men face similar social problems but not to the same degree as obese females. The extent to which the social and economic factors influence males and females is seen in prevalence rates. The prevalence of obesity is twice as high among lower-class than upper-class females but only slightly higher in lower-class than upper-class males (Stunkard, 1979). This finding suggests that obesity deters the upward mobility of women more than men.

IMPLICATIONS FOR THE 1980s

A Glimpse to the Future

We currently are witnessing a transition to less rigid sex roles and sex-role stereotypes. Changing role expectations for women are evident in the increasing numbers of women entering the paid workforce and assuming traditionally male occupational roles. If sex-role expectations influence health-related behaviors, then we can expect to see changes in the health status of women and men concurrent with their changing social and economic status. Already there is evidence that the incidence of coronary heart disease among women is increasing and that this increase is related to women's work status (Kinzer, 1979; Waldron, 1978b). Waldron (1978b) found that among women 40 to 59 years of age, high occupational status and success were correlated with the coronary-prone behavior pattern.

Changing sex roles appear to affect eating habits. As discussed, successful career women are more concerned with dieting and are less often obese than women in lower social classes. As more women become involved in successful careers, we can expect to see a lessening in the prevalence of obesity among women. Indeed, women in the United States have become somewhat thinner during the last two decades, when concern with their weight increased; men, subjected to much less pressure, are becoming heavier (Stunkard, 1979).

Changing sex roles also will influence the physical activity of women. In spite of numerous social obstacles preventing women from leading active lifestyles, recent trends suggest that female participation in athletics is increasing. Contributions to this trend include several lawsuits involving sexual discrimination in sports and the enactment of Title IX of the Educational Amendments of 1972, which bars sexual discrimination in educational settings that receive federal financial assistance (Michener, 1976; Leonard, 1980).

The relationships between eating, exercise, obesity, stress, and coronary heart disease are quite complex; therefore, it is difficult to predict how changes in these variables will affect the overall health status of men and women.

Research Implications

Large voids exist in our understanding of obesity and its relationship to morbidity and mortality. These gaps are partially the result of methodological problems in obesity research. Gaining knowledge of this complex and refractory disorder is dependent upon an improved methodology for measuring the physical and physiological concomitants of obesity. Important research opportunities also exist for continued study of proposed biological factors: genetics, adipocity, basal metabolism, and so on (USDHEW, 1979).

Investigators have begun to examine the influence of lifestyle patterns of behavior upon physical health. Sex roles and sex-role stereotypes are unusual variables of study in health research; however, the evidence presented suggests that lifestyle patterns of behavior, including food consumption, exercise, dieting, and occupational stress, derive largely from sex-role expectations. Systematically investigating the relationships of sex roles to these behaviors might help to fill the void in our understanding of obesity and its related problems.

Implications for Prevention and Treatment

Studying the influence of sex-role expectations on eating, exercise, and occupational stress might have important implications for the prevention and treatment of obesity and its medical complications.

Prevention. Early prevention of obesity entails training children in appropriate food-related activities and in physical activity. Strides can be made toward the prevention of obesity in women if children are encouraged to view such behaviors as cooking and athletics as appropriate for both males and females. The public sector and the media might contribute to this socialization process by reducing the time, money, and effort spent on urging women to achieve some unrealistic standard of physical attractiveness and redirecting it toward the realistic goal of physical fitness. This objective might be accomplished in various ways:

1. Provide females with more programs and facilities to pursue exercise.
2. Provide more extensive media coverage of women in sports.
3. Employ males more frequently as the main actors in television commercials selling food products.
4. Employ female professional athletes more frequently in advertisements and commercials.
5. Enlist women's magazines as a forum on obesity and its management (USDHEW, 1979). Magazine articles should include information on
   a. uncertainties and misconceptions of obesity
   b. probability of treatment success
   c. treatment side effects and their severity.
6. Explore the feasibility of integrating health behavior methods in the media for men and women (USDHEW, 1979).

7. Establish programs in industrial settings to
   a. provide working men and women with accurate information on the relationships between lifestyle and health
   b. offer treatment for obesity, stress, and related coronary risk factors
   c. provide working women with support groups to reexamine self- or other-imposed role expectations that contribute to stress and lack of self-esteem. Two areas for reexamination include the dual work role and pressures on women to lose weight.

Treatment.   Psychologists and health practitioners are encouraged to recognize that maladaptive lifestyle behaviors may derive from sex-role expectations clients hold for themselves and for others. To uncover potential causes of physical or psychological maladies, assessment might include evaluations of a client's sex-role orientation and expectations. If these factors appear etiologically significant, the first step toward remediation might involve educating the client regarding the influence of sex-role expectations on lifestyle behavior. A woman with poor self-esteem because of failure to lose weight might be informed that her desire to reduce stems from her expectation that she fulfill the stereotype of the beautiful female. Additionally, she might be told that society placed her in somewhat of a Catch-22 situation: On the one hand she is pressured to reduce; on the other hand, she is the family member most responsible for food-related chores, and she is discouraged from exercising.

Wooley and her colleagues (1979b) have alluded to this approach in suggesting alternative treatments for obesity. The role of a therapist should not be only to help women stay on diets. The first task of the therapist is to acquaint clients with the facts on obesity, the physiological effects of dieting, and the high probability of treatment failure. "They will be relieved to have their experience confirmed and understood, and some may be better able to withstand the difficulties knowing that they are not exclusively attributable to their own failings" (p. 20). Because of the difficulty obese women in achieving slenderness, their therapists should present them with the option of foregoing attempts to lose weight and should concentrate instead on helping them achieve greater self-acceptance. Moreover, helping the clients develop skills to combat social prejudice should be an integral part of treatment. "This means that efficacy of procedures in promoting weight loss must be balanced against the extent to which they further erode dignity and self-esteem" (Wooley et al., 1979b, p. 20).

Inherent in this alternative treatment approach is the necessity of the helping professionals' recognizing their own sex biases in prescribing treatment. Assuming that weight reduction is the major treatment goal for obese women serves to perpetuate the stereotype of the slender, attractive female. Moreover, clinical and metabolic research suggests that dieting strategies alone are iatrogenic. The woman who makes an informed decision to lose weight must be encouraged to alter lifestyle habits that may derive from sex-role expectations. She may need less exposure to food cues and much more encouragement to exercise. Professionals can avoid contributing to their clients' feelings of failure and despair by dispelling myths about obese/nonobese differences, by educating them about the probable course of their weight losses, by anticipating future difficulties, and by providing them with the behavioral and cognitive coping strategies to handle these difficulties.

REFERENCES

Al-Issa, I. *The psychopathology of women.* Englewood Cliffs, N.J.: Prentice-Hall, 1980.

Allen, D. W., & Quigley, B. M. The role of physical activity in the control of obesity. *Medical Journal of Australia,* 1977, *2,* 434–438.

Ashwell, M. A. A survey of pateints' views of doctors' treatment of obesity. *The Practitioner,* 1973, *211,* 653–658.

Bahrke, M. S., & Morgan, W. P. Anxiety reduction following exercise and meditation. *Cognitive Therapy & Research,* 1978, *2,* 323–333.

Berman, E. M. Factors influencing motivations in dieting. *Journal of Nutrition Education,* 1975, *7,* 155–159.

Björntörp, P., Carlgren, G., Isaksson, B., Krotkiewski, M., Larson, B., & Sjöström, L. Effect of an energy-reduced dietary regimen in relation to adipose cellularity in obese women. *American Journal of Clinical Nutrition,* 1975, *28,* 445–452.

Bloom, W. L., & Eidex, M. F. Inactivity as a major factor in adult obesity. *Metabolism,* 1967, *16,* 679–684.

Bodnar, L. M. Historical role of women in sports. *The American Journal of Sports Medicine,* 1980, *8,* 53–56. (a)

Bodnar, L. M. Women, sports, and the law. *The American Journal of Sports Medicine,* 1980, *8,* 290–293. (b)

Bradfield, R., Paulos, J., & Grossman, H. Energy expenditure and heart rate of obese high-school girls. *American Journal of Clinical Nutrition*, 1971, *24*, 1482–1486.

Bray, G. A. Effect of caloric restriction on energy expenditure in obese patients. *Lancet*, 1969, *2*, 397–398.

Bray, G. A. *The obese patient*. Philadelphia: Saunders, 1976.

Broverman, I. K., Vogel, S. R., Broverman, D. M., Clarkson, F. E., & Rosenkrantz, P. Sex role stereotypes: A current appraisal. *Journal of Social Issues*, 1972, *28*, 59–78.

Brownell, K. D., Albaum, J. M., & Stunkard, A. J. Evaluation and modification of activity patterns in the natural environment. Unpublished manuscript, Department of Psychiatry, University of Pennsylvania, 1978.

Brownell, K. D., & Stunkard, A. J. Physical activity in the development and control of obesity. In A. J. Stunkard (Ed.), *Obesity*. Philadelphia: Suanders, 1980.

Brownell, K. D., Stunkard, A. J., & Albaum, J. M. Evaluation and modification of exercise patterns in the natural environment. *American Journal of Psychiatry*, 1980, *137*, 1540–1545.

Brownell, K. D., & Venditti, E. W. The etiology and treatment of obesity. In W. E. Fann, I. Karacan, A. D. Pokorny, & R. L. Williams (Eds.), *Phenomenology and the treatment of psychophysiological disorders*. New York: Spectrum, in press.

Bullen, B. A., Monello, L. F., Cohen, H., & Mayer, J. Attitudes toward physical activity, food, and family in obese and nonobese adolescent girls. *American Journal of Clinical Nutrition*, 1963, *12*, 1–11.

Bullen, B. A., Reed, R. B., & Mayer, J. Physical activity of obese and non-obese adolescent girls appraised by motion picture sampling. *American Journal of Clinical Nutrition*, 1974, *14*, 211–233.

Chirico, A. M., & Stunkard, A. J. Physical activity and human obesity. *New England Journal of Medicine*, 1960, *263*, 935–940.

Craighead, L. W., Stunkard, A. J., & O'Brien, R. New treatments for obesity. Paper presented at the annual meeting of the American Psychological Association, Toronto, August 1978.

Dahlkoetter, J., Callahan, E. J., & Linton, J. Obesity and the unbalanced energy equation: Exercise versus eating habit change. *Journal of Consulting and Clinical Psychology*, 1979, *47*, 898–905.

Deischer, E., & Mills, D. The adolescent looks at his health and medical care. *American Journal of Public Health*, 1963, *53*, 1928–1936.

Dublin, L. I., & Marks, H. H. Weight and longevity. In H. E. Ungerleider & R. S. Gubner (Eds.), *Life insurance and medicine*. Springfield, Ill.: Charles C Thomas, 1958.

Dudleston, A. K., & Bennion, M. Effect of diet and/or exercise on obese college women. *Journal of the American Dietetic Association*, 1970, *56*, 126–130.

Dwyer, J. T., Feldman, J. J., & Mayer, J. Adolescent dieters: Who are they? Physical characteristics, attitudes, and dietary practices of adolescent girls. *American Journal of Clinical Nutrition*, 1967, *20*, 1045–1056.

Dwyer, J. T., Feldman, J. J., & Mayer, J. The social psychology of dieting. *Journal of Health and Social Behavior*, 1970, *10*, 269–287.

Dwyer, J. T., & Mayer, J. Potential dieters: Why are they? *Journal of the American Dietetic Association*, 1970, *56*, 510–514.

Farina, A., Fischer, E. H., Sherman, S., Smith, W. T., Groh, T., & Mermin, P. Physical attractiveness and mental illness. *Journal of Abnormal Psychology*, 1977, *8*, 510–517.

Forbes, G. B. Body composition and the natural history of fatness. In G. A. Bray (Ed.), *Obesity in America*. HEW, 1979.

Franzini, L. R., & Grimes, W. B. Skinfold measures as the criteria of change in weight control studies. *Behavior Therapy*, 1976, *7*, 256–260.

Gadpaille, W. J. Research into the physiology of maleness and femaleness: Its contributions to the etiology and psychodynamics of homosexuality. *Archives of General Psychiatry*, 1972, *26*, 193–206.

Garrow, J. *Energy balance and obesity*. New York: American Elsevier, 1974.

Glover, B., & Shepard, J. *The runner's handbook: A complete fitness guide for men and women on the run*. New York: Penguin Books, 1978.

Gordon, T., & Kannel, W. B. The effects of overweight on cardiovascular diseases. *Geriatrics*, 1973, *28*, 80–88.

Greist, J. H., Klein, M. H. Eischens, R. R., Faris, J., Gurman, A. S., & Morgan, W. P. Running through your mind. *Journal of Psychosomatic Research*, 1978, *22*, 259–294.

Gwinup, G. Effect of exercise alone on the weight of obese women. *Archives of Internal Medicine*, 1975, *135*, 676–680.

Hirsch, J., & Knittle, J. L. Cellularity of obese and nonobese human adipose tissue. *Federation Proceedings*, 1970, *29*, 1516–1521.

Hoyenga, K. B., & Hoyenga, K. T. *The question of sex differences: Psychological, cultural, and biological issues*. Boston: Little, Brown, 1979.

Johnson, A., Sex differentials in coronary heart disease: The explanatory role of primary risk factors. *Journal of Health and Social Behaviors*, 1977, *18*, 46–54.

Johnson, M. L., Burke, M. S., & Mayer, J. Relative importance of inactivity and overeating in the energy balance of obese high school girls. *American Journal of Clinical Nutrition*, 1956, *4*, 37–44.

Johnson, W. G., & Stalonas, P. Measuring skinfold thickness — a cautionary note. *Addictive Behaviors*, 1977, *2*, 105–107.

Kannel, W. B., & Gordon, T. Physiological and medical concomitants of obesity: The Framingham Study. In G. A. Bray (Ed.), *Obesity in America*. DHEW, 1979.

Kannel, W. B., & Sorlie, P. Some health benefits of physical activity: The Framingham Study. *Archives of Internal Medicine*, 1979, *139*, 851–861.

Katch, F. I., & McArdle, W. D. *Nutrition, weight control, and exercise*. Boston: Houghton Mifflin, 1977.

Keys, A. Body composition and its change with age and diet. In E. S. Eppright, P. Swanson, & C. A. Iverson (Eds.), *Weight control*. Ames, Iowa: Iowa State College Press, 1955.

Kinzer, N. S. *Stress and the American woman*. New York: Ballantine Books, 1979.

Klafs, C., & Lyon, M. J. *The female athlete*. St. Louis, Mo.: C. V. Mosby, 1973.

Krahenbuhl, C. S., Wells, C. L., Brown, C. H., & Ward, P. E. Characteristics of national and world class female pentathletes. *Medicine and Science in Sports*, 1979, *11*, 20–23.

Leonard II, W. M. *A sociological perspective of sport*. Minneapolis: Burgess Publishing, 1980.

Mahoney, M. J. Fat fiction. *Behavior Therapy*, 1975, *6*, 416–418.

Mann, G. V. The influence of obesity on health. *New England Journal of Medicine*, 1974, *291*, 226–232.

Massicotte, D. R., Avon, G., & Corriveau, G. Comparative effects of aerobic training on men and women. *Journal of Sports Medicine*, 1979, *19*, 23–32.

Mathes, E. W., & Kahn, A. Physical attractiveness, happiness, neuroticism and self-esteem. *Journal of Psychology*, 1975, *90*, 27–30.

Maxfield, E., & Konishi, F. Patterns of food intake and physical activity in obesity. *Journal of the American Dietetic Association*, 1966, *49*, 406–408.

Mayer, J. *Overweight: Causes, cost and control*. Englewood Cliffs, N.J.: Prentice-Hall, 1968.

Mayer, J., Roy, P., & Mitra, K. P. Relation between caloric intake, body weight, and physical work: Studies in an industrial male population in West Bengal. *American Journal of Clinical Nutrition*, 1956, *4*, 169–175.

Michener, J. A. *Sports in America*. New York: Random House, 1976.

Montoye, H. J. *An introduction to measurement in physical education*. Boston, Mass.: Allyn & Bacon, 1978.

Montoye, H. J., Epstein, F. H., & Kjelsberg, M. O. The measurement of body fatness: A study in a total community. *American Journal of Clinical Nutrition*, 1965, *16*, 417–427.

Neuman, J., deNeuman, M. P., Valera E., & Lindental, D. Epidemiology of coronary heart disease risk factors in a free-living population. *Preventive Medicine*, 1979, *8*, 445–462.

President's Council on Physical Fitness and Sports. *Physical fitness research digest*, DHEW, 1975.

Rand, C., & Stunkard, A. J. Obesity and psychoanalysis. *American Journal of Psychiatry*, 1974, *135*, 547–551.

Rimm, A. A., & White, P. L. Obesity: Its risks and hazards. In G. A. Bray (Ed.), *Obesity in America*. DHEW, 1979.

Rodin, J. Bidirectional influences of emotionality, stimulus responsivity, and metabolic events in obesity. In J. D. Master & M. E. P. Seligman (Eds.), *Psychopathology: Experimental models.* San Francisco: Freeman, 1977.

Rohrbaugh, J. B. Femininity on the line. *Psychology Today*, August 1979, pp. 30–42.

Rogers, T., Mahoney, M. J., Mahoney, B. K., Straw, M. G., & Kenigsberg, M. I. Clinical assessment of obesity: An empirical evaluation of diverse techniques. *Behavioral Assessment*, 1980, *2*, 161–181.

Rose, G. A., & Williams, R. T. Metabolic studies on large and small eaters. *British Journal of Nutrition*, 1961, *15*, 1.

Rose, H. E., & Mayer, J. Activity, caloric intake, and the energy balance of infants. *Pediatrics*, 1968, *41*, 18–29.

Salans, L. B. Natural history of obesity. In G. A. Bray (Ed.), *Obesity in America*. DHEW, 1979.

Schachter, S. Obesity and eating. *Science*, 1968, *161*, 151.

Silverstone, J. P., & Lascelles, B. D. Dieting and depression.*British Journal of Psychiatry*, 1966, *112*, 513–519.

Sims, E. A. H. Definitions, criteria, and prevalence of obesity. In G. A. Bray (Ed.), *Obesity in America*. DHEW, 1979.

Society of Actuaries. *Build and blood pressure study*, 1959.

Srole, L., Langner, T. S., Michael, S. T., Kirkpatrick, P., Opler, M. K., & Rennie, T. A. C. *Mental health in the metropolis: The Midtown Manhattan Study*. New York: McGraw-Hill, 1962.

Straffieri, J. R. A study of social stereotypes of body image in children. *Journal of Personality and Social Psychology*, 1967, *7*, 101–104.

Stenfanik, P. A., Heald, F. P., & Mayer, J. Caloric intake in relation to energy output of obese and nonobese adolescent boys. *American Journal of Clinical Nutrition*, 1959, *1*, 55–62.

Straw, M. Energy expenditure and weight regulation. Unpublished manuscript, 1978.

Stuart, R. B., & Davis, B. *Slim chance in a fat world: Behavioral control of obesity*. Champaign, Ill.: Research Press, 1972.

Stuart, R. B., & Jacobson, B. Sex differences in obesity. In E. S. Gomberg & V. Franks (Eds.), *Gender and disordered behavior: Sex differences in psychopathology*. New York: Brunner/Mazel, 1979.

Stunkard, A. J. The dieting depression: Incidence and clinical characteristics of untoward responses to weight reduction regimens. *American Journal of Medicine*, 1957, *23*, 77–86.

Stunkard, A. J. *The pain of obesity*. Palo Alto, Calif.: Bull, 1976.

Stunkard, A. J. Obesity and the social environment: Current status, future prospects. In G. A. Bray (Ed.), *Obesity in America*. United States Department of Health, Education, and Welfare, 1979.

Stunkard, A. J., & Pestka, J. The physical activity of obese girls. *American Journal of Diseases in Children*, 1962, *103*, 812–817.

Stunkard, A. J., & Rush, A. J. Dieting and depression reexamined: A critical review of reports of untoward responses during weight reduction for obesity. *Annals of Internal Medicine*, 1974, *81*, 526–533.

Thomas, G. S. Physical activity and health: Epidemiologic and clinical evidence and policy implications. *Preventive Medicine*, 1979, *8*, 89–103.

Unger, R. K. *Female and male: Psychological perspectives*. New York: Harper & Row, 1979.

United States Department of Health, Education, & Welfare. *Weight, height, and selected body dimensions of adults: United States 1960–1962*. Washington, D.C.: U.S. Government Printing Office, 1965.

United States Department of Health, Education, & Welfare. *Obesity and health: A sourcebook of current information for professional health*. Arlington, Va.: 1967.

United States Department of Health, Education, & Welfare. *Obesity in America*. NIH Publication No. 79-359, November 1979.

United States Public Health Service. *Skinfolds, girths, biacromial diameter, and selected anthropometric indices of adults: United States, 1960–62*. Washington, D.C.: U.S. Government Printing Office, 1970.

Waldron, I. Why do women live longer than men? Part I. *Journal of Human Stress*, 1976, *2*, 2–13.

Waldron, I. Sex differences in coronary heart disease. *Journal of Health and Social Behavior*, 1978, *19*, 119–121. (a)

Waldron, I. The coronary-prone behavior pattern, blood pressure, employment, and socioeconomic status in women. *Journal of Psychosomatic Research*, 1978, *22*, 79–87. (b)

Warwick, P., Toft, R., & Garrow, J. Individual differences in energy expenditure. In G. A. Bray (Ed.), *Recent advances in obesity research*. London: Newman, 1978.

Waxman, M., & Stunkard, A. J. Caloric intake and expenditure of obese children. *Journal of Pediatrics*, in press.

Wilkinson, P., Parklin, J., & Pearloom G. Energy intake and physical activity in obese children. *British Medical Journal*, 1977, *1*, 756.

Wilmore, J. H. Inferiority of female athletes: Myth or reality. *Journal of Sports Medicine*, 1975, *3*, 1–6.

Wooley, O. W., & Wooley, S. C. The experimental psychology of obesity. In T. Silverstone & J. Fincham (Eds.), *Obesity: Pathogenesis and management*. Lancaster: Medical and Technical Publishing, 1975.

Wooley, O. W., Wooley, S. C., & Dryenforth, S. R. Obesity and women—II. A neglected feminist topic. *Women's Studies International Quarterly*, 1979, *2*, 81–92. (a)

Wooley, S. C., & Wooley, O. W. Obesity and women—I. A closer look at the facts. *Women's Studies International Quarterly,* 1979, *2,* 69–79.

Wooley, S. C., Wooley, O. W., & Dryenforth, S. R. Theoretical, practical, and special issues in behavioral treatments of obesity. *Journal of Applied Behavior Analysis,* 1979, *12,* 3–26. (b)

Yudkin, J. Doctors treatment of obesity. *The Practitioner,* 1968, *201,* 330–335.

Zegman, M. A., Wilson, G. T., Dubbert, P., & Lamon, S. The role of exercise in the behavioral treatment of obesity. Paper presented at the annual meeting of the Society of Behavioral Medicine, San Francisco, December 1979.

■ 10
The Resocialization of Single-Again Women

JUDITH WORELL and NIKKI GARRET-FULKS

THE GROWING POPULATION OF SINGLE-AGAIN WOMEN

The childhood rehearsal of females for adult life transitions in our culture bears little resemblance to the real events that women commonly experience. Little girls frequently are urged to "play house" and "play mother" but never are encouraged to "play divorcee" or to "play single career woman." Our society has been remiss in providing role models and consequent expectations for the woman alone. Few female children are raised with the notion that they may spend half of their adult lives as single persons.

The statistics indicate, however, that the single-again adult woman constitutes a growing portion of the population. According to the U.S. Bureau of the Census (1979), in 1978 there were 1.1 million divorces and 2.2 million marriages, that is, five divorces for every ten marriages. Although the divorce rate has increased dramatically in the last 20 years, from 2.2 per 1,000 population in 1960 to 5.1 per 1,000 in 1978, it has remained fairly stable in the past five years (U.S. Bureau of the Census, 1979). If the current rates remain static, it is estimated that 40 percent of all marriages will end in divorce (U.S. Bureau of the Census, 1979; Fox-

202 : : *Special Problems of Living*

ley, 1979; Hetherington, Cox, & Cox, 1979; Rawlings & Carter, 1979).

The total number of children affected by divorce also has increased Despite declining birth rates, the number of children involved in divorce has tripled since 1956. In 1975, the total number of children involved in divorce reached a record high of 1,123,000 (U.S. Bureau of the Census, 1979), and the proportion of divorces involving children under 18 was 59 percent of the total. In over 90 percent of custody decisions, children were placed in the custody of the mother. It is not surprising that the rise in divorces involving children is paralleled by a concomitant rise in the number of one-parent families maintained by a woman. Over the past decade, female-headed households with children have grown "almost 10 times as fast as two-parent families" (Ross & Sawhill, 1975, p. 1). In 1978, 17 percent of all households with children under the age of 18 years were maintained by the mother, as compared to 2 percent by the father (U.S. Bureau of the Census, 1979).

The remarriage pattern for divorced women shows an inverse relationship between age and number of children and the probability of remarriage. Younger women are more likely to remarry than older ones, and that likelihood doubles for women who were divorced under the age of 30 compared to divorced women over 40. Women who are childless and under 30 have the greatest chance for remarriage following divorce: 80 percent of those divorced in 1972 remarried within 3 years (U.S. Bureau of the Census, 1979). The woman over 30 years old with children is more likely to remain single and more likely to continue in a single-parent role than her younger counterpart. Gender differences also are noted in remarriage patterns. Divorced men are more likely to remarry than women, and a sizable number are more likely to marry a woman ten or more years younger than themselves (Bloom, Asher, & White, 1978).

The ramifications of single-again status also affect the growing population of middle-aged widows. The Census Bureau data indicate that the increasing life expectancy for women, coupled with the traditional pattern of younger women marrying older men, increases a woman's chances of being widowed by the time she reaches middle age (Berardo, 1968; Foxley, 1979; Ross & Sawhill, 1975). The ratio of widows to widowers continues to rise and is reported to be 1 : 4 (Berardo, 1968). Gender differences also are evident in the remarriage patterns of widowed persons. Although divorced persons on the whole remarry more frequently than widowed persons, widowed men are more likely to remarry than widowed women (Bloom et al., 1978).

Despite these mushrooming statistics, researchers and counselors have spent little time or effort in exploring the ramifications and life changes involved in the single-again process (Hetherington et al., 1979; Kessler, 1976). Loss of a spouse through divorce or death necessitates dramatic role changes for the single-again woman, without clear-cut guidelines or societal sanctions for the changes. Mental health professionals need to be sensitive to the changes wrought by the transition and to the implications of these changes for clients and their social milieu.

TRADITIONAL SEX-ROLE HANDICAPS

The focus of this article is on the single-again woman and the adjustment process associated with the loss of a male spouse, as well as the resocialization process associated with the loss of the wife role. We have focused on women because the sex-role changes brought about by the loss of a spouse are far more dramatic for women than for men. The research indicates that men experience similar disorientation, loneliness, and emotional pain after divorce or loss of a spouse through death. However, men can continue to pursue their societal roles as traditional breadwinners and to enjoy the advantages of higher occupational attainment. They are more likely than their former spouses to have been full-time workers prior to divorce or widowing and less likely to have been unemployed or concentrated in low-paying, low-status, dead-end jobs. Economically, their salaries are likely to exceed that of their working former spouse by almost 70 percent (U.S. Department of Labor, 1979). In addition to the employment disparity and earnings gap between single-again women and men, women have greater difficulty with this transition process for two major reasons: (1) they are not socialized to assume unmarried roles and (2) they are not supported by society when they are single again (Aslin, 1978; Bach, 1974).

Traditionally, a woman's identity is woven inextricably into the fabric of her marriage, and the role of wife/mother is assumed to precede all other socialized adult female roles (Lewis, 1978; Sales, 1978). In Katz's (1979) life span model for development, most of the developmental tasks for women between the ages of 15 and 50 deal with the jobs of coupling, marriage, and parenting. Although both men and women experience a loss of role as a result of being single again, women may experience a "heightened sense of personal failure over not succeeding at their most important societal role" (Rawlings & Carter, 1979, p. 28). Hetherington et al. (1979) report that two of the major areas of stress for the newly divorced mother were the loss of identity and the feeling of general incompetence due to the lack of socialized cross-sex skills. Following divorce, many women are handicapped by low career aspirations, absent or inconsistent work experience, and underdeveloped job-related skills.

Although the loss of role experience is probably very similar for divorced and widowed women, two distinctions should be made between these two groups. First, the adjustment-after-loss process is characterized by the discontinuity and ambiguity in social roles and societal expectations. Widowed women have a slightly different experience than divorced women in this regard. Bereavement and mourning for the dead is institutionalized in most cultures and is invested with a structured set of expectations and prescribed roles. The finality of the death of a spouse gives structure to a widow's reactions and concomitant societal response. There is little ambiguity here, nor is there the resultant anxiety that often is elicited by ambiguous situations (Aslin, 1978).

Although society has given permission to divorce by enacting laws allowing for the dissolution of a marriage, it has not given an institutionalized structure to the divorce process (Goode, 1956). The role of the divorced person contains no clear-cut guidelines for acceptable and appropriate behavior, nor does society delineate a set of acceptable responses to the divorced person. We define divorce in such tragic terms that the individual who is relieved and happy to be out of a dysfunctional marriage may feel ashamed and guilty. Society is also at a loss for positive role models in responding to divorced individuals (Bloom et al., 1978). Although the experience after the loss of a spouse may be different for the widowed woman than the divorced woman, they both experience a similar loss of identity as a "married woman," as well as a lack of role prescriptions for single-again status.

A second reason why women have a more difficult adjustment to loss is related to prevailing societal attitudes toward women alone. Even with no-fault divorce laws and soaring widowhood rates, society continues to punish and blame single-again women. This punishment comes in the form of subtle ostracism, better known as the "fifth wheel" syndrome (Aslin, 1978; Borenzweig, 1976; Rose & Price-Bonham, 1973). Berardo (1968) reports that the widow finds herself "marooned in an environment which generally requires paired relationships as a prerequisite to social participation" (p. 196). Research indicates that divorced women receive less child-care and household help from friends and community resources than divorced fathers. Hetherington et al. (1979) found that women experienced greater dissociation from married friends than their male counterparts did, with support from those married friends decreasing rapidly after the first two months. Along with the sex-role handicaps that leave her vastly unprepared for her new status, the single-again woman finds herself abandoned by society at a time when a sense of belonging is needed most (Kessler, 1976; Rawlings & Carter, 1979).

There are four specific traditional female sex roles associated with marriage that leave the single-again woman unprepared for her new status: (1) economic dependence on a male, (2) subordination to male power, (3) reliance on a husband for social identity, and (4) investment in the supermom/superwife roles.

Economic Dependency

First, women traditionally are socialized to be economically dependent upon the male breadwinner for financial security (Aslin, 1978; Rawlings & Carter, 1977). In most marriages, the woman's career is considered secondary to that of her spouse and is regarded as a negligible source of additional income. Women who do have employment during marriage do not substitute the work role for the wife/mother role; they merely take on an additional job (O'Leary, 1974). Moreover, prevailing attitudes toward working mothers suggests to both husbands and wives that a mother's responsibility is first to her home and children (Farmer, 1978). Therefore, women's working patterns tend to be inconsistent following marriage, leaving the single-again woman unprepared to face the economic demands of singleness. Vetter (1978) reports that, in a recent sample of 4,807 women, only 16 percent were employed continuously after marriage. Further, marital status was a significant predictor of low-paying occupational status (office worker) rather than higher-paying career choices (scientific or professional) in a sample of 5,378 high-school graduates (Astin & Myint, 1978). The sex-role socialization factors in women's low achievement and career status recently were summarized by Farmer (1978) into seven variables identified in the research literature. These factors were: (1) lowered academic self-confidence; (2) fear of success in varying degrees, depending on the perceived social sanctions toward careers for women; (3) vicarious achievement motivation, which contributes both to women's contentment with wife-only status and to lower-status occupations; (4) home–career conflicts found in both working and college women; (5) work discrimination beliefs (which Farmer points out have some considerable validity); (6) low risk-taking behavior; and (7) traditional or feminine sex-role beliefs. Any or all of these sex-role orientations to career development may handicap single-again women economically in their new status.

Subordination to Male Power

A second traditional role associated with marriage is the subordinate position women assume in power relationships with men. Women have characteristically been taught to deny their anger, hostility, and competitiveness and to remain passive and unassertive in power dealings (Bach, 1974; Chesler, 1975; Johnson, 1978; Krantzler, 1973; Rawlings & Carter, 1979; Unger, 1978). Johnson (1974), as cited in Unger (1978), reports that when females were given a choice of power style they chose to use helpless/dependent power styles significantly more often than males and almost always rejected the use of expert power based on skill and competence. The inhibition of aggressiveness occurs early in the female socialization process (Kaplan, 1976). It follows then, that when a woman suddenly finds herself alone without the protection of her husband, she frequently may feel vulnerable, powerless, and helpless. Although divorce or widowhood for a woman can serve as a major catalyst for role change and a new assertive lifestyle, the sex-role proscriptions against expression of anger and power in women can be an effective handicap in the single-again adjustment process.

Reliance on the Husband for Social Identity

A third stereotypical characteristic of a married woman is her dependence on her husband for status, social contact, and identity (Aslin, 1978; Bach, 1974; Rawlings & Carter, 1977; Sales, 1978). In addition to taking his name, the woman assumes greater responsibility for adjusting to new roles and tends to center her social life around the professional associates of her husband (Barry, 1970; Hetherington et al., 1979). Her major occupational role, that of homemaker, has low social status and no pay, and therefore she achieves vicarious status through her husband's occupation and his achievements (Unger, 1978). She is likely to shape her ideals and personal traits to fit her husband's expectancies, and she frequently relocates her household to accommodate her husband's change of job (Bernard, 1972; Kaplan & Sedney, 1980).

Women are socialized to find a mate who will "complement" them (Deaux, 1976), and we believe this notion of complementarity to be destructive for women. When pairing is based on one individual completing the other, loss of one partner results in the other feeling empty and incomplete (Heikkinen, 1979). Often the void is so painful and the societal pressure for remarriage so strong that the single-again woman quickly recouples in an effort to become complete again (Kressel & Deutsch, 1977; Krantzler, 1973). Those women who opt for nontraditional roles develop a status and identity independent of significant others and develop a new support network as well. Bloom et al. (1978) found that adjustment after divorce was easier for women with nontraditional sex-role orientations.

Investment in the Supermom/Superwife Role

Lastly, the stereotypical female traits of nurturance, warmth, and familial responsibility and sacrifice lend themselves well to the traditional female role of superwife/supermom. Women have been reared to accept affiliation, warmth, and empathy as the valued major components of their central adult roles of wife and mother (O'Leary, 1974). For some women, the internal/external dictates of the wife and mother role lead to an overinvolvement with husband and children and a consequent loss of self. The literature indicates that divorced mothers consistently express anxiety about their parenting competency and children's happiness (Aslin, 1978; Hetherington et al., 1979). The consequent guilt some mothers feel about the damaging effects of divorce on their offspring often results in the overindulgence of their children at the expense of their own needs. The variety of feelings associated with the loss of this traditional female sex role range from resentment and anger to helplessness, hopelessness, and depression. For those women who can transcend their traditional sex-role socialization, the loss of the supermom/superwife role can be a catalyst for the development of more realistic relationship expectations and increased personal independence (Bach, 1974; Kressel & Deutsch, 1977).

SOURCES OF STRESS IN SINGLE-AGAIN WOMEN: RESEARCH EVIDENCE

The contributions of sex-role socialization lead to the identification of four related sources of stress experienced by single-again women: (1) economic insufficiency, (2) powerlessness, (3) social isolation, and (4) role strain. Each of these stressors may vary in intensity across groups of separated, divorced, and widowed women, as well as between those who do and do not have children under the age of 18. The single parent in particular may experience all these stressors in greater intensity than those women who do not have minor children to support and manage. As used here, the concept of stress refers to negative experiences of individuals who are facing more tasks and required behaviors than can be managed with current behavioral, skill, time, and financial resources (Blechman & Deppenbrock, 1974). The results of these multiple demands upon limited resources of the individual are subjective discomfort, tension, and increased risk for psychological and physical indicators of stress.

The evidence that marital disruption serves as a significant life stressor comes from many sources, all of which point to increases in physical and psychological symptomotology following separation, divorce, or widowhood. Using a national sample of 2,400 respondents, Douvan and Kukla (1979) found that divorced and separated women were most vulnerable to unhappiness and stress, although in these same categories men were a close second. Stress scores were determined from self-reports of happiness, immobilization (such as inability to get up in the morning), and fear of mental breakdown. In overall ratings of happiness, only 13 percent of the divorced women were affirmative, as compared to 27 percent of the single women and 40 percent of the married women in the sample. Other studies have correlated marital disruption for women with depression, alcohol and drug abuse, sleep difficulties, low work efficiency, weight loss or gain, automotive violations and accidents, inpatient and outpatient psychiatric admissions, a variety of physical illnesses and disabilities, and mortality from suicide, murder, or disease (Bloom et al., 1978; Scherman, 1979). In the following section we will discuss briefly each of the four stressors listed previously, and we will suggest some of the factors that contribute to the intensity and complexity of single-again stress.

Economic Insufficiency

The majority of widowed and divorced women are caring for dependent children in single-parent settings. In almost all cases, single-again women are existing at a lower standard of living than their married peers. In 1976, of the 4.5 million divorced and separated women in the United States, only 4 percent were receiving alimony. Single mothers fared badly also: only 42 percent of divorced mothers received any amount of child support, and only 18 percent of separated mothers did so. Poverty rates for these single-parent families approximate four times the national incidence. The median family income of divorced women who maintained families in 1977 was $9,608, or only 53 percent of the income reported for married couples (Glick, 1979). It seems clear from these statistics that a significant source of life stress comes from financial insufficiency to meet the daily living needs of the single-again family.

Economic stress is related significantly to self-reports of depression and incompetence in daily living and contributes to a sense of helplessness (Hetherington et al., 1979). In addition to insufficient funds, single-again women may be relatively uninformed about financial dealings involving insurance, taxes, mortgages, and wills. After the loss of a spouse, women may feel overwhelmed by the financial decisions and responsibilities for which they are ill prepared. Over half of the divorced women in Hetherington et al.'s (1979) sample reported discrimination in dealings with banks, mortgage institutions, and sources of credit, and many women are unaware or afraid to demand their legal rights for equal financial treatment. Vocationally unskilled and undirected single-again women lack the confidence and the skills to function autonomously (Foxley, 1979; Rawlings & Carter, 1977). Hetherington et al. (1979) note that the newly divorced woman's sense of helplessness is due not only to the reality of her diminished financial resources but to the inadequacy of her sex-role socialization in preparing her for head-of-household status. Two years after divorce, women still reported feeling anxiety over their lack of expertise in financial matters previously handled by their spouses (Hetherington et al., 1979). In a survey conducted by Parents Without

Partners (Parks, 1977), 50 percent of single-again mothers reported having financial difficulties even five years following divorce. Of all the stressors associated with separation and divorce, poverty is the most widespread and difficult to overcome (Jausch, 1977).

Powerlessness

The high rates of depression and low self-esteem reported by single-again women can be related to their perceptions of their own powerlessness (Radloff & Monroe, 1978). Deficits in effective application of power and influence appear in three contexts: power within the self, or competence in managing daily living activities; power in social situations, or ability to influence others; and power within institutional settings, or obtaining access to equitable conditions of employment and financial remuneration. Powerlessness defines the individual's inability to control important reinforcements. In all three contexts, women's tendencies to use indirect power result in failures to effectively influence self and others and consequent feelings of helplessness and despair (Johnson, 1978). For divorced women in particular, their difficulties in managing their finances, their children, their former spouses, and their social lives leave them feeling angry, rejected, incompetent, anxious, and depressed (Hetherington et al., 1979). The difficulties reported by divorced mothers in dealing with their children and former spouses will provide an example of the power struggles in which women experience themselves to be powerless and under stress.

In a longitudinal study of 96 divorcing families, Hetherington and her associates (1979) used multiple measures to assess the adjustment and well-being of the custodial mothers, their preschool children, and the noncustodial fathers over a two-year period of time. In the first year after divorce, the women reported increased family disorganization of activities and routine and decreased time spent in pleasurable activities for themselves. In their dealings with their former spouses, these women felt stress from the failure of many men to live up to their parental obligations. At the end of two years, only 19 of the 48 noncustodial fathers were seeing their child(ren) at least once a week, and one-third of the fathers were seeing their children less than once every two weeks. The mothers reported feeling helpless to intervene in the fathers' decreasing visiting patterns, while feeling increasingly stressed by having to compensate to the child(ren) with their own time and money.

In their transactions with their children, these women became increasingly more negative and less positive in their management strategies. The outcome of negative control strategies was escalated resistance on the part of the children, especially the sons, and increased stress resulting from unsatisfactory mother–child interactions. Daily diary reports of mothers' depression and negative moods were correlated with resistant and noncompliant behavior on the part of the children, particularly sons, on the previous day. It seems almost as if these women were transferring some of their helplessness patterns experienced with former spouses to their children. In particular, there was an inability to cope with the son's behavior; mothers used twice as many commands with their sons, and received less compliance, than with their daughters. In response to noncompliance, the mothers used more ignoring of noncompliant behavior, indicating a tacit acceptance of it and admission of powerlessness to control it. In return, these mothers received more reciprocal negative, demanding, complaining, and oppositional behavior from their sons, and the sons were more aggressive toward their mothers than to their noncustodial fathers. The authors comment that the divorced mother is "harrassed by her children," particularly by her son, and she receives, more than the father, excessive whining, disobedience, ignoring, dependency demands, and failure to affiliate or to attend to her. In contrast, the noncustodial father generally escapes the coercive behaviors of his children and has more opportunities for gratification outside the family unit. Fathers in this study also showed better control of their children and received less negative feedback from them. As some divorced mothers described their situation at home, it was like the "old Chinese water torture" or "getting bitten to death by ducks" (Hetherington et al., 1979, p. 121). Clearly, these are situations in which the inability of the mother to exert effective influence strategies results in increased stress and a pervading sense of helplessness and incompetence.

It is important to note here that statistics indicating the negative outcomes of divorce or separation on the adjustment of children may reflect, in part, the degree of stress and helplessness experienced by custodial mothers. Kalter (1977) reported that, in a clinic population, one-third of the referred children were from divorced families, a higher proportion than might be expected in the general population. Although the high rates of child disturbance following divorce may be attributed to the family disruption and sense of loss experienced by the child, a competing hypothesis is suggested. Divorced custodial mothers clearly are experiencing high rates of stress and powerlessness in regard to their children. Clinical referral rates may reflect maternal helplessness in managing the child's response to divorce as well as child pathology. The pathology may lie in the system that leaves the custodial mother alone and isolated to cope with increased pressure and little support. Wallerstein and Kelly (1974), for example, reported the highest postdivorce distress in those children whose parents received little emotional support from family and friends.

Social Isolation

The social isolation of the divorced or widowed woman contributes to her overall feelings of dissatisfaction and alienation from the world of the married. She experiences rejection from her former married friends, who see her as a threat to their two-parent families (Blechman & Deppenbrock, 1974; Miller, 1971). She is in conflict between her desires for new heterosexual alliances and her responsibilities to her children (Blechman & Deppenbrock, 1974). In times of rapid social change, old norms are becoming irrelevant while new ones have not been established. Norms for single-parent sexuality are not clear, and this ambiguity provides uncertainty and stress for the woman alone with children. Hetherington et al. (1979) report an intense sense of loneliness in newly divorced mothers; they have a more restricted social life than their male counterpart and frequently have little contact with other adults. As a result, they see themselves as locked into a child's world, leading to feelings of being trapped. Attempts to reduce this sense of isolation by escape into casual sexual contacts results in further feelings of low self-esteem, low happiness ratings, depression, and desperation.

The stress that accompanies isolation and abandonment by friends can be mediated by new social support systems that take over the friendship functions and offer social contact and group support, such as Parents Without Partners (PWP). However, for women who are not group oriented, these singles' institutions may have only limited capabilities for stress reduction and emotional support.

Role Strain

When the accumulation of excessive and frequently conflicting task requirements results in negative and self-deprecating evaluations of task accomplishment, we may infer the presence of role strain (Blechman &

Deppenbrock.)[1] The single-again woman is most likely to experience role strain when she is faced with multiple tasks that overburden her time and capabilities, leaving her with feelings of exhaustion and incompetence. A likely candidate for these feelings is the newly divorced custodial mother with several children at home, inadequate financial resources, conflictful relations with her former spouse, few friends or relatives to offer support, traditional sex-role socialization, and limited skills for enacting both mother and father roles. Although employment outside the home may reduce her financial and isolation problems, it also increases the number of tasks that she must complete without a coparent to share the load. Glasser and Navarre (1965) report that employed, divorced women spend more time than married women on routine household and child-care tasks and consequently devote less time to self-nurturing pleasurable activities. In the Hetherington et al. study (1979), a central theme of divorced women with preschool children was the overwhelming effects of facing too many tasks for which they had neither the time nor the energy. For women who are newly contemplating work and career activities, the stakes become even higher and the strain in meeting multiple roles with limited skills may increase.

In contrast, reported role strain was less in those women who were receiving support and assistance from close relatives and who maintained a compatible relationship with the former spouse. In these cases, certain tasks were assumed by others and problems were shared and mutually solved (Hess & Camara, 1979; Hetherington et al., 1979). In addition to family and friends, adolescent children as a support resource are not to be overlooked. On the basis of interview data, Weiss (1979) concludes that adolescents in single-again families grow up faster by assuming household and decisional responsibilities that were formerly the province of both parents. In this way, the single parent, especially the one who works full time, can share managerial responsibilities and equalize the load. Weiss suggests that equalized task and decisional responsibilities in single-parent homes may provide for positive avenues of growth in self-esteem, independence, and competence for all family members.

---

[1]It should be noted here that Blechman and Deppenbrock (1974) make a distinction between role strain and leader strain. In our estimation, this distinction is not related clearly to the multiple role assumptions required of single-again women, and we have chosen to merge the functions into a single concept of role strain.

LOOKING AHEAD IN THE 1980s: RESOCIALIZATION, REMEDIATION, AND RESEARCH

We propose that the 1980s will see a surge of interest in the single-again person, alone or with children, as divorce statistics continue to rise. Three avenues of intervention appear imperative if we are to facilitate the psychological well-being of individuals who are facing new forms of personal and family adjustment. First, we suggest a primary prevention: the resocialization of children and adults toward nonstereotyped sex roles. Second, we suggest remediation procedures in the form of counseling strategies to mediate the pain and confusion of single-again status and to promote new patterns of positive development. Finally, we see multiple possibilities for research programs that target not only the single-again woman but the social structure that continues to provide a stereotyped framework for sex-role development and behavior.

Resocialization: Education for Equal Roles

We know that stereotyped expectations about appropriate male and female behavior begin before birth and continue throughout the individual's lifespan (Worell, 1981, 1982). Although social norms for women and men in the United States have been changing at a fast pace, current evidence suggests that parents, peers, schools, the media, economic institutions, and even legal institutions continue to perpetuate gender-related distinctions. The separate and distinctive sex-role expectations for females and males contribute to the disruptive effects of single-again status.

Resocialization ideally should be functional at all levels of organized society in order to target the situational contributions to continued stereotyped practices. For practical purposes, however, we will suggest that educational intervention can provide the foundation for nonstereotyped expectations and equalized skill development in both girls and boys, as well as women and men. Although sex-role socialization is not the sole domain of the schools, we believe that schools can offer programs that equalize opportunities for information, flexible skill development, and aspirations for future roles. At the present time, only sporadic intervention programs exist for destereotyping the educational structure, personal practices, and curricula.[2]

Planned programs for educational intervention have been encouraged recently and funded by the Women's Educational Equity Act of 1974. Large and small programs are being conducted to implement one of the following four goals in schools: (1) to correct situational inequities so that all students have equal access to educational resources and activities; (2) to revise curricula, textbooks, media, test materials, and counseling practices that restrict flexible role definitions, and to develop new curricular programs that emphasize flexible roles and life span career development; (3) to modify the attitudes and values of students, teachers, school counselors, and parents toward more acceptance of flexible sex roles in family, school, and occupations; and (4) to train new behaviors in students and teachers directly that encourage sex-role flexibility (Worell, 1982).

The success of these educational programs in producing the informed and flexible individual with multiple skills who can resist situational stress has yet to be demonstrated. A particularly comprehensive life–career development program is being conducted by Hansen (Hansen, 1978a, 1978b). It begins at the first grade and proceeds throughout the school years to encourage implementation of all four goals just outlined. In addition, it has been suggested that schools implement revised family and parenting courses for high-school students (Everly, 1977). Such a course might inform students about the consequences of early marriage, low income, close spacing of children, and lack of cross-sex skill development on marital and parenting satisfaction. Everly suggests that every parent should be prepared to be a single parent!

Remediation: Counseling Model
for Single-Again Women

Resocialization as a preventative strategy is a long-range goal. What about those women who have been reared with traditional values and role models and now find themselves in a nontraditional role for which

[2]For the reader interested in current educational practices and sex-role contributions, we suggest the following references: Frazier & Sadker, 1973; Guttentag & Bray, 1976; Hansen & Rapoza, 1978; Harway & Astin, 1977; Pottker & Fishel, 1977; Sexton, 1976; Stockard, Schmuck, Kempner, Williams, Edson, & Smith, 1980; Wittig & Peterson, 1979; Worell, 1982.

there are few appropriate role models? We propose a remediation model for immediate intervention which is sensitive to the goals of resocialization as well as the psychosocial world of the newly divorced/widowed woman. Our four-pronged counseling model cuts across specific theoretical views and intervention styles in order to accommodate differing counselor preferences and skills. These four facets of intervention include the following goals: (1) offering emotional support, (2) giving cognitive structure to the single-again process, (3) providing information, (4) encouraging the development of new coping strategies and life skills.

It should be noted in the following discussion of counseling interventions with single-again women that the effectiveness of any of the techniques discussed has yet to be supported by substantial empirical research.

Offering Emotional Support.   The climate of trust and acceptance that characterizes and facilitates the client–counselor relationship is especially important when working with single-again women. Counselors dealing with this population should be knowledgeable about the grieving process and the concomitant feelings associated with the loss of a spouse. Giving clients permission to mourn, particularly in the early stages of grieving, can be a useful step in the adjustment process (Heikkinen, 1979). Since divorce is a process and not a permanent state, clients need to be reassured that the emotional roller-coaster ride will cease eventually (Kessler, 1976). Yates (1976) indicates that widowed women need to be reassured that the grief and shock will, in time, diminish.

Assisting women with the constructive ventilation and direction of anger is crucial in counseling for loss (Bach, 1974; Kaplan, 1976; Kessler, 1976; Rawlings & Carter, 1979). The socialized proscription against female expression of anger and hostility is so strong for some women that merely the identification of those angry feelings is therapeutic. Counselors should encourage working through clients' anger in the framework of counseling and/or support groups. Failure to do so may cause an increase in client self-blame or the direction of anger onto children in the form of abuse and/or withdrawal.

The counselor can be an important source of nourishment for the woman alone and should understand the client's needs to belong and be nurtured. At the same time, we believe it is important for the counselor to assist the client in developing other sources of nurturance, lest the client end up in another dependent relationship—this time with the counselor (Kaplan, 1976). To prevent this from occurring, we suggest that female clients who are recovering from the shock of uncoupling be counseled by a female professional. Feminist counselors strongly advocate all-female support groups to avoid the traditional role of subservience and dependence on males for emotional support and validation (Brodsky, 1977; Chesler, 1975; Rawlings & Carter, 1977, 1979).

The efficacy of the divorce adjustment group is widely supported in the literature, especially in regard to women's support groups (Aslin, 1978; Kessler, 1976; Krantzler, 1973; Rawlings & Carter, 1979). Women in female support groups can offer each other support, practical advice, affection, and a strong sense of identity (Rawlings & Carter, 1979). Kessler (1976) indicates that groups provide members with a safe environment for trying out new single-again roles and behaviors and for gaining emotional autonomy.

The fair-fighting techniques of Bach (1974), as well as his exercises for creative exits, can be useful methods for expression of constructive anger. In addition, various Gestalt strategies, such as finishing unfinished business, guided fantasy, and empty-chair work also have proved helpful in dealing with the grief and anger associated with loss (Heikkinen, 1979).

Giving Cognitive Structure to the Single-Again Process. Although the emotional support function of counseling is crucial to the single-again adjustment process, we believe a second component, dealing with the client's cognitions and beliefs, to be equally important. Resocializing the client to new nonstereotyped sex roles, as well as reorienting her to single status, can be facilitated by the use of several cognitive–behavioral techniques.

Cognitive restructuring refers to modifying feelings and behavior by changing clients' patterns of thoughts. If the single-again woman is to get past the hurt and anger precipitated by the loss, she must begin to shape a new life for herself by thinking differently about her experience. Single-again status can be thought of as the first step toward a new freedom rather than a painful waiting period between marriages. Similarly, reattribution or reframing involves changing the meaning and the consequences the single-again woman attaches to the loss of a spouse. Instead of seeing the divorce as a "tragedy," the client might be helped to reframe the experience as an "opportunity" for growth and discovery (Bach, 1974; Krantzler, 1973; Rawlings & Carter, 1979).

Resocializing the client to new sex roles involves not only cognitive restructuring and reattribution but modification of inculcated expectations related to female socialization. A woman does not have to be married to have an identity, social worth, and self-esteem. These types of unrealistic sex-role-stereotyped myths and irrational beliefs (e.g., "marriage is forever," "I can't live without a man," and "my children will be damaged") must be challenged and replaced with more realistic belief systems. Wolfe and Fodor (1975) believe a woman's ability to respond assertively is severely limited by these irrational belief systems internalized from stereotyped socialization. As this inability to impact on one's environment is remediated by cognitive restructuring, reattribution, and resocialization, the behavioral technique of assertiveness training may provide the necessary tools to cope with single-again status.

Any of several specific strategies for cognitive restructuring can be used, depending on counselor theoretical orientation and style preference. Rational Emotive Therapy (RET), advocated by Ellis (1962), is a particularly useful technique for identifying irrational beliefs and dispelling myths. The goals of RET are (1) to identify irrational beliefs and their maintainers, (2) to challenge the unrealistic nature of those beliefs, and (3) to develop a new belief system with more realistic and more adaptive attitudes, feelings, and behaviors (Rimm & Masters, 1974; Wolfe & Fodor, 1975).

Feminist counselors suggest sex-role analysis as a vehicle for sex-role change and personal growth (Rawlings & Carter, 1977). Sex-role analysis involves the identification of those behaviors and tasks associated with the female role which have impeded the development of autonomous and adaptive behaviors. The single-again woman typically finds herself severely handicapped by the environmentally constricting dictates of her sex role. Sex-role analysis is one method by which we might uncover the deficits brought about by these constrictions without a concomitant loss of self-esteem (Rawlings & Carter, 1977). Many of the deficits, such as unassertiveness and lack of social identity, may be attributed primarily to stereotyped socialization and not solely to personal ineptitude.

Similarly, Wyckoff (1977) has adopted the Transactional Analysis (T.A.) technique of "scripting" for use in women's problem-solving groups. Wyckoff's notion of scripting utilizes the three basic ego states used in T.A.: the parent, the child, and the adult. These states are used to analyze how individuals act and react with one another. The enduring pattern and style of those interactions develops the life script, which is shaped by parental and societal injunctions and attributions (Steiner, 1974). Wyckoff (1977) contends that this scripting is synonymous with stereotyped sex-role programming, and this programming results in unassertive and dependent women. The goal of scripting, then, is to rewrite the scripts in the supportive climate of the women's group to include more powerful and autonomous patterns and styles of interaction (Wyckoff, 1977).

Consciousness-raising (C-R) groups and assertiveness training can be important experiences for women in developing a sense of identity and in learning new skills. Brodsky (1973) contends that the role models and the sense of shared experience available to women in C-R groups have important therapeutic implications for the identity issues common to many women. Behavior rehearsal and role play are techniques counselors might use in group settings to translate insight into action in a non-threatening group environment.

Bibliotherapy can be useful for some clients, and two books in particular have proved helpful. Krantzler's book, *Creative Divorce* (1973) and Gardner's *The Boy's and Girl's Book about Divorce* (1970) are used frequently.

Providing Information. Being a source of information is a very important task for counselors working with newly widowed or divorced women. It is incumbent upon counselors to be knowledgeable about (or be able to refer clients to those individuals or agencies who are) the laws for separation, divorce, custody, and litigation (Rawlings & Carter, 1979). Counselors working with divorced populations are fast becoming facile with negotiation and mediation as nonadversarial alternatives to litigation (Kessler, 1979; Kressel & Deutsch, 1977). Counselors can be very useful in assisting clients with the decision-making process regarding custody and in supporting those clients who wish to opt for nontraditional alternatives to maternal child custody.

Where clients have custody of their children, counselors can offer valuable information regarding the effects of divorce on children as well as recommend ways to reduce the stress of divorce on the family system. Referral of clients to single-parents' groups, such as Parents Without Partners and Parents Alone, and single-parents' classes is also helpful.

The counselor should be aware of services available within the community and refer clients to appropriate contact persons. Along those lines, counselors should keep abreast of workshops, groups, and educational programs geared for remediation of skills in single-again women. Workshops dealing with legal matters specific to the needs of single-again women, such as getting credit, collecting delinquent child support, and litigating estates, are offered frequently by community interest groups. Career-related workshops are especially informative for the single-again woman and offer training in the acquisition of specific skills, for example, interviewing, resumé writing, and conducting a career search.

Encouraging the Development of New Coping Strategies and Life Skills. This particular counselor strategy is premised on long-range counseling and is not geared especially well for crisis intervention. Once the client has accepted her new status as a reality and is ready for a new beginning, the counselor can focus on ways the client can impact on her environment more effectively. Critical to developing more flexible and stable coping strategies is the ability to generate options and make autonomous decisions. Single-again women are often deficient in this skill because they characteristically relied on their husbands to make major financial, household, and career decisions. Developing decision-making strategies is one way to overcome the socialized sex-role constriction of dependency.

Since the single-again woman who opts to remain single will continue to occupy a somewhat "normless" role in society and will have few role models for her lifestyle, it may be helpful for her to develop a greater tolerance for ambiguity. Heikkinen (1979) suggests teaching clients to live in the present, the here-and-now, as a means of coping more effectively. Although we see this as especially useful in the tumultuous initial stages of marital disruption, we also advocate teaching clients planning and goal-setting skills. Hetherington et al. (1979) reported that a common complaint voiced by their sample of divorced women was role strain and an overwhelming number of new tasks. We feel that a way to minimize the resultant feelings of inadequacy engendered by the inability to manage a myriad of parental, financial, and vocational tasks is to develop methods for tackling projects in easily accomplished steps. The counselor's role in helping the client invest her energy in tasks that are meaningful to her and realistically manageable is critical (Dlugokinski, 1977; Kaplan, 1976).

The efficacy of C-R groups for women points to the therapeutic usefulness of nontraditional female role models (Brodsky, 1973). In this regard, the female counselor can serve as an important role model for the newly single woman, modeling nontraditional behaviors such as assertiveness, constructive expression of anger, and self-reliance (Bach, 1974; Kaplan, 1976; Rawlings & Carter, 1977). Assertiveness and self-reinforcement are useful coping strategies and facilitate the client's sense of control and autonomy.

Similarly, client self-nurturance and self-endorsement should be encouraged. Counselors can assist effectively in the development of this skill by modeling new ways of relating to people, by encouraging the development of new support systems, and by exhibiting confidence and respect for the client's abilities and decisions (Kaplan, 1976; Krantzler, 1973). As previously mentioned, support groups are especially facilitative in this regard.

Where clients have custody of their children and are dealing with the demands of single parenting, counselors should assist them in their attempts to develop workable relationships with noncustodial parents (Aslin, 1978). The literature indicates that children are least damaged by the trauma of divorce when both parents can create a postdivorce relationship based on cooperation, not hostility (Gardner, 1976; Hetherington et al., 1979; Kressel & Deutsch, 1977). It is incumbent upon the counselor to assist clients in negotiating workable relationships regarding visitation and child support, as well as in developing new parenting skills to meet the demands of the single-parent role (Aslin, 1978; Kessler, 1979; Kressel & Deutsch, 1977; Rawlings & Carter, 1979). As more men gain custody of their children, it will become increasingly important for counselors to be supportive of noncustodial mothers and their efforts to maintain realistic part-time relationships with their children.

A final strategy for counseling single-again women involves assistance in the decision to recouple. If the client's adjustment to loss is successful, she will exhibit ". . . increased self-understanding, the ability to form satisfying new intimate relationships, and a heightened sense of personal competence" (Kressel & Deutsch, 1977, p. 422). Remarriage is not necessarily a criterion for successful adjustment to loss (Krantzler, 1973; Kressel & Deutsch, 1977). Maintaining healthy intimate relationships without a subsequent loss of self, however, is one indication that positive growth is occurring. Single-again women who are secure in their new sex roles and new lifestyles have a greater chance for healthier, successful future relationships.

The four main counselor strategies — offering emotional support, giving cognitive structure, providing information, and encouraging new coping skills — are by no means exhaustive. They merely provide a framework from which counselors may approach counseling for loss of a spouse. Additionally, we see these strategies as ongoing and simultaneous and not developmental and hierarchical.

Research: Future Directions

Finally, we propose that new directions for research focus on the positive and proactive interventions that promise to promote individual and family well-being. It has been pointed out by a number of writers (Blechman & Deppenbrock, 1974; Everly, 1977; Hess & Camara, 1979; Hetherington et al., 1979) that too much emphasis has been given to the single family as a deviant unit. Instead, they suggest the need for additional attention to the sources of strength in single-again individuals and families and the ways in which the social structure can be modified to facilitate their positive development and growth.

Research needs concerning the single-again woman seem to fall into three categories: (1) socializing women and men in their developing years to anticipate and prepare for equal division of family and career tasks in adulthood, (2) examining the procedures and conditions of divorce and custody decisions, and (3) determining the factors that contribute to effective functioning following loss of a mate. We now will consider each of these briefly.

Socialization Research.
    1. Career development and planning in young women prior to marriage. Most of what we know about career development comes from the study of men. Theories and research on women's careers are sorely lacking.
    2. Skill development in nontraditional occupations. Fear of success in nontraditional fields, especially those involving science and mathematics, coupled with lack of necessary skill development, prevent women from engaging in higher-status and higher-paying positions. Current research on high-school girls' avoidance of mathematics needs expansion to other nontraditional areas.
    3. Education for shared marriage and parenthood. Research studies are needed to consider alternative ways to educate young men and

women to sharing marital and parenting roles. What might be the effects of dialogue among high-school students on dual-career marriages, paternity leave for new fathers, or nursery-school experiences for young men to increase their nurturing skills? Educational change strategies that target the new generation of marital partners and parents have received little research attention.

4. Examining the "mother mandate." We are only beginning to consider the variety of attitudes and personal stances that women have taken toward motherhood.[3] What are the variables that encourage the decision not to have children? Why do over 90 percent of divorcing mothers feel they need to retain sole custody of their children? The traditional sanctity of motherhood so far has escaped the researcher's probes; it needs to be opened up to objective scrutiny, so that women can feel more free to make rational decisions about motherhood and mothering responsibilities.

Divorce and Custody Research.

1. Divorce procedures that reduce interspouse conflict. In particular there is a deficit of research on alternative mediation procedures for nonadversarial solutions to support and custody decisions. Alternative mediation or conciliation models are not presently available to either the divorcing parents, to their attorneys, or to the judiciary that imposes the legal decision. Examination of effective mediation procedures might lead to local, state, or national policy planning that can relieve the stress of divorce decisions and the impact of those decisions on the lives of each family member.

2. Custody and visitation procedures that maximize family well-being. At the present time, almost nothing is known about the way in which custody and visitation decisions are made. Most parents make this decision prior to appearing in court. When the judiciary steps in to litigate disagreement, there are few divorce-impact studies to indicate which parent, if either, should retain custody and what the probable outcomes of alternative decisions will be. In particular, we need impact studies of separate, joint, and shared custody decisions and the variables that contribute to the success of each. Visitation patterns appear to be critical to the well-being of all family members and are barely touched upon in the current literature on divorce.

[3]See *Psychology of Women Quarterly*, Fall 1979, 6, for an entire issue devoted to this topic.

Research on Factors that Contribute to Effective Single-Again Functioning.

1. Separate effects of widowhood, separation, and divorce status. Here we have tended to link these individuals together because little is known about the separate experiences of each group. Research should focus on between-group characteristics and on within-group variability that lead to more or less satisfactory adjustment.

2. Single parenting and its effect on all family members. Blechman and Deppenbrock (1974) report that, in a thorough review of the literature on single parenting, only 11 percent focused on the well-being of the custodial mother. In view of the current evidence that parental variables are critical to the adjustment of the child following divorce, the focus on the child deviancy may be misplaced. Here, we need more information on the relationship between parents, the impact of differing visitation patterns, family arrangements that impede or facilitate adjustment and satisfaction, and the support systems that bridge the emotional gaps. As indicated earlier, more information is needed about how effective single-parent families function and the variables that contribute to their strength.

3. Blended, reconstituted, or step-parenting families. Since most divorcing and widowed women recouple, many of these will be faced with a new source of stress about which we currently have little research information. How can single-again women prepare for a step-parenting role, and what are the variables that determine role satisfaction or stress for blended families?

4. Interventions that facilitate single-again functioning. Although all counseling strategies require outcome evaluation, we are particularly interested in the efficacy of newer feminist models of counseling and psychotherapy. Many of the counseling interventions suggested here are relatively untried and are in need of further research to support their utility in facilitating the resocialization of single-again women.

SUMMARY AND CONCLUSIONS

The resocialization process of single-again women has been examined by means of an analysis of sex-role issues that contribute to increased psychological stress following the loss of a mate. Major factors discussed were women's economic dependency, powerlessness in dealing with men, loss of role identity and consequent social isolation, and role strain resulting from inadequate personal resources to meet excessive and conflicting task requirements for single-again status. There is some evidence that these problems are most intense for custodial mothers of young children in the two years following divorce. For all single-again women, we know that there are many mediating factors that reduce the effects of stress and there are a number of positive benefits that balance against the costs. In particular, mutual support and agreement between divorced couples regarding financial, visitation, and child-rearing decisions is an important predictor of well-being for both parents and children. Social support systems that provide companionship, child care, and renewed intimacy reduce the sense of loneliness and isolation that are common to single-again women. Three avenues of intervention were suggested to facilitate the psychological well-being of individuals who are facing new forms of personal and family adjustment. These interventions include resocialization for nonstereotyped sex roles, counseling strategies that target the focal concerns of single-again women, and research programs that begin to fill the knowledge gap concerning the possibilities for positive outcomes of single-again status. Positive benefits may include new opportunities for personal growth toward self-esteem, independence, and competence for all members of single-again families.

REFERENCES

Aslin, A. L. Counseling "single-again" (divorced and widowed) women. In L. W. Harmon, J. M. Birk, L. E. Fitzgerald, & M. F. Tanney (Eds.), *Counseling women*. Monterey, Calif.: Brooks/Cole, 1978.

Astin, H. S., & Myint, T. Career development of young women during the post high school years. In S. L. Hansen & R. S. Rapoza (Eds.), *Career development and counseling of women*. Springfield, Ill.: Charles C Thomas, 1978.

Bach, G. R. Creative exits: Fight therapy for divorcees. In V. Franks & V. Burtle (Eds.), *Women in therapy: new psychotherapies for a changing society*. New York: Jason Aronson, 1974.

Barry, W. A. Marriage research and conflict: An integrative review. *Psychological Bulletin*, 1970, 73, 41–54.

Berardo, F. Widowhood status in the U.S. *The Family Coordinator*, 1968, 17, 191–203.

Bernard, J. *The future of marriage*. New York: World, 1972.

Blechman, E. A., & Deppenbrock, M. M. A reward–cost analysis of the single parent family. Paper presented at the Sixth Banff International Conference on Behavior Modification, Calgary, Canada, April 1974.

Bloom, B. L., & Asher, S. J., & White, S. W. Marital disruption as a stressor: A review and analysis. *Psychological Bulletin*, 1978, 85, 867–894.

Borenzweig, H. The punishment of divorced mothers. *Journal of Sociology & Social Welfare*, 1976, 3, 291–310.

Brodsky, A. M. The consciousness-raising group as a model of therapy with women. *Psychotherapy: Theory, Research, and Practice*, 1973, 10, 24–29.

Brodsky, A. M. Therapeutic aspects of consciousness-raising groups. In E. I. Rawlings & D. K. Carter (Eds.), *Psychotherapy for women: Treatment toward equality*. Springfield, Ill.: Charles C Thomas, 1977.

Chesler, P. Marriage and psychotherapy. In J. Freeman (Ed.), *Women: A feminist perspective*. Palo Alto, Calif.: Mayfield, 1975.

Deaux, K. *The behavior of women and men*. Monterey, Calif.: Brooks/Cole, 1976.

Dlugokinski, E. A developmental approach to coping with divorce. *Journal of Clinical Child Psychology*, Summer 1977, 27–30.

Douvan, E., & Kukla, R. The American family: A twenty year view. In J. E. Gullahorn (Ed.), *Psychology and women in transition*. New York: John Wiley, 1979.

Ellis, A. *Reason and emotion in psychotherapy*. New York: Lyle Stuart, 1962.

Everly, K. New directions in divorce research. *Journal of Child Clinical Psychology*, 1977, 6, 7–10.

Farmer, H. Why women choose careers below their potential. In S. L. Hansen and R. S. Rapoza (Eds.), *Career development and counseling of women*. Springfield, Ill.: Charles C Thomas, 1978.

Foxley, C. H. *Nonsexist counseling: Helping women and men redefine their roles*. Dubuque, Iowa: Kendall/Hunt, 1979.

Frazier, N., & Sadker, N. *Sexism in school and society*. New York: Harper & Row, 1973.

Gardner, R. A. *The boys' and girls' book about divorce*. New York: Bantam Books, 1970.

Gardner, R. A. *Psychotherapy with children of divorce*. New York: Jason Aronson, 1976.

Glasser, P., & Navarre, E. Structural problems of the one-parent family. *Journal of Social Issues*, 1965, 21, 98–109.

Glick, P. C. Children of divorced parents in demographic perspective. *Journal of Social Issues*, 1979, 35, 177–182.

Goode, W. J. *After divorce*. Glencoe, Ill.: Free Press, 1956.

Guttentag, M., & Bray, M. *Undoing sex role stereotypes*. New York: McGraw-Hill, 1976.

Hansen, S. L. Born free: Change process evaluation of a psychoeducational intervention to reduce career sex role stereotyping for women and men. Paper presented at the annual convention of the American Educational Research Association, Toronto, 1978. (a)

Hansen, S. L. Promoting female growth through a career development curriculum. In S. L. Hansen & R. S. Rapoza (Eds.), *Career development and counseling of women.* Springfield, Ill.: Charles C Thomas, 1978. (b)

Hansen, S. L., & Rapoza, R. S. (Eds.). *Career development and counseling of women.* Springfield, Ill.: Charles C Thomas, 1978.

Harway, M., & Astin, H. S. *Sex discrimination in career counseling and education.* New York: Praeger, 1977.

Heikkinen, C. A. Counseling for personal loss. *The Personnel and Guidance Journal,* 1979, *58,* 46–49.

Hess, R. D., & Camara, K. Post-divorce family relationships as mediating factors in the consequences of divorce for children. *Journal of Social Issues,* 1979, *35,* 95–96.

Hetherington, E. M., Cox, M., & Cox, R. Stress and coping in divorce: A focus on women. In J. E. Gullahorn (Ed.), *Psychology and women: In transition.* New York: John Wiley, 1979.

Jausch, C. The one-parent family. *Journal of Child Clinical Psychology,* 1977, *6,* 30–34.

Johnson, P. Women and interpersonal power. In I. H. Frieze, J. E. Parsons, D. N. Ruble, & G. L. Zellman, *Women and sex roles: A social psychological perspective.* New York: W. W. Norton, 1978.

Kalter, N. Children of divorce in an outpatient psychiatric population. *Journal of Orthopsychiatry,* 1977, *47,* 40–51.

Kaplan, A. G. Traditional and alternative consequences of sex-role socialization. In A. G. Kaplan & J. P. Bean (Eds.), *Beyond sex role stereotypes.* Boston, Mass.: Little, Brown, 1976.

Kaplan, A. G., & Sedney, M. A. *Psychology and sex roles: An androgynous perspective.* Boston, Mass.: Little, Brown, 1980.

Katz, P. A. The development of female identity. *Sex Roles,* 1979, *5,* 155–178.

Kessler, S. Divorce adjustment groups. *The Personnel and Guidance Journal,* 1976, *54,* 251–255.

Kessler, S. Counselor as mediator. *The Personnel and Guidance Journal,* 1979, *58,* 194–196.

Krantzler, M. *Creative divorce.* New York: M. Evans, 1973.

Kressel, K., & Deutsch, M. Divorce therapy: An in-depth survey of therapists' views. *Family Process,* 1977, *16,* 413–443.

Lewis, G. L. Changes in women's role participation. In I. H. Frieze, J. E. Parsons, P. B. Johnson, D. N. Ruble, & G. L. Zellman (Eds.), *Women and sex roles: A social psychological perspective.* New York: W. W. Norton, 1978.

Miller, A. A. Reactions of friends to divorce. In P. Bohannan (Ed.), *Divorce and after*. Garden City, N.Y.: Doubleday, 1970.

O'Leary, V. E. Some attitudinal barriers to occupational aspirations in women. *Psychological Bulletin*, 1974, *81*, 809–826.

Parks, A. Children and youth of divorce in Parents Without Partners, Inc. *Journal of Child Clinical Psychology*, 1977, *6*, 44–48.

Pottker, J., & Fishel, A. *Sex bias in the schools: Research evidence*. Rutherford, N.J.: Fairleigh Dickinson University Press, 1977.

Radloff, L. S., & Monroe, M. K. Sex differences in helplessness—With implications for depression. In S. L. Hansen & R. S. Rapoza (Eds.), *Career development and counseling of women*. Springfield, Ill.: Charles C Thomas, 1978.

Rawlings, E. I., & Carter, D. K. *Psychotherapy for women*. Springfield, Ill.: Charles C Thomas, 1977.

Rawlings, E. I., & Carter, D. K. Divorced women. *Counseling Psychologist*, 1979, *8*, 27–28.

Rimm, D. C., & Masters, J. C. *Behavior therapy: Techniques and empirical findings*. New York: Academic Press, 1974.

Rose, V. L., & Price-Bonham, S. Divorce adjustment: A woman's problem? *The Family Coordinator*, 1973, *22*, 291–297.

Ross, H. L., & Sawhill, I. V. *Time of transition*. Washington, D.C.: The Urban Institute, 1975.

Sales, E. Women's adult development. In I. H. Frieze, J. E. Parsons, P. B. Johnson, D. N. Ruble, & G. L. Zellman (Eds.), *Women and sex roles: A social psychological perspective*. New York: W. W. Norton, 1978.

Scherman, A. Divorce: Its impact on the family and children. Paper presented at the American Educational Research Association convention, San Francisco, April 1979.

Sexton, P. *Women in education*. Bloomington, Ind.: Phi Delta Kappa Educational Foundation, 1976.

Steiner, C. M. *Scripts people live*. New York: Grove Press, 1974.

Stockard, J., Schmuck, P. A., Kempner, K., Williams, P., Edson, S. K., & Smith, M. A. *Sex equity in education*. New York: Academic Press, 1980.

Unger, R. K. Male is greater than female: The socialization of status inequality. In L. Harmon, J. Birk, L. Fitzgerald, & M. Tanney (Eds.), *Counseling women*. Monterey, Calif.: Brooks/Cole, 1978.

United States Bureau of the Census: *Divorce, child custody, and child support*. U.S. Department of Commerce Current Population reports. Washington, D.C.: U.S. Government Printing Office, 1979.

United States Department of Labor: Women's Bureau. *The earnings gap between women and men*. Washington, D.C.: U.S. Government Printing Office, 1979.

Vetter, L. Career development of women. In S. L. Hansen & R. S. Rapoza (Eds.), *Career development and counseling of women*. Springfield, Ill.: Charles C Thomas, 1978.

Wallerstein, J. S., & Kelly, J. B. The effects of parental divorce: The adolescent experience. In J. Anthony & C. Koupernik (Eds.), *The child in his family: Children at psychiatric risk*. New York: John Wiley, 1974.

Weiss, R. S. Growing up a little faster: The experience of growing up in a single-parent household. *Journal of Social Issues*, 1979, 35, 97–111.

Wittig, M. A., & Peterson, A. C. (Eds.). *Sex-related differences in cognitive functioning: Developmental issues*. New York: Academic Press, 1979.

Wolfe, J. L., & Fodor, I. G. A cognitive/behavioral approach to modifying assertive behavior in women. *The Counseling Psychologist*, 1975, 5, 45–52.

Worell, J. Life-span sex roles: Development, continuity, and change. In R. M. Lerner & N. A. Busch-Rossnagel (Eds.), *Individuals as producers of their development*. New York: Academic Press, 1981.

Worell, J. Psychological sex roles: Significance and change. In J. Worell (Ed.), *Psychological development in the elementary years*. New York: Academic Press, 1982.

Wyckoff, H. Radical psychiatry for women. In E. I. Rawlings & D. K. Carter (Eds.), *Psychotherapy for women: Treatment toward equality*. Springfield, Ill.: Charles C Thomas, 1977.

Yates, M. *Coping: A survival manual for women alone*. Englewood Cliffs, N.J.: Prentice-Hall, 1976.

■ 11
Sex-Role Stereotypes and Violence against Women

PATRICIA A. RESICK

With two important exceptions, men are most often the victims as well as the perpetrators of violence (Bowker, 1979; Maccoby & Jacklin, 1974). The two exceptions to the general proscription of violence against women, rape and wife battering, have been evident throughout law as well as culture. Sexual assualt and wife beating have been so well entrenched in the mores of our paternalistic society that current stereotypes of women still reflect the belief that women occasionally deserve such violence, may actually want it or need it, and are left relatively unharmed psychologically in its aftermath. Because of the taboos that have prevailed against disclosing, discussing, or studying rape and domestic violence, there has been little information available to question or counter the existing stereotypes until very recently.

The purpose of this chapter is to examine the effects of sex roles and sex-role stereotypes on violence against women. Problems with definitions and incidence estimates will be presented first, followed by a brief historical view of the relationship between violence against women and

Special thanks go to the staff of the Sexual Assault Research Project, Medical University of South Carolina, for their thoughtful comments and suggestions on early drafts of the manuscript. In particular, special thanks go to Dean Kilpatrick, Janet Paduhovich, Lois Veronen, Rebecca Hassell, and Ann Lees.

sex roles. The effects of traditional sex roles are still evident in current studies regarding violence toward women and play an important role in most current theories on the topic. Going beyond the stereotypes, recent research has begun to examine the actual effects of violence on women. Following the section on victim reaction research, suggestions for directions of research in the 1980s will be presented.

DEFINITIONS AND INCIDENCE

The first problems encountered in the study of rape and wife battering are disagreements over the definition of terms and in determining incidence. Because both types of assault are legal problems as well as topics for psychological research, definitions vary widely. Legally, in most states, rape used to be defined as forced sexual intercourse by a man against a woman who was not his wife. State statues vary, and, in some states, laws have been changed to reflect varying degrees of assault and have broadened the definition of rape to include other sex acts. Few states consider a husband forcing sex acts with his wife to be a crime. Researchers have tended to be somewhat vague and sometimes have included victims of attempted rape and other types of sexual assault in their samples. For the purposes of this paper, rape will be defined as any forced sexual act, including oral and anal sex as well as intercourse. Since the focus of the paper is on stereotypes and clinical issues, a broad definition is probably the most suitable because the intent of the acts and the impact upon the victim are of more importance here than the specific acts performed or the relationship of the assailant to the victim.

There are also some definitional problems with wife battering since such assaults vary in frequency and intensity, ranging from one event to daily occurrences over years, and from a slap to fatal blows. Most researchers have defined "wife" in a functional rather than legal sense. While the definition of beating or battering will affect the estimates of incidence and one could expect victims to respond differentially to the amount and severity of battering they have received, from a theoretical standpoint, a wide-ranging definition will be most useful. Exact definitions of rape and domestic violence used by researchers will be given throughout the paper when it is important for understanding the context of the results.

In addition to the problem of varying definitions, accurate estimates of incidence are very difficult to obtain because of the taboos that have surrounded violence against women. The prevailing beliefs concerning victim precipitation and victim blame have served to isolate and silence women who have been subjected to rape or abuse. In the past, those who did attempt to seek help often encountered male-dominated (e.g., police, medical, judicial) institutions that were not equipped for, interested in, or sensitive to the needs of victims. It has been only recently, since the feminist movement reemerged in the 1970s, that researchers and clinicians have started to become aware of the prevalence and impact of violence on women. By necessity, most research focuses upon those women who report crimes of violence to some authority; however, rape is probably the most underreported crime (Federal Bureau of Investigation, 1980), even when the assailant is a stranger. When the assailant is a spouse, as in the case of wife battering, the problem becomes further complicated by the fact that the police often refuse to or are instructed not to file complaints until injuries reach some subjective level of severity (Field & Field, 1973). Nevertheless, reported rates and victimization surveys do provide indications of the magnitude of the problem. The FBI (1980) recorded 75,989 forcible rapes in 1979, which they calculated to be one rape every seven minutes. Over the past 40 years, the increase in the rate of rape has exceeded all other serious crimes (Bowker, 1979). Determining the risk rate of rape depends on the estimate of underreporting. Katz and Mazur (1979) estimated that the chance of a woman being raped in a given year could range from one in 200 to one in 500.

In a recent issue of *Cosmopolitan Magazine* (Wolfe, 1980), over 100,000 women responded to a questionnaire regarding sexuality. Among this sample, the largest ever to respond to this type of survey, 24 percent of the respondents stated that they had been raped. While this sample is no more random or representative than Kinsey's work (Kinsey, Pomeroy, Martin, & Gebhard, 1953) or the *Hite Report* (Hite, 1976), it does represent a very large sample of urban women between the ages of 18 and 35. A rural sample was collected by Ward and Resick (1979), who randomly sampled from a small midwestern university. Among the 400 respondents, one-third indicated that they had been involved in some type of sexual assault ranging from being restrained or grabbed to attempted rape. Thirteen percent stated they had been involved in an attempted rape, while 6 percent had been raped. So even with a sample of younger, rural women, almost one-fifth had been involved in an attempted or completed rape.

Since incidents of wife battering are subsumed in police records under the category of assault, the best estimates of incidence are derived from other sources. One of the earlier studies to notice the problem of wife abuse was by Levinger (1966), who found that 37 percent of 600 divorce applicants cited physical abuse as a complaint against their husbands. Similarly, O'Brien (1971) reported that 25 of 150 divorce applicants spontaneously mentioned physical abuse during individual interviews. While marital violence often is assumed to be associated with poverty, several studies conducted at universities have found notable levels among middle-class respondents. In one such study, Adler (1977) found 34 percent of husbands and 32 percent of wives admitted to hitting, pushing, kicking, or punching their spouses. At least one person in each of the 50 couples was a graduate student. Reese and Resick (1980) administered questionnaires to 486 undergraduate students from intact homes in a variety of classes. Thirty percent of the students reported that physical aggression had occurred between their parents during their last two years of high school.

The first nationwide representative victimization survey was conducted by Straus, Gelles, and Steinmetz (1980; Straus 1977). Of over 2,000 couples who were interviewed, 3.8 percent of the respondents reported one or more attacks which could be defined as wife beating during a one-year period. Their definition did not include throwing things, pushing, grabbing, or slapping. When these findings were extrapolated to the 47 million couples in the United States, Straus (1977) estimated that 1.8 million wives were beaten by their husbands in any given year. The median frequency was 2.4 serious assaults per year.

Using a systematic random survey in the state of Texas of people who admitted to being victims of spouse abuse, Stachura and Teske (1979) concluded that *no less than* 11 percent of the women in Texas had been abused by their spouse. They also concluded that no less than 2 percent of the men had been abused by their spouse. Forty-seven percent of the victims reported they had experienced severe physical abuse, and over 80 percent of the spouse-abuse cases went unreported primarily due to a fear of reprisal.

Statistics on murder illustrate the severity of the problem of domestic violence. During 1975, 7.8 percent of the homicides reported were committed by wives against their husbands and 8 percent were committed by husbands against wives (National Center for Health Statistics, 1976). According to the FBI, one-fourth of all murders in 1969 occurred within the family and more than half of those were spouse killings (Truninger, 1971). Since wives are seven times more likely than husbands to murder in self-defense (Wolfgang, 1958), it is likely that most of the husband killings were associated with wife battering.

These estimates of the incidence of violence against women are staggering, particularly when one considers how such a severe national problem could have been ignored so long. Given these high incidence rates and the even higher nonreporting rates, clinicians should include questions concerning clients' history with violence and violence in their families in every initial interview. Clients may well refrain from volunteering information about rape and domestic violence since many of the taboos against discussing such topics are still prevalent. It also is possible that clients may not report a history of violence because they fail to see the relationship between those incidents and the later development of such problems as depression, anxiety, or agoraphobia.

SEX-ROLE STEREOTYPES: THE HISTORICAL BASIS FOR VIOLENCE AGAINST WOMEN

When there is a general proscription against violence toward women, and when men tend to aggress primarily against other men, why are there exemptions in the cases of rape and wife battering? Why are these two crimes allowed to occur at such an enormous rate? While it is true that Americans are a very violent people (Bowker, 1979), that is not sufficient to explain why rape is the fastest growing crime and wife battering continues unabated.

Bandura and his associates (Bandura, Ross, & Ross, 1961, 1963a, 1963b; Bandura & Walters, 1963) have provided compelling evidence that children learn aggression and violence through modeling as well as direct reinforcement and that male children may have a greater preparedness to imitate and learn aggression (Maccoby & Jacklin, 1974). If directly reinforced, girls imitate almost as much aggression as boys do (Bandura, 1965), but, in our society, girls are not reinforced for aggression nor have female models been available. This observation may explain why women are less aggressive but, again, does not explain why particular kinds of violence are directed toward women. The explanation for the acceptability of rape and wife battering appears to be within sex-role stereotypes and the history of sex roles.

While stereotypes of women and men affect current beliefs regarding violence against women, throughout history the roles of men and women were not maintained just through informal socialization but were legally prescribed. In her monumental book on the topic of rape, Susan Brownmiller (1975) suggests that marriage may have evolved as the one way women could protect themselves against rape. She cites the prevalent practice of bride capture that existed in England as late as the fifteenth century and exists today in some primitive societies as legal forms of kidnap and rape. Bride capture was replaced by bride price, so women subsequently were considered to be merchandise, owned by the father and sold to another man. In order to protect the value of the property, laws were introduced outlawing rape of unmarried women. The code of Hammaurabi in Babylonia, instituted 4,000 years ago, specified that a man who raped a betrothed virgin (betrothals usually occurred in early childhood) was to be punished by death. The father who committed incest with his daughter would be banished from the city. Once a woman was married and not a virgin, there was no concept of rape. No matter how an assault occurred, the woman was considered to have committed adultery, a crime punishable by death. Hebrew laws and laws through the Middle Ages were similar and reflected the belief that the injustice was done against the property of some man and showed little concern for the woman herself. During the late thirteenth century, the laws were changed and rape became a felony regardless of the marital status of the woman. From the thirteenth to the twentieth century, there was little change in the law and very little enforcement of it (Brownmiller, 1975).

Because women were considered property along with the slaves, animals, and fields, husbands were considered absolute masters and wives had few, if any, rights. Davidson (1977) and Dobash and Dobash (1977) have traced the history of wife-beating laws and pointed out that patriarchs were given not only the right but the obligation to control and chastise their wives. Throughout history, women were considered not only to be chattel but also to be morally inferior or evil and, therefore, in need of correction. The ancient customary laws in France between the thirteenth and the sixteenth centuries gave permission to husbands to punish their wives and families physically and severely treated husbands who failed to impose their authority (Flandrin, 1979). Proverbs from the sixteenth century passed on these social customs:

> A good horse and a bad horse need the spur
> A good woman and a bad woman need the stick

> *Meurier, sixteenth century; in Flandrin, 1979*

During the eighteenth century, the effectiveness of physical aggression against wives was beginning to be questioned, although it was still legal:

> He who strikes his wife is like he who strikes a
> sack of flour: the good goes, and the bad remains.

> *Proverb, 1786; in Flandrin, 1979*

That proverb carries some interesting assumptions still concerning women who stay in a battering relationship, assumptions that may be subscribed to today.

Over the eighteenth and nineteenth centuries, laws concerning chastisement began to be modified to restrict the amount and type of violence used against one's wife. As late as the nineteenth century, the English common law specified the "rule of thumb" in which it was legal for a husband to "chastise" a wife with a rod not thicker than his thumb. By the late 1800s in the United States, women were allowed to divorce their husbands for cruelty but only two states rescinded their laws against the "ancient privilege" of wife beating (Davidson, 1977). Today, the states allow a woman to bring criminal action against her abusing spouse but not to the same extent that criminal laws protect a third party against injury. However, a woman cannot sue her husband for damages. She must resort to criminal action or divorce (Calvert, 1974). A woman who is cohabiting but not married has even less legal protection. Courts and police are reluctant to interfere in the private matters of the family, so much violence is overlooked. Many police departments have "stitch rules" that suggest that the officer not make an arrest until the wounds require a set number of stitches (Field & Field, 1973).

Together, both rape and wife beating have served as two sides of the same coin, the subjugation of women. Rape has punished the unattached woman, whereas wife beating (as well as incest and child abuse) has served to punish and control within the family. By the time the laws changed, these forms of violence against women were so entrenched in the culture that it made very little difference. Unfortunately, Freud and his followers developed theories of personality that failed to consider that society could have an impact on personality development. They accepted the status quo as the natural order of things and therefore right, and they began to search for intrapsychic explanations for the nature of women and men. When Freud was told by a number of his women patients that they had been molested or raped by their fathers as children, he rejected the idea that this actually happened. He developed the theory that childhood assault was a fantasy to disguise the woman's guilty wish to sleep with her father (Freud, 1905). This was probably the beginning of the victim-blame theories of rape and abuse. Psychoanalytic thought, beginning with Freud and elaborated upon by Deutsch, fostered the belief that women are subject to biologically based masochism (Waites, 1977). Deutch, in her volumes on the psychology of women (1944, 1945), maintained that the mature feminine personality is accepting of the pain of intercourse and childbirth and is, therefore, passive and masochistic. The transfer of erogenous sensations from the immature clitoris to the mature vagina was accomplished by the woman's surrender to an act of rape. Brownmiller (1975) points out that, in the late 1940s and 1950s, popular magazines and books quoted Deutch's pronouncements to teach women to accept their female role, and her theory was accepted by sex-crime experts who explained away violence against women.

In keeping with the prevalent attitudes regarding sexual assault, Kinsey, Pomeroy, Martin, and Gebhard (1953) found that 24 percent of their sample of 4,441 female subjects reported some kind of molestation experience with an adult male during their preadolescence, but he minimized any harm in such experiences. Although 80 percent of the assaulted group stated they had been emotionally upset or frightened, Kinsey et al. insisted it was cultural conditioning rather than the experience itself that caused the reaction. To support this contention, he cited earlier articles that proposed that children didn't report such events to their parents because of their guilt feelings at the pleasure of the experience. He finished the section by blaming the parents of the assaulted child for the child's fear reaction. The assailant is not mentioned particularly. Along the same vein, Abrahamsen (1960) wrote an analysis of a Rorschach study on the wives of eight rapists in which he blamed the wives and mothers of the rapists for driving the men to the crime by their alternating masochistic and aggressive behavior. In one of the first studies to examine wife battering, Snell, Rosenwald, and Robey (1964) again looked to the woman's role and dynamics of the couple. Essentially, they felt that there was some role reversal; the husbands were passive, indecisive, and sexually inadequate, while the wives were masculine, aggressive, and frigid. The bouts of battering served to release the man from feeling castrated by his wife while they at the same time gave the wife some masochistic gratification.

In summary, from the beginning of history until the mid 1970s, there has been an almost unbroken line of thought regarding violence toward women. While not permissible, sexual assault against women was tolerated and, through attitudes if not laws, condoned. Women were held responsible for their own chastity and respectability but were given neither the resources nor the power to protect themselves. Because of this powerlessness, women fell under the jurisdiction of men who were given legal permission to use physical force against them as they saw fit. While laws have changed slowly to reflect more humane attitudes, violence against women was not considered an appropriate topic for psychological research until the late 1970s.[1]

ATTITUDINAL AND THEORETICAL RESEARCH

Current research on rape and domestic violence has evolved in different directions. The rape literature has focused heavily on studies of societal attitudes, including jury studies and studies of victim reactions. Because the domestic violence field has been dominated largely by sociologists, the majority of that research has been attempting to construct theories of violence and explain why battered women remain in violent relationships. Relatively little of the domestic violence research has focused on victim reactions or therapeutic issues.

It is not surprising that public attitudes regarding sexual assault and

[1]In 1976, as I completed my graduate work and began looking for an academic position, I was advised by several of my professors to pick a more legitimate area of research than a "womens' topic." Fortunately, the federal government decided that rape was a "legitimate" topic and began awarding research grants to study the problem. Where money goes, respectability follows.

wife abuse have not changed substantially, since the topic was all but ignored until the mid-1970s. Stark and McEvoy (1970) found that between
20 percent and 25 percent of adults surveyed for the National Commission on the Causes and Prevention of Crime and Violence felt it was acceptable for spouses to hit each other under certain circumstances. It has
been argued (Straus, 1976) that 25 percent is likely to be a considerable
underestimate of proviolence norms, since the opposite might be perceived as more socially acceptable. Straus pointed out that observational
studies might be more revealing than attitude surveys and referred to a
study in which confederates were seen to be fighting by passers-by on the
street. Men would stop to help a male victim who was being assaulted by
either another man or woman or would aid a woman being attacked by
another woman. However, no man interfered when a woman was being
attacked by a man (cited in Pogrebin, 1974). This was interpreted by
Straus (1976) to be evidence of the general phenomenon of male hostility
toward women.

There has been much more extensive research on attitudes regarding rape than regarding domestic violence. A number of studies have focused on sex differences, sex-role attitudes, and victim blame. While
several studies have found that people have multidimensional attitudes
toward rape, such as victim blame, assailant blame, and societal blame
(Feild, 1978; Resick & Jackson, 1981; Ward & Resick, 1979), there is
substantial evidence that sex-role stereotypes strongly influence perception of rape victims (Burt, 1980; Feild, 1978; Krulewitz & Payne, 1978;
Stewart & Sokol, 1977; Williams, 1979). Using a variety of sex-role stereotyping scales with various rape scales or experimental vignettes, interesting and consistent findings have emerged.

For example, Burt (1980) conducted a study to examine acceptance
of rape myths, false beliefs that create a climate hostile to victims. (Examples of such myths are: any healthy woman can resist rape; women
unconsciously want to be raped; only bad girls get raped). She found
that many Americans do believe many rape myths. More than half of her
sample of adult women and men ascribed to the belief that, in the majority of cases, the victim of rape was promiscuous or had a bad reputation
and that, in the majority of cases, the woman reported rape as an attempt to get back at a man she was angry with or to cover up an illegiti-
mate pregnancy. She found that the higher a person's sex-role stereotyping or the more he or she believes that sexual relationships are adversarial or accepts interpersonal violence, the greater his or her acceptance of

rape myths will be. She also found that younger and more educated people held less stereotypic beliefs regarding both sex roles and rape.

Burt's concept (1980) of adversarial sexual beliefs, in addition to sex-role stereotypes, may be important for understanding acquaintance rapes. The belief that sexual relationships are fundamentally exploitative leads to distrust and miscommunication in dating. When clear communication is lacking, it is likely that people will rely on stereotypic expectations to guide their interactions. One common stereotypic belief is that women don't know what they want, or that they want to be "seduced" into having sex. If a man proceeds despite her protestations, based on stereotyped expectations rather than what he is being told, the woman may experience rape, with the concomitant sequelae, while he assumes he has engaged in consensual sex. Burt concluded that "rape is the logical and psychological extension of a dominant–submissive, competitive, sex role stereotyped culture" (1980, p. 229).

Feild (1978) factor-analyzed an "attitudes toward rape" questionnaire and compared the responses of several groups of people. He, too, found that traditional attitudes toward women were correlated with victim blame and the belief that, because the "property is now used," a raped woman is a less attractive person. Aside from sex-role stereotyping, he also found a sex difference, with women having a much more negative view of rape than men, who ascribed to more stereotypic views. In comparing the attitude of a group of citizens with the attitudes of police, rapists, and rape crisis counselors, Feild found the attitudes of citizens and police to be much closer to those of the rapists than those of the counselors. Similar to the Field study, King, Rotter, Calhoun, and Selby (1978) found that another group likely to have contact with victims, emergency-room physicians, were also more likely to ascribe blame to the victim than were rape crisis counselors.

In a study of nurses' attitudes, Alexander (1980) found that the nurses were likely to judge the victim's role in the assault based on their perceived character (marital status, dress, amount of resistance) in interaction with their status as rape victims. More "respectable" victims were viewed as less responsible for their assault. This finding was particularly true of nurses who strongly subscribed to adherence in societal norms. In one other study, Resick and Jackson (1981) found that male psychologists were somewhat more likely to blame the victim for her rape than female psychologists. It is quite likely that the attitudes of professionals who interact with victims of rape can affect their recovery.

These studies and others that demonstrate victim blame for rape (Jones & Aronson, 1973; Smith, Keating, Hester, & Mitchell, 1976) support the theory that rape is the direct result of sex-role socialization and societal acceptance of violence. In addition to Brownmiller (1975) and Burt (1980), Russell (1975) has concluded that "rape is the ultimate sexist act. It is an act of physical and psychic oppression. Eradicating rape requires getting rid of the power discrepancy between men and women, because abuse of power flows from unequal power" (p. 265).

Theories regarding the causes of wife battering have been more varied and multidimensional than the theories of rape. While a complete analysis of current theories and supporting research on domestic violence is beyond the province of this paper, even a cursory examination reveals the enormous impact of sex-role stereotypes from the societal level on down to the individual level. Straus (1973, 1977; Straus et al., 1980) has developed a multivariate theory of wife beating which, when expanded, can encompass all of the other theories. Straus' theory (1973) views violence as a systematic product of antececent variables and precipitating variables followed by various consequences. For the purposes of this chapter, the antecedent variables will be divided further into general, or sociological, antecedents and the more individualized, or psychological, antecedents. These are shown in Table 11–1. Sex-role stereotypes pervade both types of antecedents.

Among the general sociological antecedents are cultural norms of sexual inequality. Straus (1980b) has delineated a number of ways in which society helps to create and maintain high levels of marital violence. This norm is helped when men marry women who are younger, less intelligent, educationally inferior, smaller, and less economically productive than themselves. When such arranged superiority is not the case, men may feel almost compelled to fall back upon physical force to maintain their status. Prior to Straus, O'Brien (1971) hypothesized and supplied some evidence that violence occurs when individuals of superordinate status find their positions threatened. Allen and Straus (1980) also have provided support for this hypothesis.

A second societal factor cited by Straus (1980b) is the sexist economic and occupational structure of society, which enforces the dependence of women upon men. Data on discriminatory practices against women are so abundant that it probably is unnecessary to delineate them here. When women are not economically independent, their options for leaving a violent relationship are considerably reduced. Child-care

242 : : *Special Problems of Living*

TABLE 11-1. Multivariate theory of domestic violence

I.   General Antecedents (sociological variables)
      A. Historical precedents
      B. Cultural norms of inequality between sexes
      C. Sexist economic structure of society
      D. Acceptance of violence in culture

II.   Specific Antecedents (psychological variables)
      A. Individual and family characteristics
      B. Inability to cope with stress
      C. Status inequality theory
      D. "Compulsive masculinity"
      E. Learned helplessness

III. Precipitators
      A. Stress
      B. Alcohol
      C. Work problems
      D. Marital disruption
      E. Problems with children

IV.   Short-Term Consequences
      A. Reinforcement for assailant
      B. Punishment of victim's behavior
      C. Cycle theory
      D. Stockholm Syndrome (bonding of victim to assailant)

V.   Long-Term Consequences
      A. Marital and family dysfunction
      B. Abused children
      C. Homocide
      D. Psychological dysfunction of victim
      E. Reinforcement of societal norms

Note: This table is a synthesis of most of the current theories of domestic violence organized here within a social learning theory framework. A number of other variables and an infinite number of situational precipitators could be added to those listed.

problems, beliefs in the inappropriateness of single-parent child rearing, and strong beliefs in the preeminence of the wife role for women also help maintain the dependent role of women upon men.

Two studies support the observation made by clinicians that violent families have more traditional sex roles. Frieze, Knoble, Zomnir, and Washburn (1980) found some evidence that severely battered women were more traditional than either mildly abused or nonbattered women.

They married at a younger age, had more children, and were restricted in the places they went and in the money they had access to. Based on semistructured interviews of battered women, Star, Clark, Goetz, and O'Malia (1979) also observed that these women had very traditional marital and sex roles. After giving a "family environment" scale to university students, Reese and Resick (1980) found that violent homes were more likely to be hierarchical, with one member assuming control of the family.

Another factor influencing marital violence is the generally high level of violence in society, which carries over into the family realm (Straus, 1977); however, perhaps the most important factor that serves to justify marital violence is family socialization in violence. Stark and McEvoy (1970) have found that physical punishment is almost universal and approved of. Children are raised to believe that violence at the hands of loved ones is acceptable, with the consequent association of love with violence. Since women are in an inferior role and are considered "child-like," they, too, become appropriate people to punish physically in order to teach. Straus (1980a) has concluded from his research that the marriage license is a hitting license. The role of modeling in wife battering has been supported by several researchers who have found that a high proportion of batterers came from violent homes (Frieze et al., 1980; Gayford, 1975; Hilberman & Munson, 1977; Rounsaville, 1978).

The specific or psychological antecedents are the logical consequences of societal sex-role stereotypes, norms, modeling, and direct reinforcement. Individual and family characteristics as well as the ability to cope with stress would be the specific antecedents in a battering relationship. In order to explain the violence of modern men, Parsons (1947) derived the concept of "compulsive masculinity." Since boys are raised almost exclusively by women, with few male role models available in the traditional family in which the father works long hours and the mother stays home, Parsons hypothesized many boys would have problems with masculine identification. He further hypothesized the exaggerated toughness in preadolescent and adolescent males to be from the unconscious need to repudiate a natural identification with their mother, hence, "compulsive masculinity."

A social-learning-theory explanation might be that, in the absence of appropriate modeling by fathers, male teachers, and the like — boys turn to the extreme stereotypes in the media where violence is extolled. Whether or not male models are present in the environment, boys learn that, for them, violence works; violent behavior tends to be reinforced positively since the aggressor usually gets what he wants (Patterson, Littman, & Bricker, 1967). If he is punished for aggression, it is typically by means of more aggression, and another lesson is learned. Violence is acceptable if you are the biggest person and if you deal it out under the guise of discipline. There is evidence that boys receive more punishment as well as more praise than girls, so there is ample opportunity for them to model aggression (Maccoby & Jacklin, 1974). When threatened with the loss of some possession, violence or the threat of violence could serve as an effective means of retaining the possession and establishing dominance. Among battering husbands, extreme jealousy appears to be almost universal (Rounsaville, 1978; Walker, 1979). The violence they use appears to function as a method of maintaining exclusive ownership over their wives.

One of the major theories that has been proffered to explain why women remain in a battering relationship is learned helplessness. Walker (1979) has drawn a parallel between Seligman's theory (1975) of learned helplessness and the experience of battered women. The noncontingent aversive events (battering), combined with the lack of community support and pressure from the extended families and society to hold the family together, effectively immobilize battered women. While the women may believe they have at least a limited ability to control their husband's violence, they express hopelessness and helplessness over the possibility of extricating themselves from the battering relationship. Since women often define their wife role as "helper," they often feel guilt over their failure to help their husbands change over time. The subsequent depression further immobilizes them.

Precipitating events, the triggering conditions for violence, have not been examined much in the research but are often the events that are cited as "causing" the episode by those involved: alcohol, stress, work problems, marital dysfunction, a burned dinner, and so on. In a recent attribution study, Richardson and Campbell (1980) found that, when the husband was drunk and involved in violence, relatively more blame was assigned to the alcohol and less to him. However, when the wife was drunk, she was blamed more for the incident than when she was sober. It is probable that even a minor stressor could serve as the triggering event, the excuse for violence, if the general and specific antecedents are present in the couple's relationship.

Aside from the obvious negative consequences of the violence to the victim, the family, and society, there are some consequent events that may serve to prolong and maintain the battering relationship. After interviewing 120 battered women, Walker (1979) developed the cycle theory of violence. She observed that battering episodes tend to follow a three-stage process. First, there is a period of building tension for the batterer, during which the wife attempts to placate him. The tension-building phase culminates in an acute battering episode. Following the battering incident, the husband is mortified over what he has done and attempts to make it up to his wife. He becomes attentive, affectionate, and giving. She develops a false sense of hope that his considerate behavior is permanent. This third phase may serve to reinforce the wife for staying with the husband and may allow her to believe that all will be better in the future. While the cycle theory has not been tested empirically thus far, it holds promise in explaining one important variable for why battered women remain in periodically violent relationships — a strong schedule of intermittent reinforcement.

Another possible explanation for the continuing attachment of the battered woman to her batterer is somewhat more cognitive. There are some parallels between battered women's responses and the reactions of terrorists' hostages, a phenomenon that has been named the Stockholm Syndrome. Ochberg (1978) hypothesized that hostages need to deny their continuing danger throughout their captivity. Having successfully denied their danger, the hostages are overwhelmingly grateful to the terrorists for giving them life. They focus on the captors' kindnesses rather than their acts of brutality. The syndrome, including the feelings of fondness toward one's captors, often lasts for years after the incident is over. Perhaps battered women, who also may be captives in much the same way as hostages, develop cognitive coping strategies similar to the Stockholm Syndrome. Because their husbands didn't kill them or hurt them worse than they did, the women are grateful and are bonded to them more than before.

The development of a multivariate theory of battering will be an important contribution to the fields of psychology and criminal justice as more supporting evidence is established. As the public and professionals become aware of the nature of battering relationships, more support and service should become available for the victims rather than the typical disgusted response of "Well, why doesn't she just leave him? I would." It will be an important area of research and therapy development in the 1980s.

VICTIM REACTION RESEARCH

The emphasis on victim reaction in the rape literature has been to demonstrate that rape is, in fact, a traumatic life event, rather than a stereotypic sexual act that a woman should/could lie back and enjoy. Among the first reports of victim reaction were interview studies by Sutherland and Scherl (1970) and Burgess and Holmstrom (1974b). While not controlled, systematic studies, these reports provided important descriptive information that has inspired subsequent research. Several large-scale studies have been conducted within the past several years and now are yielding surprisingly consistent data.

Because of the almost universal use of weapons and/or threats of physical violence (Katz & Mazur, 1979; Resick, Calhoun, Ellis, & Atkeson, 1980), rape is clearly perceived by the victim as a life-threatening event. It is not uncommon for the victim to depersonalize or black out during the event (Veronen, Kilpatrick, & Resick, 1979). It has been hypothesized (Kilpatrick, Veronen, & Resick, 1979a, 1979b) that sexual assault is sufficiently traumatic to condition fear reactions to any stimuli present during the situation. Paired with the avoidance behavior which victims invariably engage in after the assault, there is a good probability of the development of phobic reactions. In two separate longitudinal studies comparing victims' reactions with matched groups of nonvictims, supporting evidence has been obtained. Kilpatrick et al., (1979a, 1979b; Kilpatrick, Resick, & Veronen, 1981; Veronen & Kilpatrick, 1980) have found that rape-related fear reactions are present in many victims for at least one year following assault. Typical fears include fears of being home alone, of the dark, of walking alone, of men, and of violence in the media. Calhoun, Atkeson, and Resick (1981), in a similar but larger longitudinal study, also have found significantly greater fear reactions in victims than nonvictims. In a study of 27 victims who had been raped from 1 to 16 years ago, Ellis, Atkeson, and Calhoun (1981) found no significant differences between the victims and individually matched comparison subjects on the Veronen-Kilpatrick Modified Fear Survey, which was used in all the preceding studies. However, when victims of stranger rapes were compared with victims of acquaintance rapes, strong differences emerged. Women who were assaulted by strangers had much higher scores on the Modified Fear Survey and showed continued elevation of rape-related and vulnerability cues.

Aside from fear reactions, victims appear to have a strong initial crisis reaction, as observed by Burgess and Holmstrom (1974a, 1974b) and supported by more recent research efforts (Atkeson, Calhoun, Resick, & Ellis, 1982; Frank, Turner, & Stewart, in press; Kilpatrick et al., 1979a). Scores on almost every kind of psychological measure that has been administered are elevated to clinical levels, indicating an acute traumatic reaction. Depression, confusion, and anxiety appear to be the most frequent reactions. Interpersonal functioning is frequently disrupted also (Resick, Calhoun, Atkeson, & Ellis, 1981). Reactions of significant others toward the victim can both exacerbate or help alleviate these acute symptoms (Resick, Calhoun, Ellis, & Atkeson, 1980).

Between two and three months postrape, the strong initial reaction subsides, but problems remain for some victims. Besides the fear reactions, work adjustment is often a problem for almost a year following assault (Resick et al., 1981), and some victims continue to show problems with depression, pervasive anger (particularly focused on the criminal justice system), psychophysiological reactions, or relationships with men (Ellis et al., 1981). Problems with sexual functioning have been found by both Ellis et al. (1981) and Feldman-Summers, Gordon, and Meagher (1979).

If psychological reactions to rape may be quite severe for some rape victims and at least temporarily life disrupting for almost all rape victims, what then of the women who are the victims of continued physical, sexual, and psychological abuse for years at the hands of their husbands; what of the battered women? Well-controlled research on the subject is almost nonexistent. Methodological problems are even more rampant than for research on rape. A good definition or way to discriminate battered women from other less severely affected victims of marital violence is lacking. Length of the battering relationship and frequency of episodes as well as severity should be taken into account. An even more serious problem is to determine whether any psychological patterns that emerge in research predate the battering or reflect responses to the violence. Some psychological characteristics could serve as antecedents for battering inasmuch as some women may be more accepting of violence or more submissive initially. Nevertheless, from clinical and interview studies, a psychological profile of battered women and their reactions is beginning to emerge. Besides the obvious outcomes of marital problems and potential homicide, there do appear to be some parallels to the typical rape reaction. Hilberman and Munson (1977) found that, in a 12-month period, half of all the women referred for psychiatric evaluation by

the medical staff of a rural health clinic were found to be victims of marital violence. In only four of 60 cases was the marital violence known to the
referring physician. The authors drew the parallel to rape victims except
that the stress was unending. They described agitation and anxiety bor-
dering on panic. They also noted a high rate of prior psychological dysfunction among these women and numerous somatic concerns.

Hilberman and Munson, as well as most other researchers on the
topic, also point out the high incidence of depression. Prescott and Letko
(1977) found that 75 percent of 40 battered women reported depression.
Over half of the women reported feeling helpless, and one quarter felt
guilty. These findings give some support for Walker's (1979) theory of
learned helplessness in battered women. Rounsaville and Weissman
(1977–1978) gave the CES-D scale to determine the incidence of depression among 37 battered women. They found 20 percent to be asymptomat-
ic, 60 percent to be moderately depressed, and 20 percent to be severely
depressed. Using *DSM-II* diagnoses, they classified 52 percent as depressed, 12 percent as overtly or latently schizophrenic, 6 percent as drug
or alcohol abusers, and 29 percent without any notable psychopathology.

Jens (1980) also reported on the use of the CES-D with battered
women. Women who were the victims of repeated violence and who, for
the most part, had left the battering relationship were included in the
sample. The 434 battered women scored significantly higher on the depression scale than the norms of community surveys. Over 50 percent
scored above the cutoff established for clinical depression.

Two studies have used the 16PF in order to derive a personality profile of battered women. Star (1978) gave the 16PF and the Buss-Durkee
Hostility Guilt Inventory to 58 women in a battered women's shelter. All
of the women had been abused mentally and emotionally, and 46 had
been abused physically. She compared those women who had been physically abused with those who had not and found that they differed on
one factor of the 16PF. Both groups of women were low on ego strength,
but the nonbattered yet emotionally abused women scored significantly
lower. Low scores indicate being easily annoyed, generally dissatisfied,
and unable to cope with life's demands. On the other inventory she
found that the physically battered women were more likely to deny hostility but were higher in irritability. The nonbattered women were more
likely to be openly' oppositional.

The other study, also by Star and her associates (Star et al., 1979)
reported on the use of the 16PF and the Clinical Analysis Questionnaire

with 50 battered women. Overall, the sample fell within the average range but differed from norms on six personality traits and three clinical factors. The profile of the group of women revealed tendencies toward shyness and introversion; feelings of being unable to cope; a reserved, cautious manner; tendency to withdraw and avoid interpersonal contact; self-sufficiency; tension and frustration; paranoia (probably realistic); and a tendency to retreat from reality.

Overall, these findings depict strong psychological reactions in women who have been victims of violence. A proportion of women, perhaps 20 percent to 25 percent, appear able to cope and recover from the violence in a reasonably short period of time (within two or three months). Those women with a poor premorbid history seem more vulnerable to the effects of assault. It is questionable, though, whether any woman, even one who previously was strong and healthy, could emerge completely unscathed from a prolonged relationship with psychological and physical battering. In the end, the violence seems to serve its function. Women who have been victimized most often fulfill the traditional stereotypes society holds for women: depressed, anxious, helpless, and vulnerable people.

CLINICAL AND RESEARCH ISSUES IN THE 1980s

It should be evident from the preceding material that violence against women is not just an isolated clinical problem but an immense societal problem that will not be alleviated until men and women are no longer raised within the shadow of traditional sex-role stereotypes and until women are treated as respected equals in society. While the enormity of the task of changing an entire society is rather overwhelming, there is much that clinicians and researchers can do to have an impact on the problem.

First, there must be an awareness of the extensiveness of the problem. Clinicians will continue to believe that violence and abuse are relatively rare events if they rely on the unsolicited complaints of victims. Questions concerning past and present experience with violence should be included in all client interviews and protocols. Agencies need to begin to compile statistics of incidence and document rehabilitation efforts.

Second, while the interface between violence and sex-role stereotypes appears accurate in theory, much more research will be necessary on the correlations between them and the potential causal role of gender stereotypes in violence. As men and women adopt more androgynous roles, their participation in violent behavior also should be examined. If a clear causal connection can be established, researchers, clinicians, and educators will need to determine the best ways to teach nonadversarial and nonviolent sex roles. Burt (1980) has suggested that egalitarian sex roles may be accomplished best by fighting sex-role stereotyping with young children, before such stereotyping is complicated by sexual as well as sex-role interactions.

More research also needs to be focused on nonviolent methods of child rearing as well as methods of changing prevalent attitudes regarding the "benefits" of spanking. The generational nature of violence in families indicates that new child-rearing techniques are needed. Those adults who are nonviolent and well adjusted are probably so in spite of, rather than because of, spanking and corporal punishment.

A leftover from psychodynamic theory that is held almost universally is the "catharsis" model of aggression. There appear to be widely held beliefs among many professionals as well as the public that anger should be "gotten out of the system" by hitting some *thing* or yelling. The value/necessity of displacing anger through aggressive means has not been established. Contrary to such a hypothesis, correlations have been found between verbal and physical aggression (Owens & Straus, 1975; Reese & Resick, 1980). Practicing physical aggression does not decrease, but is likely to increase, the probability of further aggression (Bandura & Walters, 1963). The public needs to understand that anger should be reduced, not displaced. Some anger-management procedures have been developed (Novaco, 1975, 1976; Frederiksen & Rainwater, 1979), but more research, particularly with abusive and violent populations, is needed. Marital therapies need to focus on conflict reduction rather than leveling and some other potentially inflammatory methods that have been advocated (e.g., Bach & Goldberg's *Creative Aggression*, 1974) in the pop psychology field.

While recent research and clinical findings point to the traumatic and possibly long-term effects of violence on women, relatively little attention has been given to treatment of victims beyond informational and supportive counseling immediately following the incident. While crisis intervention is important and needs to be established in all communities, there is sufficient evidence that, for some victims, brief intervention may not be enough. There have been only a few single case studies that have suggested biofeedback (Blanchard & Abel, 1976), systematic desensitization (Wolff, 1977), or stress inoculation (Kilpatrick, Veronen, & Resick, 1980) for fear reactions in victims of assault. There have been no empirical investigations of the efficacy of treatment methods for battered women. An important effort in the 1980s will be to develop appropriate therapeutic procedures for women who have continuing problems with fear, depression, self-concept, and interpersonal relationships following violent relationships or sexual assault.

Since only the tip of the iceberg has been exposed in the 1970s, the 1980s should prove to be a period of increased understanding and sophistication on this important clinical and societal problem. Federal funds for research and services are becoming increasingly available. More professionals are needed to augment and lend their research and clinical expertise to the efforts of the grassroots organizations that have done an excellent job drawing national attention to the problem and offering increased services to victims of violence. Through the combined efforts of more professionals in the social sciences and those of the grassroots feminist movement, much more could be accomplished and it could prove to be an exciting decade.

REFERENCES

Abrahamsen, D. *The psychology of crime.* New York: Columbia University Press, 1960.

Adler, E. S. *Perceived marital power, influence techniques and marital violence.* Paper presented at the Annual Meeting of the American Sociological Association, Chicago, September 1977.

Alexander, C. S. The responsible victim: Nurses' perceptions of victims of rape. *Journal of Health and Social Behavior*, 1980, *21*, 22–33.

Allen, C. M., & Straus, M. A. Resources, power and husband–wife violence. In M. A. Straus & G. T. Hotaling (Eds.), *The social causes of husband–wife violence.* Minneapolis: University of Minnesota Press, 1980.

Atkeson, B. M., Calhoun, K. S., Resick, P. A., & Ellis, E. M. Victims of rape: Repeated assessment of depressive symptoms. *Journal of Consulting and Clinical Psychology*, 1982, *50*, 96–102.

Bach, J. R., & Goldberg, H. *Creative aggression.* New York: Avon Books, 1974.

Bandura, A. Influence of models' reinforcement contingencies on the acquisition of imitative responses. *Personality and Social Psychology*, 1965, *1*, 589–595.

Bandura, A., Ross, D., & Ross, S. A. Transmission of aggression through imitation of aggressive models. *Journal of Abnormal and Social Psychology*, 1961, *63*, 575–582.

Bandura, A., Ross, D., & Ross, S. A. Imitation of film mediated aggressive models. *Journal of Abnormal and Social Psychology*, 1963, *66*, 3–11.(a)

Bandura, A., Ross, D., & Ross, S. A. Vicarious reinforcement and imitative learning. *Journal of Abnormal and Social Psychology*, 1963, *67*, 601–607.(b)

Bandura, A., & Walters, R. H. *Social learning and personality development.* New York: Holt, Rinehart & Winston, 1963.

Blanchard, E. B., & Abel, G. G. An experimental case study of the biofeedback treatment of a rape-induced psychophysiological cardiovascular disorder. *Behavior Therapy*, 1976, *7*, 113–119.

Bowker, L. H. The criminal victimization of women. *Victimology: An International Journal*, 1979, *4*, 371–384.

Brownmiller, S. *Against our will: Men, women and rape.* New York: Simon & Schuster, 1975.

Burgess, A. W., & Holmstrom, L. L. *Rape: Victims of crisis.* Bowie, Md.: Robert Brady, 1974.(a)

Burgess, A. W., & Holmstrom, L. L. Rape trauma syndrome. *American Journal of Psychiatry*, 1974, *131*, 981–986.(b)

Burt, M. R. Cultural myths and supports for rape. *Journal of Personality and Social Psychology*, 1980, *38*, 217–230.

Calhoun, K. S., Atkeson, B. M., & Resick, P. A. *Fear reactions in rape victims: A chronic problem?* Unpublished manuscript, University of Georgia, 1981.

Calvert, R. Criminal and civil liability in husband–wife assaults. In S. K. Steinmetz & M. A. Straus (Eds.), *Violence in the family.* New York: Harper & Row, 1974.

Davidson, T. Wifebeating: A recurring phenomenon throughout history. In M. Roy (Ed.), *Battered women: A psychosociological study of domestic violence.* New York: Van Nostrand Reinhold, 1977.

Deutsch, H. *The psychology of women.* Vol. I and Vol. II. New York: Grune & Stratton, 1944, 1945.

Dobash, R. E., & Dobash, R. P. Wives: The appropriate victims of marital violence. *Victimology: An International Journal*, 1977, *2*, 426–442.

Ellis, E. M., Atkeson, B. M., & Calhoun, K. S. An assessment of long-term reactions to rape. *Journal of Abnormal Psychology*, 1981, *90*, 263–266.

Federal Bureau of Investigation. *Uniform Crime Reports – 1979.* Washington, D.C.: U.S. Government Printing Office, 1980.

Feldman-Summers, S., Gordon, P. E., & Meagher, J. R. The impact of rape on sexual satisfaction. *Journal of Abnormal Psychology*, 1979, *88*, 101–105.

Feild, H. S. Attitudes toward rape: A comparative analysis of police, rapists, crisis counselors and citizens. *Journal of Personality and Social Psychology*, 1978, *36*, 156–179.

Field, M. H., & Field, H. F. Marital violence and the criminal process: Neither justice nor peace. *The Social Service Review*, 1973, 47, 221–240.

Flandrin, J. L. *Families in former times: Kinship, household and sexuality*. Cambridge, England: Cambridge University Press, 1979.

Frank, E., Turner, S. M., & Stewart, B. D. Initial response to rape: The impact of factors within the rape situation. *Journal of Behavioral Assessment*, in press.

Frederiksen, L. W., & Rainwater, N. *Explosive behavior: A skill development approach to treatment*. Paper presented at 11th Annual Banff International Conference on Behavior Modification, Banff, Canada, March 1979.

Freud, S. Femininity, no. 33 (1933). *New introductory lectures on psychoanalysis*. New York: W. W. Norton, 1965.

Frieze, I. H., Knoble, V., Zomnir, G., & Washburn, C. *Types of battered women*. Paper presented at the Annual Research Conference of the Association for Women in Psychology, Santa Monica, Calif., March 1980.

Gayford, J. J. Wife battering: A preliminary study of 100 cases. *British Medical Journal*, 1975, *1*, 194–197.

Hilberman, E., & Munson, K. Sixty battered women. *Victimology: An International Journal*, 1977, *2*, 460–470.

Hite, S. *The Hite report: A nationwide study on female sexuality*. New York: Macmillan, 1976.

Jens, K. S. Depression in battered women. Paper presented at the Annual Meeting of the Rocky Mountain Psychological Association, symposium on *Personality Characteristics and Battered Women*, Tucson, Arizona, April 1980.

Jones, C., & Aronson, E. Attribution of fault to a rape victim as a function of respectability of the victim. *Journal of Personality and Social Psychology*, 1973, *26*, 415–419.

Katz, S., & Mazur, M. A. *Understanding the rape victim: A synthesis of research findings*. New York: John Wiley, 1979.

Kilpatrick, D. G., Resick, P. A., & Veronen, L. J. Longitudinal effects of a rape experience. *Journal of Social Issues*, 1981, *37*, 105–122.

Kilpatrick, D. G., Veronen, L. J., & Resick, P. A. The aftermath of rape: Recent empirical findings. *American Journal of Orthopsychiatry*, 1979, *49*, 658–669.(a)

Kilpatrick, D. G., Veronen, L. J., & Resick, P. A. Assessment of the aftermath of rape: Changing patterns of fear. *Journal of Behavioral Assessment*, 1979, *1*, 133–148.(b)

Kilpatrick, D. G., Veronen, L. J., & Resick, P. A. *The brief behavioral inter-*

vention procedure: A new treatment for recent rape victims. Paper presented at the 14th Annual Convention of the Association for Advancement of Behavior Therapy, New York, November 1980.

King, H. E., Rotter, M. V., Calhoun, L. G., & Selby, J. W. Perceptions of the rape incident: Physicians and volunteer counselors. *Journal of Community Psychology*, 1978, *6*, 74–77.

Kinsey, A. C., Pomeroy, W. B., Martin, C. E., & Gebhard, P. H. *Sexual behavior in the human female.* Philadelphia: W. B. Saunders, 1953.

Krulewitz, J. E., & Payne, E. J. Attributions about rape: Effects of rapist force, observer sex and sex role attitudes. *Journal of Applied Social Psychology*, 1978, *8*, 291–305.

Levinger, G. Physical abuse among applicants for divorce. *American Journal of Orthopsychiatry*, 1966, *36*, 804–806.

Maccoby, E. E., & Jacklin, C. N. *The psychology of sex differences.* Stanford, Calif.: Stanford University Press, 1974.

National Center for Health Statistics. *Vital statistics report.* Vol. 24. Washington, D.C.: National Center for Health Statistics, 1976.

Novaco, R. W. *Anger control: The development and evaluation of an experimental treatment.* Lexington, Mass.: Lexington Books, 1975.

Novaco, R. W. Treatment of chronic anger through cognitive and relaxation controls. *Journal of Consulting and Clinical Psychology*, 1976, *44*, 861.

O'Brien, J. E. Violence in divorce-prone families. *Journal of Marriage and the Family*, 1971, *33*, 692–698.

Ochberg, F. The victim of terrorism: Psychiatric considerations. *Terrorism: An International Journal*, 1978, *1*, 147–168.

Owens, D. M., & Straus, M. A. The social structure of violence in childhood and approval of violence as an adult. *Aggressive Behavior*, 1975, *1*, 193–211.

Parsons, T. Certain primary sources and patterns of aggression in the social structure of the western world. *Psychiatry*, 1947, *10*, 167–181.

Patterson, G. R., Littman, R. A., & Bricker, W. Assertive behavior in children: A step toward a theory of aggression. *Monographs of the Society for Research in Child Development*, 1967, *32*, serial no. 113.

Pogrebin, L. C. Do women make men violent? *Ms.*, 1974, *3*, pp. 49–55 & 80.

Prescott, S., & Letko, C. Battered women: A social psychological perspective. In M. Roy (Ed.), *Battered women: A psychosociological study of domestic violence.* New York: Van Nostrand Reinhold, 1977.

Reese, D. J., & Resick, P. A. *Perception of family social climate and physical aggression in the home.* Unpublished manuscript, University of South Dakota, 1980.

Resick, P. A., Calhoun, K. S., Atkeson, B. M., & Ellis, E. M. Social adjustment in victims of sexual assault. *Journal of Consulting and Clinical Psychology*, 1981, *49*, 705–712.

Resick, P. A., Calhoun, K. S., Ellis, E. M., & Atkeson, B. M. *Patterns of assault and prediction of reactions in victims of rape.* Unpublished manuscript 1980.

Resick, P. A., & Jackson, T. J. Attitudes toward rape among mental health professionals. *American Journal of Community Psychology*, 1981, 9, 481–490.

Richardson, D. C., & Campbell, J. L. Alcohol and wife abuse: The effect of alcohol on attributions of blame for wife abuse. *Personality and Social Psychology Bulletin*, 1980, 6, 51–56.

Rounsaville, B. J. Theories in marital violence: Evidence from a study of battered women. *Victimology: An International Journal*, 1978, 3, 11–31.

Rounsaville, B., & Weissman, M. M. Battered women: A medical problem requiring detection. *International Journal of Psychiatry in Medicine*, 1977–1978, 8, 191–202.

Russell, D. E. *The politics of rape: The victim's perspective.* New York: Stein & Day, 1975.

Seligman, M. E. P. *Helplessness.* San Francisco: W. H. Freeman, 1975.

Smith, R. E., Keating, J. P., Hester, R. K., & Mitchell, H. E. Role and justice considerations in the attribution of responsibility to a rape victim. *Journal of Research in Personality*, 1976, 10, 346–357.

Snell, J., Rosenwald, R., & Robey, A. The wifebeater's wife. *Archives of General Psychiatry*, 1964, 11, 107–112.

Stachura, J. S., & Teske, R. H. C. A special report on spouse abuse in Texas. Survey Research Program, Criminal Justice Center, Sam Houston State University, Huntsville, Texas, 1979.

Star, B. Comparing battered and nonbattered women. *Victimology: An International Journal*, 1978, 3, 32–44.

Star, B., Clark, C. G., Goetz, K. M., & O'Malia, L. Psychosocial aspects of wife battering. *Social Casework: The Journal of Contemporary Social Work*, October 1979, 479–487.

Stark, R., & McEvoy, J. Middle class violence. *Psychology Today*, 1970, 4, 52–65.

Stewart, A. J., & Sokol, M. *Male and female conceptions of rape.* Paper presented at Annual Meeting of the Eastern Psychological Association, Boston, April 1977.

Straus, M. A. A general systems theory approach to a theory of violence between family members. *Social Science Information*, 1973, 12, 105–125.

Straus, M. A. Sexual inequality, cultural norms and wife beating. *Victimology: An International Journal*, 1976, 1, 54–70.

Straus, M. A. Wife beating: How common and why? *Victimology: An International Journal*, 1977, 3, 443–458.

Straus, M. A. The marriage license as a hitting license: Evidence from popular culture, law and social sciences. In M. A. Straus & G. T. Hotaling (Eds.), *The social causes of husband–wife violence.* Minneapolis: University of Minnesota Press, 1980.(a)

Straus, M. A. Sexual inequality and wife beating. In M. A. Straus & G. T. Hotaling (Eds.), *The social causes of husband–wife violence.* Minneapolis: University of Minnesota Press, 1980.(b)

Straus, M. A., Gelles, R. J., & Steinmetz, S. K. *Behind closed doors: Violence in the American family.* New York: Anchor/Doubleday, 1980.

Sutherland, S., & Scherl, D. J. Patterns of response among victims of rape. *American Journal of Orthopsychiatry*, April 1970, *40*, 503–511.

Truninger, E. Marital violence: The legal solutions. *Hastings Law Journal*, 1971, *23*, 259–276.

Veronen, L. J., & Kilpatrick, D. G. Self-reported fears of rape victims: A preliminary investigation. *Behavior Modification*, 1980, *4*, 383–396.

Veronen, L. J., Kilpatrick, D. G., & Resick, P. A. Treatment of fear and anxiety in victims of rape: Implications for the criminal justice system. In W. H. Parsonage (Ed.), *Perspectives on victimology.* Beverly Hills, Calif.: Sage, 1979.

Waites, E. A. Female masochism and enforced restriction of choice. *Victimology: An International Journal*, 1977, *2*, 535–544.

Walker, L. E. *The battered woman.* New York: Harper & Row, 1979.

Ward, M. A., & Resick, P. A. *Relationships between attitudes toward rape and sex role perception.* Paper presented at 87th Annual Meeting of the American Psychological Association, New York, September 1979.

Williams, J. E. Sex role stereotypes, women's liberation and rape: A cross-cultural analysis of attitudes. *Sociological Symposium*, 1979, *25*, 61–97.

Wolfe, L. The sexual profile of that *Cosmopolitan* girl. *Cosmopolitan*, 1980, *189*, pp. 254–257, 263–265.

Wolff, R. Systematic desensitization and negative practice to alter the after effects of a rape attempt. *Journal of Behavior Therapy and Experimental Psychiatry*, 1977, *8*, 423–425.

Wolfgang, M. E. *Patterns of criminal homicide.* Philadelphia: University of Pennsylvania Press, 1958.

■ four
CONCLUSION

■ 12
Concluding Comments, Criticism, and Caution: Consistent Conservatism or Constructive Change?

VIOLET FRANKS and ESTHER D. ROTHBLUM

It is important to consider this last chapter as a sequel to the introductory section. In chapter two, Kelly introduced the concepts of sex-role stereotypes versus androgyny, reviewed the major research developments, and discussed the implications for psychological disorders. Subsequently, Weinraub and Brown (chapter three) reviewed the development of sex-role stereotypes, and Kirsch (chapter four) reviewed sex roles and language uses. The introductory section paved the way for subsequent chapters; the present chapter will attempt to integrate these chapters by discussing the overall conclusions made by the contributors regarding feminine sex-role stereotypes and their influence on mental health. Special emphasis will be placed on implications for mental health professionals of the 1980s.

CONTRIBUTORS CLARIFY: WHAT ARE
FEMININE SEX-ROLE STEREOTYPES

As we, the editors, received initial copies of chapters from contributors, we were intrigued by the different perspectives used to describe sex-role stereotypes. Some chapters (Kelly, Brehony, Rothblum, and Muehlenhard), emphasized sex-typed traits commonly ascribed to males and females. Thus, such characteristics as submissiveness, passivity, dependency, nurturance, tact, and emotionality were viewed in relation to the symptoms of agoraphobia, depression, and unassertiveness. Other chapters (Rothblum, Brehony, Zegman, and Worell and Garret-Fulks) focused on the traditional sex roles of women as wives, mothers, and homemakers. For example, the role of housewife was related to obesity in light of increased food cues, grocery shopping, cooking, food-related television commercials, and decreased physical activity (Zegman). Brehony described agoraphobia as the "extreme and exaggerated version of the stereotypic feminine role."

Sex-role stereotypes were described in a developmental framework by Weinraub and Brown, both in terms of children's awareness of sex-appropriate behavior and in their conformity to such roles. The chapter discusses the role of teachers, peers, and television as they influence stereotypes. Other authors pointed out differential responses by adults to boys and girls (Brehony) and the false expectations provided for girls regarding marriage (Worell and Garret-Fulks).

Myths surrounding women were the focus of chapters by Tevlin and Leiblum, Zegman, and Resick. Myths about female sexuality suggest that women are asexual, innocent, modest, passive, and romantic and that physical beauty is equivalent to sexual attractiveness (Tevlin and Leiblum). Resick describes myths surrounding rape, including "any healthy woman can resist rape; women unconsciously want to be raped; only bad girls get raped." Zegman discusses the myth that physical activity is harmful to women.

Finally, some perspectives defy categorization. Resick presents an elaborate historical description of rape and physical aggression toward women, beginning in Biblical times, with relevant legal developments of violence against women. Kelly and Muehlenhard discuss the problem of the ineffectiveness of the feminine sex-role stereotype. Zegman and Rothblum rule out greater biological susceptibility as constituting the main determinant for sex differences in the areas of obesity and depression, respectively. The role of society is discussed by Resick as serving to "maintain high levels of marital violence," by Worell and Garret-Fulks as promoting marriage as a social identity for women and divorce as social isolation, and by Zegman as excluding women from athletic competition. Brehony states at the outset of her chapter that her focus on sex-role stereotypes reflects the perspectives of current feminist thinking.

Thus, stereotypes pervade all aspects of society, including the media, the law, education, employment, marital roles, and social functioning. The unique focus of contributors influences the flavor of each chapter and provides ten separate perspectives on the function of sex roles. It is clear from all chapters that sex-role stereotypes continue to influence behavior in the present, as they have in the past.

IS IT NORMAL TO BE NORMAL? CONSEQUENCES FOR MENTAL HEALTH

We may learn a lesson from history:

> Charlotte Anna Perkins was born in Hartford, Connecticut, on July 3, 1860. . . . In 1884, after much vacillation, she reluctantly married Charles Walter Stetson, a local artist. Katharine Beecher, their only child, was born a year later. Soon after, Charlotte Stetson became so deeply depressed and despondent that she consulted S. Meir Mitchell, the well-known Philadelphia neurologist who specialized in women's nervous disorders. Mitchell's famous 'rest cure' forbade Charlotte Stetson ever to write and sharply limited her reading time. The treatment almost drove her mad. She ultimately rejected his regimen, as she was all her life to reject 'expert' advice, and fled to California, away from husband and child. There the depression lifted. [Lane, 1979]

What was normal for women in 1880s resulted in depression for Charlotte Perkins Gilman. It inspired her to write *The Yellow Wallpaper*, a name taken from the color of the nursery in which she "rested." What are the consequences of "normal" stereotypes for women in the 1980s, 100 years later? The preceding chapters present the following conclusions for mental health:

1. The combination of women's roles in society and learned help-

lessness results in depression, including lowered mood, feelings of worth-lessness, loss of energy, and possible suicide (Rothblum). About two-thirds of all depressed individuals are women.

2. Expectations about women's roles and lack of autonomy among women may result in the housebound syndrome of agoraphobia, with long-lasting avoidance of and panic concerning social situations (Brehony). Eighty-five percent of agoraphobics are women.

3. Women are conditioned to associate sexual activity with shame and guilt, to adopt a passive role in sexual encounters, and to blame themselves for sexual problems of the couple (Tevlin and Leiblum). A large proportion of women experience difficulties with sexual interest, arousal, and orgasm.

4. As a result of feminine sex-role stereotypes regarding tact, passivity, submission, and dependence, women experience difficulty behaving assertively, including requesting change, expressing dissatisfaction, and standing up for one's rights (Muehlenhard). Women appear less assertive than men on all self-report surveys.

5. Women's greater exposure to food-related cues, combined with society's deemphasis on women's athletics and its focus on women's physical beauty, results in increased "social hazards" of obesity among women (Zegman). Sixty-three percent of obese individuals are women.

6. The focus on societal roles of women as wives and homemakers and of marriage as "social identity" for women results in major adjustment problems for single-again women, including social isolation, role strain, economic difficulties, and negative perceptions by society (Worell and Garret-Fulks). Women are more likely than men to remain single following divorce and to become widowed, and they constitute about 90 percent of all single parents.

7. Society both produces and maintains high levels of violence against women and holds women responsible for their "chasity and respecability" (Resick). Nearly all victims of rape and spouse abuse are women.

MALE STEREOTYPES HAVE A LONGER SHELF LIFE

This book will be criticized for its omission of corresponding male-dominated disorders, such as alcoholism, drug abuse, and certain personality disorders. The omission was intentional. Too often, textbooks on issues affecting both sexes include a chapter or section on how the particular topic affects women. One is led to conclude, then, that all preceding material must refer specifically to men. To illustrate, a recent book appropriately entitled *Models of Man* includes as a final chapter the essay "Are Models of Man Models of Women?" (Beloff, 1980). Beloff states: "When there has been a model of women it has been given to us. And that given model has been patronizing." The goal of the present book is to focus on women — not by default or by comparison with men, but through *women's* mental health concerns that are particularly influenced by feminine sex-role stereotypes in society.

Additionally, it can be argued that male sex-role stereotypes are currently more adaptive. Masculine-ascribed traits such as independence, aggressiveness, objectiveness, dominance, activity, competence, logicality, worldliness, directness, adventurousness, self-confidence, loudness, and ambition (Broverman, Broverman, Clarkson, Rosenkrantz, & Vogel, 1970) are not incompatible with men's roles at work or outside of work. Most have positive connotations, contrary to feminine traits such as emotionality, subjectiveness, malleability, sneakiness, tearfulness, vanity, and submissiveness (Broverman et al., 1970). It becomes apparent from the list of male-ascribed traits that masculine sex-role stereotypes may result in coronary proneness, alcoholism, and delinquency, just as feminine sex-role stereotypes lead to more "passive" disorders such as agoraphobia, depression, and sexual dysfunction. That constitutes a separate agenda.

Finally, a common criticism toward advocates of research on women's health is "but women live longer than men anyway." As the preceding chapters have illustrated, the salient difference is the *quality* of life. According to the President's Commission on Mental Health (1978), women earn 56 percent of men's incomes, occupy the lowest-paying jobs, compose the majority of single parents, perform most of the housework, and comprise nearly all of rape or spouse-abuse victims.

WHAT THE FEMINISTS NEVER TOLD YOU: CONSEQUENCES OF NONTRADITIONAL SEX ROLES

The 1970s indicated that women should be like men. In her popular book, *Games Mother Never Taught You*, Betty Lehan Harrigan (1977) describes the lack of preparation women receive to survive and compete in business. She provides strategies for women to escape the secretarial pool, understand the power tactics of men, and gain promotion to positions of power themselves. The decade was marked by unprecedented numbers of women entering law, medical, and graduate schools. Corporations publicized the exceptional female vice-president or board member. Women similarly entered blue-collar jobs traditionally reserved for men. Finally, in the mental health field, Broverman's research (Broverman et al., 1970) pointed out that ascribed characteristics of men and of mentally healthy individuals were identical.

It is too early to know the consequences of women entering nontraditional roles; however, preliminary results are disquieting. Assertive women are perceived by others to posess negative personality traits (see chapters by Kelly and Muehlenhard). High-school boys consider even casual social initiation by high-school girls to constitute willingness to engage in sex (see chapter by Muehlenhard). Fully half of female physicians and one-third of female Ph.D.s are clinically depressed (see Rothblum), and the suicide rate for female physicians is four times the rate of white women in general (Rothblum). Finally, women are told "you can be *anything*"; the reality is "you must be *everything*" as women struggle to combine the roles of full-time, success-oriented career woman, homemaker, mother, and wife.

Thus, women cannot "act like men." First of all, they still are responsible for housework and children in addition to new career roles; the new superwoman role provides new stress. Second, women in nontraditional jobs experience prejudice and discrimination. Finally, women who behave in nonstereotypic ways are perceived negatively by others.

IMPLICATIONS FOR THE 1980s:
CONSISTENT CONSERVATISM

We may be shouting. The clangs of feminist demands in the 1970s have been deafening. However, who is listening? A decade after the woman's rights movement reemerged, and a decade after, affirmative action and consciousness raising, the following sex differences still exist:

1. In *employment*, the income gap between men and women is

widening. This is true of all income levels and types of occupation.

2. In *education*, children are reinforced for engaging in sex-appropriate behavior (see chapter by Weinraub), and textbooks portray women in stereotypic roles (President's Commission, 1978).
3. In *athletics*, only two percent of the budget in college sports is allocated for women (President's Commission, 1978).
4. In *politics*, women comprise only a minute fraction of political figures.
5. The *media* continue to promote sex-role stereotypes of women as passive, submissive, and unassertive (see chapter by Weinraub), and the number of women engaged in sex-role stereotyped tasks on television is increasing (see chapter by Muehlenhard).
6. Positions of *leadership*, power, and fund-allocation still are held primarily by men.

There are constant trends in the way stereotypes are acquired and perpetuated — in schools, at the job, through the media. Moreover, the institutions through which society prescribes behavior for people have not changed. The pressures on women to adhere to traditional sex-role stereotypes are equivalent to the importance of the institution demanding such adherence. We cannot be optimistic about the overall probability of change in the next decade.

IMPLICATIONS FOR THE 1980s: CONSTRUCTIVE CHANGE

Are there any possible strategies and tactics with which mental health professionals can intervene? Contributors made the following suggestions and recommendations for treatment and social change:

1. Change existing practices in school systems and education. This includes educating children against violence (Resick), developing more appropriate and flexible skills in children (Weinraub and Brown), continuing and expanding sex education (Tevlin and Leiblum), and preparing children for nontraditional future roles (Worell and Garret-Fulks). Schools are urged to revise and update portrayal of women and of society

in textbooks (Muehlenhard; Worell and Garret-Fulks) and to increase physical activity and athletic programs for girls (Zegman).

2. Advise parents on child-rearing practices that better prepare children for flexible roles (Worell and Garret-Fulks), nonviolence (Resick), and increased physical activity (Zegman). Parents should serve as models of nonstereotypic sex roles and recognize and point out possible consequences and obstacles of such sex roles to children (Weinraub and Brown).

3. Therapy should provide a relearning process to help women assume more responsibility for their lives. Therapists and mental health professionals can model more adaptive behavior for women (Kelly). They should offer emotional support, acceptance, and self-reliance and provide information, community services, and career help (Worell and Garret-Fulks). Assertiveness training was mentioned most often as a specific intervention, although Kelly and Muehlenhard point out that women also must be trained in effective ways to deal with the consequences of assertion in work and social situations. Other interventions included helping women identify their sexual needs (Tevlin and Leiblum); crisis intervention for rape and spouse-abuse victims (Resick); specific interventions for single mothers, widows, and other at-risk population (Rothblum); flooding (Brehony); and use of significant others in therapy (Rothblum). Whenever possible, individual problems should be interpreted within the context of society (Brehony).

4. Provide support groups to bring together individuals with similar problems (Brehony; Worell and Garret-Fulks), and set up programs in work settings (Zegman).

5. Train colleagues and other professionals regarding the extensiveness of the problem (Tevlin and Leiblum; Resick).

6. Use the mass media to change stereotypes and educate the public. Finally, there are impossible stereotypes such as "be independent but take care of the house"; "stay thin but cook the meals"; and "stay young." Women must be aware of these Catch-22s; therapists need to challenge irrational beliefs.

Mental health professionals need to understand the pressures society places on women and realize that they are not treating patients in a vacuum. It is important to differentiate between feminist values and traditional values. Preceding chapters have pointed out that stereotypes are maladaptive and can result in pathology, yet conforming to stereotypes also can be appropriate and effective. One function performed by helping professionals will be to help women discriminate.

CONCLUSION: OUR MESSAGE

A decade of women-oriented research and feminist therapy has passed. Ten years ago there were few data on women's mental health; there had been little systematic research. One reason for this book was that we felt there was a need to integrate the literature.

Feminists (e.g. Chesler, 1972) have claimed that psychopathology among women is the result of sex-role biases of mental health professionals; that men and women are allocated clinical diagnoses according to gender. The current book disproves this. Women who come in for treatment *are* depressed, agoraphobic, sexually dysfunctional, and so on. Whatever processes led to the symptoms of emotional distress happened before diagnosis and treatment. Additionally, the present book points out that even today there is pervasive influence of sex-role stereotypes and sex differences during childhood and throughout adulthood.

Furthermore, the mental health field puts more emphasis on the role of patients' rights. This has resulted in new research directions, including conceptualizations of women's roles and socialization as they affect psychopathology. The developments have been sporadic, however. Research in the areas of women and depression and sexual dysfunction has been extensive and results have extended to the popular press and to television. Research on other areas, such as agoraphobia and problems facing single women, is still in its infancy. Thus, our knowledge about most aspects of mental health awaits further investigation.

As the 1980s begin, two constrasting social movements face society. The first, the "pro-family movement," attempts to "strengthen the American family and to remove those Federal Governmental policies which inhibit its strength and prosperity" (Family Protection Act, 1980). This includes proposals to forbid schools to use educational materials which "tend to denigrate, diminish, or deny the role differences between the sexes as it (*sic*) has been historically understood in the United States" and to limit "intermingling of the sexes in any sport or other school-related" activity (Family Protection Act, 1980). Furthermore, proposed legislation would expand the parent's role "in supervis-

ing and determining the religious or moral formation of his (*sic*) child,"
override all current laws "relating to spouse abuse or domestic
relations," and provide funds for child-abuse programs only if a state
"specifically authorizes such a program" (Family Protection Act, 1980).
Finally, "no program may receive Federal funds unless, prior to providing a contraceptive device, abortion counseling, or an abortion to an
unmarried minor, the agency notify the minor's parents or guardian"
(Family Protection Act, 1980). Recently, the *New York Times* summarized the "new right" advocates as stressing " . . . broad agreement on
the so-called 'profamily issues'— antiabortion, antiequal-rights amend-
ment, antibusing, pro-prayer in the schools — and a free-market conservatism on economic issues. They favor limited Government spending
on social programs but more for defense" (Range, 1981, pp. 23–24).

Funding cuts will severely curtail progress on research in sex roles
and women's mental health, since these topics have not been considered
"priority" issues in the past and will not be supported when allocations
are limited. Additionally, any conservatism, whether in the economy or
in social policy, will limit change in women's roles, in their social conditions, and, ultimately, in their mental health.

A second, conflicting, social movement represents those individuals
who argue that the nuclear family no longer represents the norm and
that policy and economic changes need to incorporate the new living
styles. Advocates of this movement argue that current institutions in society, which were designed to meet the needs of an employed husband,
housewife, and two children, cannot serve effectively the requirements
of increasing proportions of the never-married two-career couples, the
elderly, single parents, and other nontraditional family compositions.
Alvin Toffler, author of *Future Shock*, represents this viewpoint in his
latest book, *The Third Wave* (1980, p. 9):

> A new civilization is emerging in our lives, and blind men everywhere are
> trying to suppress it. This new civilization brings with it new family styles;
> changed ways of working, loving, and living; a new economy; new polit-
> ical conflicts; and beyond all this an altered consciousness as well. Pieces of
> this new civilization exist today. Millions are already attuning their lives to
> the rhythms of tomorrow. Others, terrified of the future, are engaged in a
> desperate, futile flight into the past and are trying to restore the dying
> world that gave them birth.

Toffler's recommends the following:

> The decision to live outside a nuclear family framework should be made easier, not harder. Values change more slowly, as a rule, than social reality. Thus we have not yet developed the ethic of tolerance for diversity. . . . [we are] firmly taught that one kind of family is "normal" and others somehow suspect, if not "deviant," [hence] vast numbers remain intolerant of the new variety in family styles. Until that changes, the pain of transition will remain unnecessarily high. [p. 224]

We end, therefore, on a note of "cautious optimism," to use Tevlin and Leiblum's term. Society is in an agony of transition; pressures to conform and to reform face women in particular and society in general. There is room for effective change, just as there are pressures to maintain traditional norms. The 1980s will determine the outcome of that choice, but they follow a decade of great progress and new ways of conceptualizing traditional roles. It was during the 1970s that we gained the "liberation rights" for oppressed groups — gay rights, black civil liberties, advocacy groups for various minorities. Will this new wave of conservative reaction stultify progress made in accepting new methods of dealing with old stereotypes? Or has the progress and change of the 1970s solidified enough to lead to permanent change? One hopes that the "feminine mystique" will not reenter as a "feminine mistake." If the reappraisal of values we have experienced recently will leave a permanent effect on womankind and mankind, then both sexes can use their strengths for mutual benefit and growth. If not, everyone may be the loser, man, woman, and child.

REFERENCES

Beloff, H. Are models of man models of women? In Chapman, A. J. & Jones, D. M. (Eds.), *Models of man*. London: British Psychology Society, 1980.

Broverman, I. H., Broverman, D. M., Clarkson, F. E., Rosenkrantz, P. S., & Vogel, S. R. Sex role stereotypes and clinical judgments of mental health. *Journal of Consulting and Clinical Psychology*, 1970, *34*, 1–7.

Chesler, P. *Women and madness*. New York: Avon, 1972.

Family Protection Act (S.1808, H. R. 6028), Section-by-section summary and constitutional analysis. Washington, D.C.: Library of Congress, 1980.

Harragan, B. L. *Games mother never taught you: Corporate gamesmanship for women*. New York: Warner Books, 1977.

Lane, A. J. Introduction. In Gilman, C. P. S., *Herland*. New York: Pantheon Books, 1979.

President's Commission on Mental Health. Task panel reports. Report of the special population subpanel on mental health of women, February 1978, 1022–1116.

Range, P. R. Thunder from the right. *New York Times*, February 8, 1981, pp. 23–84.

Toffler, A. *The third wave*. New York: Bantam Books, 1980.

Index

Adult occupations, children's awareness of sex differences in, 37–39
Adult possessions, sex differences in,
33–35
Aggression and aggressiveness, 23–24
sexual, 137–141
See also Assertiveness; Violence
against women
Agoraphobia, 22–23, 262
defined, 113
description of, 114–115
directions for clinical and research
activities, 124–125
feminine sex-role stereotype and,
116–119
mechanisms leading to, 119–123
overview of, 112–113
sex differences in, 115–116
Agoraphobia Research Questionnaire
(ARQ), 117–118
Androgyny, 9, 15–19, 259
Anxiety disorders, 22–23
Arousal dysfunction, 130, 133–134
Assertion, definitions of, 154–156
Assertion training, 153
Assertiveness, 21–22, 153–154, 262
assertion, definitions of, 154–156
changing the feminine stereotype,
167–168
changing women's behavior, 168–
169
data on consequences of behaving

assertively, 162–166
feminine sex-role stereotype and,
156–158
implications for the 1980s, 167–
169
negative assertion, 155, 157, 158–
160, 163–164
positive assertion, 156, 157–158,
160–161
review of research on, 158–162
social initiation, 156, 157–158,
161–162, 164–166

Behavioral skills, sex roles and, 18–19
Bem Sex-Role Inventory (BSRI), 15,
16, 18, 117–118

Caloric intake, reducing, 180–181
Child custody, research on, 223
Children, development of sex-role
stereotypes in, 9, 30–32, 260
adult possessions, sex differences in,
33–35
agoraphobia and, 120–122
awareness of sex differences, 33–39
factors influencing, 45–49
keeping sex-role stereotypes in their
place, 49–51
language patterns and, 69–72
occupational preference and,
43–45
peer influence, 46–47

271

agoraphobia and, 115–116
depression and, 91–94
See also Single-again women
Marriage, traditional sex-role handicaps of, 203–208
Masturbation, 135–136
Mental health, sex-role stereotypes and, 11–12, 259–262
aggression, 23–24
agoraphobia, 22–23, 112–125
anxiety disorders, 22–23
depression, 21, 83–107
language use and sex roles, 61, 74–77
new formulations of sex-role style, 14–18
psychological treatment and sex-role change, 24–26
sex roles as behavioral skill repertoires, 18–19
traditional models of sex-role development, 12–14
unassertiveness, 21–22, 153–169
M-F scales, 13–18
Models of sex-role development
new formulations, 14–18
traditional, 12–14
Morbidity, obesity and, 188–189
Mortality, obesity and, 188–189
Motherhood, depression and, 95, 96–98

Negative assertion
data on consequences for women, 162–164
defined, 155
feminine-stereotype characteristics and, 157, 158
review of research on, 158–160
Nontraditional roles for women, consequences of, 263–264

Obesity, 172–173, 262
age and, 175
behavioral model, 180
biological theories of, 176–178

causes of, 176–180
contributions of sex roles and sex-role stereotypes, 185–190
double standard of physical attractiveness, 189–190
eating habits and, 186–187
exercise and, 182–185
implications for the 1980s, 190–194
medical implications of, 175–176
morbidity and mortality, 188–189
physical activity and, 187–188
prevalence of, 174–175
prevention of, 192–193
problems of definition and measurement, 173–174
psychological factors in, 178–179
race and, 174
reduction of caloric intake, 180–181
remedial efforts, 180–185
research on, 191–192
sex-role stereotypes and, 185–190
social class and, 174–175
treatment of, 193–194
Occupational preference of children, 43–45
Orgasmic dysfunction, defined, 130
Overweight, 173–174. *See also* Obesity

Parental responsibility, depression and, 95, 96–98
Passivity, sexual, 137–141
Personal Attributes Questionnaire (PAQ), 15, 16, 18
Personality characteristics, children's awareness of sex differences in, 35–37
Physical activity, obesity and, 187–188
Positive assertion
defined, 156
feminine-stereotype characteristics and, 157, 158
review of research on, 160–161
Powerlessness, as source of stress in women, 210–212
PRF ANDRO Scale, 15, 16, 18